A Child's Geography
Explore the Holy Land

Ann Voskamp and Tonia Peckover

"Go into all the world..."
~ Mark16:15

A Child's Geography is an endeavor of which a portion of profits support
World Vision, *an internationally recognized Christian relief,*
development and advocacy organization dedicated to
working with children, families and communities
to overcome poverty and injustice.

"Circle... take her measure... gaze long... climb ...
Then you can tell the next generation, detail by detail, the story of God." *~Ps. 48 12*

BRAMLEY BOOKS
www.bramleybooks.com
A Division of Knowledge Quest, Inc.

Published in the United States of America by:
Bramley Books
A Division of Knowledge Quest, Inc.
P.O. Box 789
Boring, OR 97009

www.achildsgeography.com
www.knowledgequestmaps.com/achildsgeography.htm
Copyright 2006 by Ann Voskamp and Tonia Peckover
First Edition, Published 2006
Second Edition, Revised and Published 2008 by Knowledge Quest, Inc.
All rights reserved.
ISBN # 1-932786-33-3 / 978-1-932786-33-0

Cover design by Jeremy Conn of Conn Creative Media – www.conncreativemedia.com
Template designs for CD-ROM by Tonia Peckover
The copywork passages were graciously and competently compiled by Crystal Eddy

Publisher's Cataloging-in-Publication data

Voskamp, Ann.
    A child's geography : explore the holy land / Ann Voskamp and Tonia Peckover.
    p. cm.
    "Second edition"
    Series: A Child's Geography, Vol. 2
    ISBN 978-1-932786-33-0
1. Bible--Geography--Juvenile literature. 2. Palestine--Historical geography--Juvenile literature..
3. Jordan--Historical geography--Juvenile literature. 4. Israel--Description and travel--Juvenile
literature. 5. Bible--History of Biblical events--Juvenile literature. I. Peckover, Tonia. II. Title.
III. Series.

BS633 .V67 2008
220.9121--dc22   2008921557

Explore the Holy Land
Table of Contents

Before Embarking….

There is nothing nicer than curling up with a good book and your children. You are invited. Come. Snuggle. Explore. Discover. Delight. Worship our Creator. **Here are just a few thoughts before we "Explore the Holy Land" together…**

Scheduling

"Explore the Holy Land" offers you a ticket to an unforgettable adventure through six countries in sixteen chapters. Each chapter is divided into two sections by narration prompts (*Field Notes*) and followed by mapping activities (*Travel Logs*), ending with music, art, poetry, book, and food suggestions (*Bringing It Home*).

The curriculum can easily be spread out over a school year. Some options to consider:
~2 weeks per chapter: Read the entire chapter in one sitting and narrate. The following week do mapping and optional activities.
~2 weeks per chapter: Read half a chapter a week and narrate. Divide the optional activities over each week.
~3 weeks per chapter: Read half a chapter a week and narrate. The third week do mapping and optional activities.
~Unit Studies: Cover 3 countries a term. Use *"Explore the Holy Land"* as a spring board to immerse yourselves in each country. Use the internet, library and local resources to stay in this country for as long as you like.

Readings

Whether you gather the kids around for a read-aloud or your older students read alone, it is best to study geography with visual aids. Make sure to have an open atlas and/or a globe at hand to look up all the places you'll be exploring. Each chapter is divided into two sections. These sections may be too long for younger readers or too short for older readers. Feel free to adapt the length to fit **your** family.

Field Notes

At the end of each chapter section we have offered narration prompts in the form of *"Field Notes."* Just like modern day explorers, we ask the child to talk into an imaginary recorder and tell of his or her discoveries. We have offered the prompts to stimulate their memories – **but these are not mandatory!** Let your child talk about what captured his or her imagination. You may be surprised at what they've learned!

Travel Logs

Every good explorer keeps a record of his journey. After each chapter, your child will be asked to draw a map of the country we have been studying and label important cities and regions, along with some of the sights we've seen along the way. Finally, they will write a short entry of their own observations. A three-ring binder and plastic sleeves may be appropriate for storing maps and log entries or you may want to get creative and make your own authentic travel logs to record your journey!

Bringing it Home

Each country offers a world of culture for us to explore. We have tried to offer a taste of all these lands by sharing music, simple art projects, suggested reading lists, poetry and recipes that allow you to bring each country into your own home. **All of these activities are optional.** We have tried to keep these activities as simple as possible, thus making them accessible for busy homeschooling families.

Many of the activities are found on-line. All the links specified in the text can be found at our website for your convenience: www.achildsgeography.com.

Prayer Walk

Our deepest desire in writing a Christ-centered geography is to help young children develop a love for each of the countries and cultures we study. We hope you will join us at the end of each country study as we pray for the beautiful peoples God has created across the world. Each Prayer Walk is written as a prayer and includes specific requests for that particular country. You may want to pray along with us at the end of each of your lessons.

With all the details taken care of, we are ready to embark on our journey. Grab your kids and let's go!

"The whole earth is full of His glory!" ~Isaiah 6:3

Directions to Eden, Please?

Turkey ~ Part 1~

When I was young and summer days grew warm and long, I used to swim in the cool of the Maitland River, fish in its murky shadows, and canoe under its leafy canopy. The Maitland River isn't well-known so you've probably never heard of it. But perhaps you *have* heard of these four well-known rivers from the beginning of time, written of in Genesis 2:10-14: *"Now a river flowed out of Eden to water the garden; and from there it divided and became four rivers. The name of the first is Pishon... The name of the second river is Gihon...The name of the third river is Tigris..."*

Wait! Now imagine that the Bible then named the very river that coursed near your home. *"And the fourth river is the ...."* Wouldn't you catch your breath if you read that verse in the Bible and realized, "That's the very river I swim in on summer afternoons!"? There *are* children today who do indeed read in the Bible of the river that streams just outside their house! The stories of the Bible happen in real, actual places on Earth. God's story, through the ages, is rooted in **geography**. The words of Scripture are firmly rooted in the ground of our world, places you can see and touch and experience today. I can't wait to experience those rivers and mountains and lands with you!

Of course, geographers pack their bags before embarking on a Holy Land exploration, but the most important elements of a journey simply cannot be tucked into a suitcase. Firstly, wise travelers have observing *eyes* that are focused to truly see the sights. Secondly, astute adventurers nurture strong *memories* to net their adventures and keep them as their own. And thirdly, sensible geographers carry with them a healthy *faith*. A growing faith gives our heart the eyes to see the evidence and glory of God everywhere we travel. With our trio of essentials, let us depart!

The Bible begins with the story of geography: the story of Earth, and its creation...and it begins with a garden. The Bible reads, *"Then the Lord God planted a garden in Eden in the east"* (Gen. 2:8). This is the first mention of an exact, geographical location on our Earth. It speaks of a real garden that once existed: the Garden of Eden. If I cracked open my Bible, could I find a map that told me where the Garden of Eden is today? No! No modern map can show us where to find the ancient Garden of Eden. Perhaps we could, however, gather some ideas regarding its location from the Bible and its clue of those four rivers: *"Now a river flowed out of Eden...and became four rivers..."* (Gen. 2:14). Since Eden means "delight" in Hebrew, we will need to look for a place of delight! Let's begin in a place where children today can eat a candy called "Turkish Delight." These children live in the Middle Eastern country of Turkey...and one of the rivers that flowed through the Garden of Eden begins in that country. Might Earth's very first inhabitants, created masterfully by God's own hand, have walked through the dark green valleys of this country? Why not hop on a flying carpet to see where the Garden of Eden may have been in Turkey?

The Turkish Flag: The star and crescent are Muslim symbols.

More than 250,000 people visit the 4,000 shops of Istanbul's Grand Bazaar every day, the world's most famous bazaar. The oldest part of the Bazaar was built in 1461 under Mehemt the Conqueror. Today's shoppers carry home purchases of goods such as jewelry, pottery, spices and carpets.

Tales of *flying* carpets are merely the stuff of fantasy, but our carpet is as real as the Garden of Eden once was. We'd find such a carpet in Turkey...but where exactly are we? Hold a globe in your hand and spin till you find where God has intersected the Mediterranean Sea, and the continents of Europe and Asia; there you will pinpoint Turkey. Now that you've landed, let's make our way to the crowded Turkish Grand Bazaar in the city of Istanbul. (Can you locate Istanbul in the northwest corner?) A **bazaar** is the Persian word for market, and it is here in the Grand Bazaar of Istanbul that we would find our ornate Turkish carpet called a **_kilim_** (KEE-lim). Here, in alleys so narrow one can hardly squeeze through, stringing along more than 65 streets, merchants from over 4,000 shops shout out to passing shoppers trying to sell their colorful wares. Some shopkeepers of the Grand Bazaar grab our arms, tugging us into their stalls, while others tickle our ear with whispered prices especially negotiated for us. In one shop selling carpets, I imagine our fingers reaching out to feel the dark hues and naturally dyed colors. Perhaps the shopkeeper, Ahmet, may roll the kilim out for us, chuckling, "*Evet, evet,*" (Yes, yes in Turkish) teasing us that our carpet may float away, sweeping us up over the Grand Bazaar and all of the city of Istanbul. Imagine: a dip and a dive, a launch and an upward lunge, and here we would be, on our own kilim, looking down at the country of Turkey below us!

With your eye on your globe and Turkey far below, what image can you form out of the shapes you see? I imagine a strange creature with the Sea of Marmara as an eye. Can you pinpoint where Istanbul and the Grand Bazaar might be?

Turkey covers an area of 301,400 square miles [780,626 square kilometers] which is about the size of the states of Texas and Virginia combined. While we may have an easy overview of the entire country from our carpet, Turkey actually spans about 1000 miles [1, 609 km] from end to end. We'd have to start driving before the sun rose and drive long after sunset, to cross the entire country.

From your carpet perch, you would surely have noticed the four great bodies of water bordering Turkey: the Mediterranean Sea, the Aegean Sea, the Sea of Marmara and the Black Sea. What makes these bodies of water *sea*s and not oceans or lakes? A **sea** is a stretching expanse of salty water that is usually a reaching arm of ocean, butting into a continent of land. If you look carefully, you'll find that the Mediterranean Sea, for instance, is really just an arm of the Atlantic Ocean that God has allowed to reach into the lands of Africa, Europe and Asia. Out of the Mediterranean Sea stretches another arm, the Aegean Sea...and out of the Aegean Sea extends the arm of the Sea of Marmara....which reaches out even further as the Black Sea. This arm of seas from the Atlantic Ocean is a long-reaching arm indeed! (Our travels will lead us to seas that are *not* connected to oceans at all, but are entirely surrounded by land, called **land-locked seas**. Such a body of water is nearly always a body of *salty* water. [An exception is the Sea of Galilee.] A lake, on the other hand, is a large body of usually fresh water surrounded by land.)

Wave-tossed by this quartet of seas, the country of Turkey is actually like a bridge between the two continents of Asia and Europe. Yes, all that separates these two continents is a sliver of water—with the city of Istanbul on either side of the ribbon of blue waves. Istanbul, Turkey's largest city of 9.5 million people, is the only city in the whole wide world built on *two* continents! (You may have heard of Istanbul's ancient name, Constantinople, in your history studies.) That thread of water, which separates the city into East Istanbul and West Istanbul; and separates Europe from Asia, is one of the most important trade waterways in the world: the Bosphorus Strait. It is the connecting waterway for ships from the Black Sea to sail on out to the Sea of Marmara, then to the Aegean Sea…and onto the Mediterranean Sea, and out into the Atlantic Ocean.

This is a photograph taken of Turkey from a satellite up in space. Looking down from way above, what shapes do you see in Turkey's geography? The different shades of green tell us where plants, trees and vegetation are growing in the landscape. The blue areas are the seas and lakes. The white areas above the land are clouds. *Photo courtesy of visibleearth.nasa.gov*

Although the Bosphorous is a **strait** of water, that doesn't mean it flows perfectly straight, without winding around bends and curves. Actually, the word **strait** has nothing to do with "straight" lines, but means it is a narrow channel of water that God created between two landmasses. This narrow strait joins two larger bodies of water. Try thinking of it this way: have you ever squeezed on a long, thin balloon? Just as a skinny balloon bulges out into large shapes when you squeeze it in the middle, so the strait of water "squeezed" by the two landmasses swells into two larger bodies of water on either side! Looking at your globe, or map, of Turkey, can you determine which two larger bodies of water bulge out of the squeezed (only 0.5 to 2.8 mi. [660 to 4,500 m.] wide!) Bosphorus Strait? Yes, the Sea of Marmara and the Black Sea!

Recall that little Maitland River that I used to play in? Big old Hereford cattle use to wander down its banks to lap up the thirst-quenching cool water or sometimes splash across to the other side of the river. The Greeks had a story about their god Zeus supposedly hiding a cow in the silvery, narrow waters of the Bosphorus Strait. Thus, in the Greek language, "Bosphorus" means the "the cow crossing-place." (That makes it rather easy to remember that the Turkish city of Istan**bul,** is on the Bosphorus strait—the *cow* passage!) You are not likely to not see any cows swimming down there in the Bosphorus Strait but you will probably see streams of cars crossing over top of the strait on the Bosphorus Bridge, the 12th longest suspension bridge in the world. This stretch of steel allows you to drive from the continent of Europe right into Asia.

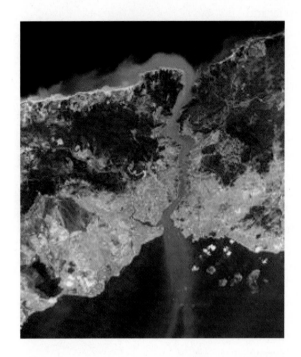

God drew a thread of blue water, the Bosphorous Strait, to separate the continents of Europe and Asia. Bridges now span the Bosphorous Strait, but a. 4,593 feet [1, 400 m] rail tunnel, running 180 feet [55 m] underneath the Strait, is currently being built.
Photo courtesy of visibleearth.nasa.gov

Named after the "cow crossing-place," a cow would no longer have to swim the Bosphorous, but could be driven across one of the massive bridges that span the Bosphorous Strait!

Field Notes

What an amazing start to finding the Garden that was there in the beginning! Are you enjoying your carpet ride? Have you ever seen someone perched on a floating carpet speaking tales of adventure onto a mini-recorder? You may stay seated on the carpet and I'll be the mini-recorder, listening to your field notes!

Press Record and talk to me...

~ **about how the geography of Earth connects to the stories of the Bible**: What important place from the Bible might have been located in Turkey? What are three essentials that a geographer brings to every exploration?

~ **about Turkey's location on a globe**: What does the country look like from above and what of its size? What bodies of water border Turkey? Which continents? Tell me what you learned about seas. Tell me more about where you found your kilim.

~ **about the Bosphorus Strait**: What does its name mean? What is a strait? What does a strait connect? Name the bodies of water the Bosphorus Strait connects. What kind of bridge spans the Bosphorus Strait?

The Black Sea region of Turkey is beautiful and temperate. The seasons are not extreme, but moderate, and rain is plentiful. Hasn't God created excellent growing conditions for many crops such as hazelnuts, tea, tobacco and cherries?

While you may not see any cows crossing the Bosphorous Strait, if you look across Turkey *(see previous arial photograph of Turkey on page 7)*, can your keen eyes determine where you might find cows in this country? Cows in Turkey like to chew exactly what cows like to chew along the banks of my little Maitland River: lush, green grass. Rich green grass is waiting for us if we soar east from Istanbul up along the northern coast of Turkey. You will notice how the skies are gray with rain clouds here but the coastal mountains below us are deep green. Indeed, here along the Black Sea you may actually see many cows grazing to produce Turkey's very best milk and butter. The climate of this area of Turkey is what we call **temperate.** A **temperate climate** is an area with weather that is not too cold and not too hot - but just right!

In temperate regions, like here on the Black Sea coast of Turkey, changes between seasons are not extreme with searing hot days followed by freezing cold days, but subtle, with moderately warm days giving way to moderately cool days.

As the warm air blowing in off the Black Sea rises over the north coast of Turkey, rain clouds are formed, which creates rainfall year round, almost 8 feet [2.4 m] of rain during a year; four to six times the rainfall in other regions of Turkey. (That amount of rain is as high as you sitting on your Dad's shoulders!) The rain clouds that God sends off the Black Sea make these steep mountain slopes verdant and lush with grass and crops. Imagine looking over our carpet's edge to see the Turks on this mountainous northern coast bringing in harvests of cherries from what some believe to be the world's oldest cherry orchards, the gathering of billions of hazelnuts, and expansive tea and tobacco plantations. Four in every ten Turks live by working in God's land growing crops or grazing herds of livestock such as goats or cattle. As we peer over carpet's edge, deeply inhaling those aromas of teas and drying tobaccos, drifting in on the sea breezes up through this garden-like area of Turkey, we can't help but sing praise to our God who owns *"the cattle on a thousand hills"* (Ps 50:10), and who *"care[s] for the land and water[s] it…enrich[ing] it abundantly"* (Ps. 65:9)!

Speaking of fertile, lush gardens, can you spot the Tigris and Euphrates Rivers down there in the southeast part of Turkey? Recall these words from God's Word *"Now a river flowed out of Eden to water the garden; and from there it divided and became four rivers…The name of the third river is Tigris; …And the fourth river is the Euphrates"* (Genesis 2:10,14). Today, we know very little of the first two-mentioned rivers of Eden but we may ponder over the two other named rivers, the Euphrates and Tigris. The name Euphrates itself comes from a root word that means "to gush forth" and we can see that it does just that as the river winds and meanders its way through steep canyons and gorges. As you gaze down on the Euphrates, one can imagine how Abraham must have felt when God said to him *"Unto thy seed have I given this land …unto the great river, the river Euphrates"* (Genesis 15:18). This great river is the northeastern boundary of the Promised Land and the site of such great historical events as the battle between Nebuchadnezzar II of Babylon and Pharaoh Necho II of Egypt in 605 B.C. (Jer 46:2).

The course of the Euphrates River is one border of Mesopotamia, "the land between two rivers." The Euphrates River also marked one of the boundaries of the land promised by God to Abraham and his descendants. In the Old Testament, the very important Euphrates River is referred to simply as "The River" (*ha-nahar*).
Photo courtesy of holylandphotos.org

The Tigris River, on the other hand, comes from a word that means "the river that goes," which it certainly does, coursing throughout Turkey faster and with a greater volume of water, than the Euphrates The Euphrates and Tigris Rivers both begin high up in a rugged region of Turkey called Anatolia. (Can you locate the Anatolian Plateau stretching across the center of Turkey?) From way up in space, we see this vast central region of the Anatolia as dry and rolling. Thus, we aren't surprised that in the Greek language Anatolia means: "Land of the Mother Sun." The Anatolia is what geographers refer to as a plateau.

A **plateau** is like a mountain without a peak. Similar to a mountain, the center Anatolian Plateau of Turkey rises high into the air; but unlike a mountain, God creates plateaus with a relatively flat top. A plateau can be regarded as a flat-topped mountain, or an oversized table of land rising up out of the landscape. Think of the Anatolian Think of the Anatolian Plateau as a table rising up out of the central interior of Turkey, a *tableland*, where the Tigris and Euphrates Rivers begin and course down through its rugged terrain.

The lands that lie in between the winding Tigris and Euphrates Rivers are known as the Mesopotamia. **Mesopotamia** literally means "the land between two rivers." Often times the word Mesopotamia is also referred to as the "Cradle of Civilization." I picture this part of Anatolia, meaning "the land of the mother sun," as having two arms, the Tigris and Euphrates Rivers, which cradled Earth's very first towns, farms and society, born here in the Mesopotamia, "the land between the two rivers."

Take a look down there at the southeastern Anatolian Plateau where historians believe that our planet's very first homes were built and farms were cultivated. Ever since the dawn of time, this sweeping Anatolian Plateau has been the birthplace of a chain of civilizations and peoples whom God has used in mighty ways to write the world's history. The Hittites of the Bible lived here. The Persians, Romans, and Byzantines ruled here. It was in the Mesopotamia that the first metal was ever made. Copper, the first metal ever used by mankind is still mined here in Turkey, near the Tigris River. When we read in the Bible of how Adam and Eve's son was a farmer and that their great-grandson's great-grandson worked with metal, we wonder if the Garden of Eden itself was once indeed here, somewhere in Turkey, lying between the Tigris and Euphrates Rivers. Did the very first people ever to walk the dust of this earth, Adam and Eve, indeed first walk here, in the Turkish Mesopotamia, between the Euphrates and Tigris Rivers? In all truth, we simply do not know. The global flood of Noah's day dramatically and catastrophically changed the landscape of our world. Are these two rivers of Turkey the same rivers of the Biblical Garden of Eden? Some suggest not: The Tigris and Euphrates Rivers of Turkey today flow on top of thousands of feet of fossil sediments believed to be from Noah's Flood. Thus, it is argued, these two rivers are not the same rivers of the Garden of Eden. Then why do they have the same names, you ask? The Maitland River that coursed near my house was named after a long ago Governor, Sir Maitland. And it may be that the families who settled this part of Turkey after the flood named these two rivers after the long-ago rivers they remembered flowing out of the Garden of Eden. The original Tigris and Euphrates Rivers of the Garden of Eden fed and watered Adam and Eve's paradise, just as the modern Tigris and Euphrates Rivers do today for great areas of Turkey.

Ataturk Dam dramatically alters the original flow of the Euphrates River. The dam may benefit some in Turkey with hydroelectric power and water to irrigate farms, but it has left others below the dam with much less water. What a difference this dam has made!

Peer over our carpet's edge and perhaps you may see a young girl dipping her pail in the Euphrates; or watch two boys watering their cattle at river's edge and another man netting mullet fish. Since the beginning of time, water has been necessary for living. All rivers, like the meandering Maitland River or the great Euphrates and Tigris Rivers, provide drinking water for livestock and people, irrigation for crops, a means to transport goods, travel waterways, and a source of food. Thus, all throughout history, humans have built towns, which have grown into prospering cities, close to where God has provided running water.

Industrious beavers often built dams of sticks and mud across my Maitland River. But what we see as we gaze carefully down from our floating kilim, are definitely not beaver-built structures stretching across the rivers. Nor were these here in the day of Adam and Eve. Do you see the massive concrete dams spanning the width of the rivers? More than 20 such dams are built over both rivers to generate electricity for the Turkish people and to irrigate over 17 million square miles [44 million sq km] of Turkey's land in need of water. While the Tigris and Euphrates Rivers may be dammed up to benefit families in Turkey, dams actually leave *less* water for other families down river.

How God created our Earth—geography—weaves through the stories and peoples of the past, powerfully effects where and how people live on this globe today, and influences the family of humanity's future. The God-designed geography of Turkey, with its Bosphorous Strait, its Anatolian Plateau, its temperate coastlines, and the course of its rivers, such as the Tigris and Euphrates, determines where families live, what they eat around their tables, how they work and what they do. God formed humanity out of the dust of the Earth, and for all of our days, we are intimately connected to the dust under our feet, to the geography of Earth.

We've explored some of the highlights of Turkey's geography, but we have yet to visit Turkey's highest—and most secretive—point, its whirling dervishes, its underground cities to crawl through, its magnificent churches and its camel wrestlers to shake your heads over. So hold on to your carpets—oh, the places we'll go!

Field Notes

I can't wait to hear your memories and field notes from our first ride through Turkey! **Press Record and talk to me...**

~ about the Black Sea Region:
What of its climate? What is grown in this region?

~ about the Tigris and Euphrates Rivers:
Do you remember what their names mean? Where do they begin? Tell me what you think about these rivers and the rivers of the Garden of Eden. How do the rivers help the people of Turkey today?

~ about plateaus (or tablelands): Once you have described a plateau – what famous plateau lies in the center of Turkey? Can you find it on your map?

~ about Mesopotamia: What does its name mean? What else is it sometimes called? Why? Can you name some of the people groups that started here?

Travel Log

Using your globe or atlas, draw an outline map of Turkey.

As we travel, let's make record in our very own travel log of the places we've visited and the unusual sights we've seen! Make your map large enough to hold all of your discoveries!

Don't worry about making a perfect map, just do your best. Drawing the basic shape yourself will help you remember it better. Or you can use the map provided for you on the CD-ROM.

Map Notes: Let's record the locations of:

- **Istanbul**
- **Sea of Marmara**
- **Mediterranean Sea**
- **Aegean Sea**

- **Black Sea**
- **Bosphorous Strait**
- **Anatolian Plateau**

Optional:
- **Tigris River**
- **Euphrates River**
- **Mesopotamia**

If you'd like, draw pictures or symbols on your map representing:

The Grand Bazaar *(perhaps a picture of your own floating kilim?)*
Bosphorus Bridge *(if you draw a cow in the river, that may help you remember the story of the river's name!)*
Cherry trees or baskets of tea on the Black Sea coastline *(Do you recall that this is one of the oldest orchards in the world?)*
Dams on the Tigris and Euphrates Rivers

Travel Notes: Geographers write what they've seen in order to share the adventure with others—and so they can revisit the places in their memories! On the next page of your travel log, record three important sights you want to remember from your tales of Turkey.

~art ~books ~food ~music ~poetry
. . . .

Bringing It Home
Simple ideas to bring the world to your door

Art

The Turks are known for their brilliant colors and intricate geometric designs in textiles and tiles.

Perhaps you'd like to try weaving your own kilim:

http://www.allfiberarts.com/library/aa01/aa040201.htm

Or, try your hand at decorating a Turkish Tile:

http://www.papermandalas.com/turkishtile.htm

Music

Music captures so much of a land and people. Introducing your children to Turkish music is a simple way to transport yourselves around the world: a bit like your own flying carpet! Why not check out these sites while your young geographers notebook and map and let the music play while they recount their travels?

You can hear a wide selection of Turkish music at these sites:

(The Republic of Turkey Ministry of Culture)
http://www.discoverturkey.com/english/kultursanat/muzik.html

(National Geographic)
http://worldmusic.nationalgeographic.com/worldmusic/view/page.basic/home
(Click on Middle East and then Turkey)

Also, you can check your local library for Turkish classical music (called *sanit*) or traditional folk music.

Houses for sale:
An Ark, a Beehive, a Fairy Chimney, and a Salt Pan!

Turkey ~ Part 2~

Tucked in the corner of a high cupboard in my kitchen is a red, heart-shaped plate, the perfect plate on which to eat birthday cake, or Valentine's Day cookies, or just "I love you" meals. The back of the plate reads in black letters: "Made in Turkey." Somewhere in Turkey, a Turk made the heart-shaped plate on which I eat. The Turk and I have never met, but I think of him every time I pull down that red heart dish. And I think I, too, am falling in love with God's land of Turkey and her people. Are you?

I doubt that Noah and his family had any heart-shaped plates, but I would hazard a guess that they loved this land more than you and I both! Who wouldn't, after rocking and rolling on the waters of a worldwide flood for months and months and months?! When God caused the flood waters to recede, I imagine Noah and his family fairly tumbled out of that ark to kiss the land of Turkey, for this grateful family had landed on top of…well, there it is right now!

Pull-up on the carpet, so we don't collide with that magnificent snow-capped mountain, down there along the northern border of Turkey! That icy, craggy peak below us is the highest mountain in the country: the Great Mount Ararat. While we may never know where the Garden of Eden bloomed on Earth, or where the first Tigris and Euphrates rivers once coursed, Turkey's Mount Ararat is the very first geographical place referred to in the Bible that we can locate today with any degree of certainty. Mount Ararat is the location the Bible records as the resting place of Noah's Ark after the Global Flood. Genesis 8:4 reads, *"In the seventh month, on the seventeenth day of the month, the ark rested upon the mountains of Ararat."*

Mount Ararat is known in Turkey as *Aghri Dagh*, which means the Mount of the Ark. Rising up near Turkey's border with the neighboring country of Iran, the Iranian call the mountain *Koh-I-Nuh*, meaning the Mountain of Noah. *Photo courtesy of allaboutturkey.com*

Now, strain your eyes for a glimpse of ancient wooden beams. Very recent pictures of Mount Ararat taken from a satellite in space have discovered an ark-like shape submerged in the ice and snow. The description in the Book of Genesis tells us the ark was six times longer than wide (300 cubits by 50 cubits). The irregular shape seen in the satellite photographs of Mount Ararat is very similar to that 6:1 proportion! Perhaps the space pictures have merely captured an image of an unusual rock formation—or maybe we are very close to uncovering Noah's ark after all this time!

The children who live today at the base of the looming, volcanic Mount Ararat, in the village of Dogubayazit, tell visitors that they indeed live in Noah's countryside. (Can you imagine saying that?) For down through the ages, fathers and mothers in this region of Turkey have gathered children on their knees to tell them the story of Noah and the ark with its cargo of antelopes and gorillas and butterflies and flamingos, and all the other marvels of the animal kingdom, perched high atop Ararat. This story of God's goodness and His love for Noah—and of all humanity—leaves the Turkish children of today, living in the shadow of the mountain, to exclaim all good things as being the "the luck of Noah!" I think Noah would rather call such good things the "Grace of God!"

Lake Van is Turkey's largest lake. Fed by sulfur springs, the lake is very salty, making the water unusable for drinking or farming. Would you be surprised to see a cat swimming here?

At home on my childhood farm, we marveled at the grace of God experienced by our barnyard cats. Incredibly, those cats survived all manner of near scrapes and accidents. Our travels now take us to a strange occurrence that is far more incredible than nine-lived farm cats. It is a glorious feat of our Creator God!

South of Turkey's highest mountain, Mount Ararat, we find Turkey's largest and deepest lake, the triangular-shaped Lake Van. It's not surprising that few cities dot this desolate region of Turkey; yet it is unusual to find so few cities surrounding an all-important water source. That is because Lake Van is one very salty body of water and salty water does little to help thirsty animals or crops in the fields. Since Lake Van is fed by **sulfur** springs and has no apparent outlet to flow into, it keeps growing saltier and saltier! In the chill of winter, you won't find any ice skaters on Lake Van as you would at many frozen lakes. Although the winters in this part of Turkey are bitterly cold, the high salt content keeps the lake from freezing.

However, if you squint your eyes, you may catch a glimpse of something that is most startling and incredible here at Lake Van. Look closely and you may see a white and red-haired cat swimming down there among the islands. Known as the Swimming Cat, or named a *van kedi* in Turk, Van cats, as they are called, are one of the rarest breeds of cats in the world. In this region of temperature extremes, you may never see skaters on a blustery winter day, yet the relentless summer heat may allow one to witness Van cats cooling off with a dip in the salty Lake Van water. Yes, a cat that likes to swim!! Our God is a God of surprises! While other cats have three types of hair, God especially created the Van cat with only one type of hair, which feels like soft cashmere or rabbit fur that dries quickly when wet—which is especially beneficial if you are a swimming cat with an unusual love for water! When the bitter winter descends in this region of Turkey, the Van cats grow a thick coat to withstand the harsh weather. If a Van cat down there in the lake turns to catch a glimpse of you up on your carpet, you'll never forget its gaze—for a Van kedi has one amber eye—and one blue eye! Our incredible Creator God has created a cat with a penchant for swimming—and an astonishing, unforgettable set of

The beautiful and unusual *van kedi* has bi-colored eyes.
Photo courtesy of allaboutturkey.com

two-colored eyes. Such multi-colored creation sets us in mind of the rainbow that God once arched across this Turkish sky and Noah's Ark up on Mount Ararat, doesn't it?

The village of Haran, where Abraham and his family once lived, still has beehive-shaped mud houses, just as it would have thousands of years ago. *Photo courtesy of holylandphotos.org*

Slipping further south now, deep down into the Turkish Mesopotamia, we gaze down on the treeless plateau. A dark haired boy and his father herd a flock of Angora sheep to a muddy waterhole for a drink outside a small rural village. A mother wearing a white hair kerchief walks down a dusty dirt street with a baby propped on her hip. This is Haran, one of the oldest continuously inhabited places on Earth—and the home of Abraham. God's word reads *"Terah took his son Abram, his grandson, Lot, son of Haran, and his daughter-in-law, Sarai, the wife of his son Abram...to Haran [and] they settled there"* (Genesis 11:31). Abraham's address once read: Abraham: Haran, Turkey.

At one time the junction of the Damascus road and the highway between Nineveh and Carchemish, Haran was also the place where Abraham's father, Terah died, (Genesis 11:32), where God spoke to Abraham about following Him to a promised land, where Rebekah's brother, Laban once had his home (Genesis 27:43), and where Jacob fled to escape the fury of his brother, Esau (Gen 27:41-43). In captivating Turkey, children like you live today where Noah first climbed from the ark and walk on the same dirt streets of Haran where Abraham and his descendants once walked with their flocks!

As you look across the landscape from Haran, you will see rolling hills, horse-drawn carts, goats, and sheep, and girls in brightly colored dresses, their hair covered in scarves. (Some say there may now be more farm animals than people in Haran!) What you won't see in Haran are trees. Without trees, you will not find any houses built of wood. So, how do the families of Haran build their homes? It is thought that for at least the last 3,000 years houses in Haran have been built the same way: out of the dirt of the Earth. People use what God has given them where they live, to build their homes and make a living. Without trees, people make houses of mud!

These beehive houses stay cool in summer and warm in winter. Some houses even have electricity and cable television! *Photo courtesy of holylandphotos.org*

As a kid, I made mud pies, mud balls, mud cakes, but never mud houses! The mud houses of Haran are the most memorable houses you may ever see. Not square, not with flat roofs, or with peaked roofs, but like...beehives! For thousands of years the mud houses of Haran have been built like beehives with conical roofs. These homes seem to be an extension of the land they are settled on, growing right up out of the dirt. Why do the people of Haran build such seemingly strange houses?

Again, the geography of a place determines how people live: Haran is very hot in summer and cold in winter—and these beehive-shaped homes stay cool in summer and warmer in winter. Do not be fooled by the rustic appearances, however. These mud houses have electricity and some even have cable television! If we stepped out of the beating sun of Haran's streets and into the cool shade of a bee-hive house, we would find Turkish carpets hanging on the walls, and laying on the floors. We could sit as Turks traditionally sit, on pillows on the carpet, and share with this family a simple lunch: a hunk of cheese made from sheep's milk, a few slices of salami with **pide**, a broad, round and flat kind of bread made of wheat, washed down with the traditional Turkish drink, **ayran**, made of yoghurt and water. (If you were to walk into a McDonald's in Istanbul, you could order ayran alongside your Big Mac! Or you could also order the Turks other favorite drink: a coke!)

Care to have an Ayran? In Turkey's rural areas, a host's standard drink for guests is an ayran. "We have come to drink your ayran" say the guests.

Field Notes

What a fascinating ride we've had so far! Are you imagining life in a beehive house as I am? I'm so excited to hear about what you have seen!

Press Record and talk to me...

~ **about Mount Ararat and the ark:** What is that region like today? Has the ark been found? Can you locate Mount Ararat on your map?

~ **about Lake Van:** What is unusual about Lake Van? Why don't more people live around the lake? Can you ice skate there in the winter? Why not? Tell me about the amazing creature that swims in the lake.

~ **about Haran's mud houses:** What do they look like? Why do the people build them in this way? How does geography affect where people live? Who in real life once lived in or passed through Haran? Describe life in Haran today.

After lunch, we swoop further to the West, where we find the bustling city of Tarsus. The Turkish town of Tarsus was once an important sea port on the brilliantly blue Mediterranean sea but because of the **silting** up, Tarsus is now located some 9.3 miles [15 km] away from the lapping waves of the Mediterranean Sea and its sandy beaches. Over time, God's command of the winds and waters actually shapes and changes the geography of this world!

Cleopatra's Gate named for the Egyptian Queen who visited Tarsus around 40 B.C. It is believed that Cleopatra disguised herself as the Greek goddess Aphrodite and sailed through the gate to meet Marc Antony, a Roman leader. The city of Tarsus is also the birthplace of the Apostle Paul. *Photo courtesy of holylandphotos.org*

You may have read of the bustling city of Tarsus before? This city of narrow, cobblestone streets rising up out of the cotton fields of the Mediterranean region of Turkey was the birth place of the Apostle Paul. In Acts 21:39, Paul says, *"I am a Jew of Tarsus in Cilicia, a citizen of no insignificant city."* Tarsus was certainly a significant city, hosting such famous historical figures as Alexander the Great, Cleopatra, Marc Antony, Julius Caesar and Cicero! Leaning over the edge of our carpet, we see Tarsus situated on the edge of a fertile plain, cedar groves surrounding its rising buildings. A **plain** is an expanse of level, or nearly level, land. (Do you remember what we geographers call a plain that rises up out of the landscape like a table? Yes, a plateau or tableland!) In general, plains may be more suitable for farming than elevated plateaus like the Anatolia or steep mountains, such as the rugged Taurus Mountains running like a fence between these narrow Mediterranean coastal plains and the Anatolia. Orange and lemon trees, lush banana trees, and waving fields of wheat and barley grow up out of the rich soil. Rice and cotton are also bountiful where precious water is irrigated upon the land. In the fields where the Apostle Paul once walked, we may now see **combines** harvesting soft white balls of cotton to make **textiles**, fabric and clothing, one of Turkey's most important industries. (One of my favorite pair of cotton pants has a tag reading: Made in Turkey. I'm amazed to think that those pants first began as a cotton plant growing up out of this Turkish dirt!)

As we fly over the Mediterranean coast, white sails wave at us from boats bobbing on the brilliant blue water, and numerous productive farming villages quietly dot the coastline. Dropping closer, strange, bizarre shapes rising up out of the landscape catch our eye…stranger than mud houses, stranger than beehive-shaped houses. We've stumbled into the land of the Fairy Chimneys in the Cappadocia region of the Anatolian Plateau. (Look for Lake Tuz, and the area between Konya and Kayseri on your map of Turkey.)

No bees lived in the beehive houses of Haran, and neither do any fairies live in the Fairy Chimneys of Cappadocia, but if you imagined there were such things as fairies, would they have houses with chimneys like these strange rock formations? Only our imaginative Creator God could have dreamed up anything as fantastic as these cone-shaped rocks in the Cappadocia!

If you've ever worn a cap outside to protect yourself from the sun's beating rays and pelting raindrops, you'll understand a bit of the structure of these unique formations.

God created these strange Fairy Chimneys from the deposits spewed forth from volcanoes on the Anatolian Plateau: first a thick layer of ash fell, then a dust that compressed into a stone called tuff and, lastly, a thin layer of lava that hardened into a sturdy **basalt** stone. Over time, God has allowed the outer layer of basalt to crack, and His winds and waters have weathered and washed away the stone into strange shapes. Finally, He sculpts a fairy chimney when a small cap of the original basalt sits atop a cone of tuff. Like when you don a cap, God leaves a cap atop the cone to protect it from eroding or weathering away. When He eventually sends winds that undercut the cap, the cap falls off the fairy chimney, and the chimney itself soon weathers away into nothing….which, thankfully, does not happen to you when you take off your cap!

Cappadocia's "fairy chimneys" are a popular tourist destination. Made of basalt, these conical structures are shaped by wind and water through a process called erosion.

Ironically, the Fairy Chimneys are in a region of Turkey called Cappadocia—a name which actually has nothing to do with caps but means "the land of beautiful horses." Let's slide off our floating kilim and ride a sleek thoroughbred horse up through what some consider Turkey's most spectacular scenery. If you feel afraid in dark, small places, you may want to stay with our beautiful horse instead of exploring into the shadows of the Fairy Chimneys.

When I was young, my brother, sister and I would head up to the haymow in the barn to make mazes of tunnels and secret rooms dark and deep within the mountain of bales. Riding our horse up through Cappodicia, we would hardly imagine that underneath these mountains and towers of Fairy Chimneys lay tunnels eight levels deep with whole cities of underground rooms!

The Hittites of the Old Testament were the first people to carve into the soft rock of the Fairy Chimneys to create granaries for their grain stores. Geography, how God forms the land, benefits people down through the ages; the constant cool of the dark caves was the perfect temperature to preserve grains. But no one dug out actual houses in which to live in this brittle, tawny-colored tuff until after the time of Jesus, when persecuted Christians sought hiding places from the Roman Empire. In the three hundred years after Jesus, tens of thousands of new Christians carved bedrooms and stables and churches and flourmills into the Fairy Chimneys—and deep down away into massive underground cities. Perhaps as many as 60,000 New Testament Christians lived in the mazes and labyrinths of low twisting passages leading to room upon room: a whole community of people, living deep underground! The Fairy Chimneys became the Christian's chimneys. God had created the geography of the land to provide perfect homes for these new believers. In the hot Turkey summers, these caves and tunnels were a cool relief, and in bitter winters, the Fairy Chimneys and underground cities of Cappodocia provided protection from the winds and cold.

If you'd like to experience what those early Christians felt living in the underground Cappodocian cities, there are Fairy Chimney hotels that will let you even sleep here in an underground room of your own! What do you think that would be like?

The Fairy Chimneys with their "caps." In this same region are amazing underground cities, originally developed by the ancient Hittites.

Before we check in for the night, let's sail a bit further north into the Central Anatolian Plateau to Tuz Golu, where you will see a sight that simply must not be missed. As the sun is setting pink in the sky, do you notice the lake below, gleaming with its own hues of white and pink? If you could speak Turkish, you'd know that Tuz means "salt" and Golu means "lake." Tuz Golu is Turkey's second largest lake, after Lake Van, but it is one of the largest salt lakes in the world! Lake Tuz is fed by salt springs and, with no drainage outlet, the salt content keeps increasing as water evaporates, leaving the salt behind. While saltier than Lake Van,

it is much shallower, with a depth of only 3-6 feet [1-2 m]. In the summer, the sun's heat evaporates much of the water making it possible to walk across the whole lake, hardly getting your legs wet! Don't forget your shoes though; otherwise you'll spend your day shrieking "Ow! Ow! Ouch!" as those sharp, hard salt crystals poke at the bottom of your feet. Because it is not very deep, the salt crystals caked to the bottom of the lakebed gleam a brilliant white, making Tuz Golu look like a huge salt pan—with a pink haze hanging over it. The haze comes from particular pink **algae** that grow in this water, the only life that can live under such salty conditions. People however, do live near Lake Tuz, working in mines to process most of the salt that is used in Turkey. God's

imaginative geography not only creates beauty—like that glorious pink hue of Tuz Golu mirroring the brilliance of the sunset— but also provides families and peoples with the resources necessary for living—from the time of Noah, to today.

From the dizzying heights of Mount Ararat, to the dark depths of underground cities and houses carved into the rock of Fairy Chimneys, Turkey is the home of new beginnings. Stepping out on Mount Ararat, Noah and his family begin a new life in the new world after the Global Flood. From his mud, beehive-shaped house in Haran, Old Testament Abraham made a new start in his quest after God. Setting out from his coastal village of Tarsus, New Testament Apostle Paul brought a new religion of hope to ears that had never heard. And deep within the Fairy Chimneys of Cappadocia, early Christians hid from old

Doesn't our view from a spacecraft window clearly show how Lake Tuz is like a salt pan? Two major rivers, groundwater, and surface water feed Lake Tuz, but the lake has no drainage outlet. The lake becomes very salty during the summer with most of water in the lake drying up, leaving an average of a foot [30 cm] thick salt layer! Three mines near the lake process and refine the salt for people to use. *Photo courtesy of visibleearth.nasa.gov*

powers and ways to grow a strong faith in a world after Jesus. With such fascinating stories, who wouldn't pull down their heart-shaped, Made-in-Turkey plate, and feel a genuine love for the country of Turkey—and He who created it all, our Glorious God?!

Field Notes

Weren't those Fairy Chimneys amazing? I'm not sure I'd want to sleep underground though. Would you? I'm ready to hear all about your trip!

Press record and talk to me...

~ about Tarsus and the Mediterranean coastal plains: What is a plain? What crops grow in this region? Which Apostle was born in Tarsus? Can you name any other famous people who visited there? How has God changed the geography of Tarsus over time?

~ about the Fairy Chimneys: Describe one to me. How does God form a Fairy Chimney? Can you name the region in which they are found? Tell me about the underground cities. Who lived there? Why?

~ about Toz Golu: What color is it? Why? What other unusual characteristics does the lake have? Why do people live near Toz Golu? Tell me about salt. Take me on an imaginary walk across the lake.

Travel Log

Using your globe or atlas, let's add the following locations to your map of Turkey. We've seen things today that simply must be mapped, so that they will never be forgotten!

Don't worry about making a perfect map, just do your best. Drawing the basic shape yourself will help you remember it better. Or you can use the map provided for you on the CD-ROM.

Map Notes: Let's record the locations of:

- **Mt. Ararat**
- **Lake Van**
- **Haran**

- **Tarsus**
- **Cappadocia**
- **Tuz Golu**

If you'd like, draw pictures or symbols on your map representing:

> **The Ark** *(perched right on top of Mt. Ararat)*
> **Van kedis or Van cats** *(swimming in Lake Van!)*
> **Beehive houses**
> **Fairy chimneys**
> **Crops growing on the coastal plains** *(there are a lot to choose from, just pick a couple of your favorites)*
> **Underground cities**
> **Salt shaker** *(on the shallow Lake Tuz)*

(Challenge Mapping: Can you point out the following regions on your map: Black Sea Region, Central Anatolian Region, And Mediterranean Region)

Travel Notes: Geographers write what they've seen in order to share the adventure with others—and so they can revisit the places in their memories! **On the next page of your travel log, record three important sights you want to remember from your tales of Turkey.**

~art ~books ~food ~music ~poetry

. . . .

Bringing It Home

Simple ideas to bring the world to your door

Books

The Hungry Coat *by* Demi

In this Turkish folk tale, Nasrettin Hoca (a medieval philosopher and folk hero) finds his friends treat him differently when he is wearing an old coat and decides to teach them a funny lesson. *all ages*

The Tigris and Euphrates Rivers *by* Melissa Whitcraft

Follow the Tigris and Euphrates through the Middle East, learning history and geography along the way. **Read aloud or older readers*

Turkey *by* Tamra Orr

Take an indepth look at Turkey's history, peoples and places. **Read aloud or older readers*

Poetry

The aim in learning is
To understand God's Truth.
Because without knowledge
It is wasted hard labour.   ~Yunus Emre (1238-1320)

(Yunus Emre was a thirteenth century whirling dervish from Anatolia.)

Wandering and Wrestling, Whirling and Worshiping

Turkey ~ Part 3~

Izmir is the third largest city in Turkey. First built around 3,000 years ago, its ancient name was Smyrna. Revelation 2:8 reads: *"And unto the angel of the church in Smyrna write..."* The last book of the Bible is speaking about the church in this very city!

Not far from where I live stands a town with a church, a post office and store fronts. You can park anywhere you'd like and you won't find any of the sidewalks crowded. That's because no one lives in the town anymore. That grey, dilapidated town, no more than an empty shell of lonely buildings, is called a ghost town. But really, not even ghosts live there!

Today is the perfect day to hop on our floating *kilim* and wander through a Turkish ghost town—one that thousands of people visit every day!

Kindly navigate our carpet up the Aegean Coast of Turkey, where waves lap warm on the coastline. (Can you locate the Aegean Coast of Turkey on your map?) The many cities along the Aegean, like the bustling Izmir, (Can you find Izmir?) are hard at work, manufacturing clothing and cars. Vineyards and groves of olive trees flourish in the sunshine. From our carpet seats, we can certainly agree with the historian Herodutus who wrote that the Aegean Region of Turkey has "the most beautiful skies and the best climate in the world."

In the midst of the cities, towns and peoples of the Aegean coast stands Turkey's most famous ghost town: Ephesus. No one lives or sleeps or works in Ephesus, but Ephesus' streets swarm with people: tourists and explorers like you and me! For this abandoned town of Ephesus is a town like none other. Ephesus was built **2,000** years before Jesus was born. And a hundred years after Jesus ascended into heaven, Ephesus was a city of nearly a half million people!

After Jesus returned to heaven, his mother Mary and the Apostle John are believed to have come and lived here in Ephesus. Did you know that you probably have a letter in your house that was written to the people who once lived in Ephesus? No, your mailperson did not mistakenly deliver the letter to your house. Open up your Bible and you'll find that letter! Remember the Apostle Paul who was born in the Turkish

The **Library of Celsus** contained approximately 15,000 scrolls. It was built 110 A.D. to honor Celsus Polemeanus, a Roman senator, who was buried beneath the library floor.
Photo courtesy of holylandphotos.org

25

city of Tarsus? In 50 B.C. he wrote a letter to the Christians in Ephesus. His letter is in your Bible as the book of Ephesians—for that is what the hundreds of thousands of people who lived in Ephesus were called. Paul actually came to live in the city for awhile and during that time, wrote another letter you'll find in your Bible: 1ˢᵗ Corinthians. If you turned to the last book of the Bible, Revelation, you'll read how an angel spoke to the Apostle John, saying, "*Write in a book what you see, and send it to the seven churches: to Ephesus and to Smyrna and to Pergamum and to Thyatira and to Sardis and to Philadelphia and to Laodicea*" (Rev. 1:11). Every single one of those seven churches spoken of by the angel were once located in the country we now call Turkey! And did you take note of the first church mentioned? Yes, the church of Ephesus!

In these old stone walls of Ephesus we will not find a church building, but oh, the buildings we do find! For wandering through ruins, Ephesus is better than Rome itself!

The library in my hometown is a simple, one-story building, but the library of Ephesus' towers three stories high. Standing in front of this stone structure and its reaching columns, we can almost imagine the librarian from 2,000 years ago, handing out scrolls to inquiring readers, and Ephesians sitting in the reading rooms facing towards the East. Can you guess why the library reading room faces to the East? Yes, so that the rising morning sun might stream in and light those darkened rooms. God's design of Earth determines the details of our lives.

Just a short walk from the Ephesian library is Ephesus' amphitheater. A dramatic sight to behold, the theater in Ephesus took 60 years of digging to create more than 25,000 stone slab seats for people to sit on and behold spectacular plays! Though no one lives in Ephesus any more, tourists and visitors still arrive in hordes to see live plays performed on the same stage where the Apostle Paul himself once spoke out against the worship of false idols.

All that remains of the Temple of Artemis is a lone marble column (located in the foreground of this picture). Archaeologists have found evidence that the Temple was destroyed and rebuilt at least four times.
Photo courtesy of holylandphotos.org

Ephesus was indeed a city of idol worship. The Ephesians built a temple to the false goddess Diana, the Temple of Artemis, which was one of the Seven Wonders of the Ancient World. A man named Anitpater who stood before this Ephesian Temple of Artemis over 2,000 years ago exclaimed, "When I saw the house of Artemis that mounted to the clouds, those other [Seven Wonders of the World] lost their brilliancy, and I said, "Lo, apart from Olympus, the Sun never looked on aught so grand!" The Apostle Paul obviously cared little for the Temple's status as one of the Seven Wonders, and from the stage of the Ephesian theater he "*persuaded and turned away a considerable number of people [from the worship of the false goddess Diana], saying that gods made with hands are no gods at all!*" (Acts 19:26)

Today, as we peer down at where the splendid Temple of Artemis once stood, a brilliant Wonder of the Ancient World, we see not much of anything at all. One lone column rising out of the marshland is all that remains of the monumental building; the first in the world to be constructed entirely of marble. The Apostle Paul was right, wasn't he? Diana's temple has been reduced from a celebrated Wonder of the world to one disappointing stone column. The truth of God still stands: *"Heaven and earth may pass away, but my Word will never pass away."* Only stones and ruins now testify to this once bustling Turkish city. As you leave Turkey's most famous vacant town, think on how *"all the gods of the peoples are idols, But the LORD made the heavens"* (1 Chron. 16:26).

Field Notes

A ghost town, a library and a theater…Oh, do tell me all about the wondrous sights you've just seen! **Press Record and talk to me…**

~ **about the Aegean Sea Region**: Where do we find this region in Turkey? What city do we find in this area? Describe some of the sights of this region. What is produced in this area of Turkey?

~ **about Ephesus**: The Apostle Paul wrote a letter to the people of Ephesus. If we wanted to read that letter today, where would we look? What would it be like to visit Ephesus today—and how is it different than it once was? What was the library once like? And what is it like today? How was Ephesus' amphitheater built? Does it look the same today? Tell me about the Temple of Artemis. What do we read about this temple in God's Word? What remains of this Wonder of the Ancient World today?

Turkish oil wrestling, called Yagli Gures (literally, "oiled wrestling,") dates back to the 1600's. Wearing tight short leather trousers called "Kispet," wrestlers cover themselves, and their heavy shorts made of water buffalo leather, with olive oil. What do you think that feels like? *Photo courtesy of allaboutturkey.com*

When I was young, a memorable Sunday School picnic game was to slather a pig in oil and compete to be the first to cleverly wrestle down the slippery, fast-as lightning hog. Any Turkish child could have outwitted us for Turks know all about wrestling and oil and they do it like no other peoples you've ever seen!

A long time ago, to protect themselves from the mosquitoes on the Anatolian plain, Turks slathered themselves with olive oil. When a dispute broke out, they often ended up "oil wrestling!" Today, dressed in short leather trousers made from the heavy hide of water buffalo, young boys, not just from here in the Aegean, but from all over Turkey, learn the art of wrestling by apprenticing under the tutelage of a master oil-wrestler.

As if watching the spectacle of oiled men glistening in the sun as they wrestle each other for 40 minutes weren't surprising enough, here in the city of Selcuk, not far from the once grand Ephesus, you may see the butting heads and wrestling of elaborately dressed camels! Milky saliva runs from the mouth and nostrils of the excited camels which aggressively lean on each other until one gives in and charges off into the crowd! Watch out! Spectators hurriedly scramble out of the way of nearly 1 ton [1,000 kilogram] charging camels!

Camel wrestling is more for fun than for sport. The camels are elaborately dressed and their owners have great fun bragging about the strength of their animals. Part of the fun for the crowd is racing to get out of the way of a runaway camel!

A day of oil and camel wrestling may be very entertaining, but I think Turkey's Children Day may be the most amusing day of all for Turkish children. I knew a little boy who often asked, "If Mother's Day is in May and Father's Day is in June, when is Children's Day?" In Turkey, Children's Day is celebrated every year on April 23rd with a holiday off school, candies and treats, and week-long festivities! Children, dressed in brilliant costumes, perform their traditional dances and parades in huge stadiums for the whole country to observe! Other children from around the world even travel to Turkey for Children's Day to represent their own cultures alongside the Turks. Turkish parents and grandparents gather around their television sets to watch these colorful performances of children from different countries all over God's globe!

An Islamic mosque in Turkey. Notice the tall minaret where the muezzin calls the faithful to pray. How is this building different or the same as where you gather to worship?

Have you ever dreamed of becoming the President of your country? On Children's Day, Turkish children get to do just that. The President, Prime Minister, and provincial governors gather in Turkey's capital, the city of Ankara, on the Anatolia (can you find that on your map?), and allow children to govern the country for the day! What worthwhile endeavors would you undertake if you were made President of Turkey on Children's Day? Today's children are indeed the future governors of their countries. May you grow to be a man or a woman with a voice to help your *"nation come and worship before Lord, and glorify [His] name"* (Ps 86:9)!

Nearly all the peoples of Turkey follow the teachings of the Qu'uran, written by Muhammed, the founder of the religion of **Islam**. As Muslims, Turks worship in buildings called **mosques**. Early in the morning darkness, from all over the country of Turkey, men called **muezzins** climb the mosque's towers, or **minarets**, and shatter the stillness of dawn with the loud song, *"Hayya-la-l-faleahHayya la-l-faleah."* Having heard the Call to Prayer, called the *"Athan,"* Turks rub sleep from their eyes, kneel down on their prayer mats and offer up prayers to **Allah**, whom they worship. The name Islam actually means "submission to Allah," which Muslims believe they do by practicing the Five Pillars of Islam.

A faithful Muslim believes and practices these five pillars or five core beliefs:

1. Allah alone is worthy of worship and Muhammad is Allah's Prophet.
2. Pray five times daily.
3. Care and give to the poor.
4. Purify through fasting.
5. If at all possible, make the pilgrimage to the city of Mecca once during one's life.

A Turkish worshipper at an Islamic mosque. Notice that the man has removed his shoes before kneeling to pray.

Turkish Muslims also believe that submitting to Allah includes refusal to eat pork (which is why you will find many wild hogs in some regions of Turkey). During the month-long celebration of **Ramadan**, Turkish Muslims also fast every day from sunrise to sunset. But don't fret: at the close of the fast of Ramadan, they celebrate **Seker Bayrami**, meaning the Sweet Fest in Turkish, when they feast for three grand days on chocolates and candies!

Have you ever known a little girl who loved to wear a dress that whirled gloriously about her if she twirled around and around and around? That kind of whirling and twirling is exactly what we will see if we turn our Turkish kilim back to where we began, Istanbul, and into the only Muslim Dervish lodge in the city. The word **Dervish** refers to a certain group of Muslims who are known for their simple lifestyles and indifference to material possessions. One group of these Muslim Dervishes in Turkey, called the Whirling Dervishes, tries to meditate through a spinning dance - and if we hustle into the Dervish lodge with the other tourists, we may catch a glimpse of the whirling Dervishes and their seven centuries-old tradition of twirling! The beat of the drum and the melody of the reed flute fill the large room. Cloaked in long white robes, tall brown hats perched on their heads, the men spin round and round with their arms crossed. Spinning faster, their bell-like skirts unfurl, their arms rising up. The rush of the Whirling Dervishes, their skirts billowing, is like a gust of wind blowing through the hall, sweeping us up.

The Dervishes' effortless-looking spinning comes with much practice. Spinning for a quarter hour at a time to the drone of ancient Islamic hymns, the dervishes whirling is a prayer trance to Allah.

Photo courtesy of allaboutturkey.com

Marveling at the spinning rotation of the circling dancers, one question begs an answer: how do they do whirl like that and not fall over with dizziness? The answer lies in the black shoes under their floating white skirts: for years they carefully practice the work of keeping their right foot planted on the floor as their left foot pumps them counterclockwise. After the ceremony closes, a Dervish turns to us and proclaims, "If Islam is the main body of the [Turkish] tree, we are the flower on that tree." Let us say goodbye and leave the whirling Dervishes to their bell-like

Don't you think the Church of the Hagia Sophia (meaning Church of Divine Wisdom in Greek) is beautiful under this fresh powdering of snow? Considered the finest example of Byzantine architecture in the world, the church was constructed by the Emperor Justinian in 537 A.D. With a force of 10,000 workers, the dome atop the church of Hagia Sophia was built in record time: it took just five years, ten months, and four days to complete! Today, it is the fourth largest cathedral in the world. *Photo courtesy of allaboutturkey.com*

blooming and sweep over to one of the most magnificent buildings ever built!

From our carpet's edge, gaze down there past the children playing in the fountain, past the street vendors selling postcards, to what is sometimes referred to as the eighth Wonder of the World, the Church of the Holy Wisdom. This church, or the **Hagia Sophia** (*hagia* meaning "divine" or "holy" and *sophia* meaning "wisdom"), was a church built more than 1,500 years ago but is today one of the most popular sights to see in all of Turkey. No wonder, considering the 30 million tiny gold tiles decorating its interior, and its immense, flat dome that still leaves architects scratching their heads in wonder.

Hagia Sophia was ordered built by the Christian Emperor of the Holy Roman Empire, Justinian, in 537 A.D. If we leave our kilim outside and step into the cool, dim oasis inside, we are taken by this magnificent dome hovering 180 ft [54 m] in the air over us. The forty windows that circle the dome's base make it seem as if the dome is floating, as if heaven has descended upon us, like a magnificent umbrella held above an open room, light entering all around. When Emperor Justinian first stood in this breathtaking space, on a Christmas night, he is said to have whispered, "Glory to God that I have been judged worthy of such a work. Oh Solomon! I have surpassed thee!"

On the very same spot, almost one thousand years later, Mehmet the Conqueror, who had just captured Constantinople (what we now call Istanbul) from the Christians, ordered that the great Church of the Holy Wisdom no longer be a place of Christian worship to God, but become a Muslim mosque. This explains why the Church of the Holy Wisdom today has 4 slender minarets at her corners, each once used to call Muslim Turks to daily prayer. Muslims were so intrigued by the beauty of this Christian church that many of their mosques the world over are patterned after the Church of the Holy Wisdom. Neither Christians nor Muslims worship here now for today the Hagia Sophia is a museum for visitors and explorers to come from all over the world and wonder in its age, its colored history and its spectacular architecture.

We've wandered and wrestled and whirled and worshiped our way around Turkey, from Istanbul by the Bosphorus, up through the wet, verdant Black Sea Region, and across the Eastern Anatolia (with the Tigris and Euphrates Rivers and Mount Ararat). Then down we swooped through Southern Anatolia (can you remember who once lived in this region in his mud beehive?), and over into the Mediterranean coastal

The interior of the Hagia Sophia is known for its colorful, light-enhanced beauty. With the light streaming in from the forty windows around its dome, doesn't it create the illusion that the dome actually floats over the church?

plain (with cotton now growing where Paul once lived). Next we sailed up into the Central Anatolia and Cappadocia (what strange place did we visit here?) and over into the Aegean sea region (with Izmir and Ephesus, and wrestling and warm breezes), only to return back to teeming Istanbul with its whirling Dervishes and breathtaking, world-renowned Church of the Holy Wisdom. What a whirlwind trip of Turkey! Are you out of breath? Let's return our kilim to the Grand Bazaar and Ahmet. The memories of Turkey we've netted with our keen eyes and vibrant faith, will always be ours.

Field Notes

Don't you find Turkey an amazing country of the most unusual sights?! Let's record every detail of our unforgettable trip!

Press Record and talk to me...

~ **about oil and camel wrestling**:
In which region of Turkey would we find such an event? Tell me about the experience!

~ **about Children's Day**: What special privilege does the President give to children on this day? What other privileges do the children experience? What is the name of the capital city of Turkey and in which region is it found?

~ **about the Whirling Dervishes**: Where in Turkey would we see the whirling Dervishes? What do they wear? How do they keep from falling? Why do they whirl?

~ **about the Hagia Sophia**: In what city will we find the grand building ? What does it look like? Tell me about Emperor Justinian.

Travel Log

Using your globe or atlas, let's finish your map of Turkey.

We've seen things today that simply must be mapped, never to be forgotten!

Map Notes: Let's record the locations of:

- *Ephesus*
- *Izmir*
- *Selcuk*

If you'd like, draw pictures or symbols on your map representing:

- *A Dervish Lodge* (perhaps a whirling circle to represent the spinning dance?)
- *Hagia Sophia* (a great dome?)
- *Camel-wrestling* (with their colorful costumes?)
- *Ephesian library* (maybe a scroll?)
- *Ephesian ampitheatre* (how about a cheering crowd?)
- *Temple of Artemis* (one lone pillar?)

Travel Notes: Geographers write what they've seen in order to share the adventure with others—and so they can revisit the places in their memories! **On the next page of your travel log, record three important sights you want to remember from your tales of Turkey.**

~art ~books ~food ~music ~poetry
. . . .

Bringing It Home
Simple ideas to bring the world to your door

Food

~ The Turks love their tea!

Turkish tea, *çay* (CHAH-yee) is brewed in a **samovar** (a metal urn with a spigot) and served boiling hot. It is a beautiful red-tinted tea that looks lovely served in the traditional tulip-shaped glasses.

Let's brew a pot and imagine we are relaxing on our kilim with our Turkish friends. If you want, spread a rug or tablecloth on the floor and gather pillows and cushions to sit on.

- Bring a kettle of water to a boil and brew your tea. (Use tea bags or loose tea.) The Turks allow their tea to steep for 10 – 15 minutes, so wait patiently!
  When you are ready, fill your cup half way with the strong, dark tea and fill the rest of the cup with hot water. You may have your tea **açik** (ah-CHUK) weak, or **koyu** (koh-YOO) dark.
- Serve with sugar and lemon (if desired) – but no milk! Our Turkish friends would not approve!
- Enjoy!

Dessert always goes well with tea. Perhaps you might like to make some Turkish Delight or Noah's Pudding?

Turkish Delight

Known in Turkey as **Rahat lokhoum,** the name of this irresistible sweet comes from an Arabic phrase that translates "soothing to the throat." Do you think you may be like C.S. Lewis's Edmund who *"thought only of trying to shovel down as much Turkish delight as he could, and the more he ate, the more he wanted?"* That is exactly how the first taste-testers experienced Turkish Delight! This is the legend:

More than 300 years ago, a Turkish Sultan living in the Instanbul palace of Topkapi ordered the greatest candy makers in Turkey to create a dessert so mouth-watering that the members of his household would cease squabbling as they were savoring the delectable dessert. Candy maker Hadji Bekir looked around his home in the Anatolian mountain town of Kastamonu and concocted a simple recipe that the Sultan couldn't resist—and neither will you!

2 cups Sugar
2 Tbl Cornstarch
1 cup Water
1/2 tsp Cream of tartar
1 Tbl flavoring (extract) (such as lemon, orange, rose)

Food coloring (appropriate to flavor, such as yellow for lemon)
1/2 cup toasted almonds or pistachios, chopped
Confectioners' sugar

Dissolve sugar and cornstarch in water and add cream of tartar. Bring to a boil and heat to 220 degrees F. [104 C] (Use a candy thermometer to check the temperature.) Cover the pot during the last 5 minutes of cooking. Add flavor and food coloring, then nuts.

Grease a shallow pan. Pour candy into prepared pan. When cool, cut into squares and roll in sifted powdered sugar. Store in plastic bag.

Noah's Pudding

Also known as Asure, this is one of the best-known desserts in Turkey. Traditionally shared with friends and family, we invite you to serve up bowls of Noah's pudding while recounting unforgettable stories about a man, a mountain in Turkey and a marvelous promise God wrote all over the sky!

1 cup barley
1 cup canned white kidney beans, washed and drained
1 cup canned chickpeas, washed and drained
1 cup sugar
1 tsp vanilla extract

10 cups water
10 dried apricots, soaked in water overnight, cut in pieces
10 dried figs, cut in pieces
1/2 cup raisins

Garnish:
1/4 cup walnuts, crumbled

Place 4 cups of water and barley in a large pot over high heat. Bring to a boil. Immediately, turn heat down to medium-low and cook for approximately 30 minutes. Add beans, chickpeas, vanilla, apricots, raisins, figs, sugar and 6 cups of hot water. Cook another 45 minutes on medium-low, stirring occasionally. Pour into a large bowl and let cool. Keep refrigerated. When serving, garnish with crumbled walnuts.

Go into all the world...

a walk of prayer

As we've journeyed through Turkey we've caught a glimpse of an amazing landscape, and customs and lifestyles that are different from our own. Yet the boys and girls who live there are not so different from us at all. They were created by a God who loves them dearly—just as He loves you.

Will you and your family join me in praying for the Turkish people?

Lord, give us Your love for the peoples of the world, and help our family to live in a way that shows our love for them.

Father, we remember the **earthquakes that devastated northern Turkey** near Istanbul in 1999, leaving many dead and many more homeless. You, Father, know how the country and families are still suffering the effects of these earthquakes. Lord God, provide for these mothers and fathers and children who still need help and homes.

~We pray too, Lord, for the **Kurds**, thought to be descendants of Biblical Medes (Dan. 5,6), that large people group living throughout the Middle East and comprising a significant portion of the Turkish population. They have no homeland of their own and have faced persecution in many different countries. How we pray for the Kurdish people to know peace. We pray that they will be protected from persecution. Lord, show Christian workers in Turkey how to show Jesus' love to the Kurds.

~We uphold **Turkish Christians** before Your throne. We pray that You will strengthen them to follow the Lord, and You will grant them access to Bibles. Please bring other Christians to Turkey to fellowship and worship with these believers.

~There are hardly any **Christian witnesses** in Turkey. God, please raise up **pastors** who will lead Turkish Christians; provide for their needs and strengthen their faith. Give them Your wisdom to teach the Word of God.

We love you, Lord, and the people who are living in Turkey, today. May the Light of our Savior dawn over all nations today. Draw us all closer to You, Father. In Jesus name, Amen.

We dance with these Turkish folk dancers. **"*Let all the inhabitants of the world stand in awe of Him*" Ps. 33:8.**

The Land of Milk and Honey

Israel ~ Part 1 ~

On a farm not far from here, I know a boy named Ivan who rises early in the beginning dark of day, and treads out to the barn with his Father and brothers to milk their herd of goats. After the streams of warm goat's milk have been collected into the large tank, Ivan tends to the beehives, gathering pails of sweet, sticky honey. Carrying a pail of honey in one hand, and a pail of milk in the other, Ivan slowly walks to the house with the bounty of his family's farm. It is almost as if Ivan's farm actually flows with milk and honey.

The Bible tells of another such country: *"On that day I swore to them that I would bring them…into a land…flowing with milk and honey, the most beautiful of all lands"* (Ezekiel 20:6). I wonder what Abraham and his family imagined in their minds' eyes when God forever promised them this land? While the Bible speaks figuratively of this land flowing with milk and honey, I always literally envisioned a land of rivers coursing with foamy, white milk, meadows humming with the buzz of bees, and fields awash with golden, gooey honey.

Think of it: this land is the most beautiful of all lands. Who can resist traveling to the most breathtaking, most picturesque, most scenic land on this spinning orb? I can hardly wait!

Our search takes us to the center of the world. If you place your finger on the Mediterranean Sea and then slide due east, you will find the country we seek: Israel. Not only is Israel literally in the "middle" of the world, near the **convergence**, or meeting, of the three **continents** of Asia, Africa and Europe, but Israel is also in the center of the world's news almost every day. If you read today's national newspapers — or yesterday's — or tomorrow's — you will invariably read some news about Israel. The land flowing with God's blessings is a sought after land for which the peoples and powers of the world continue to wrestle. Israel also lies at the heart of three of the world's most noted religions: **Christianity, Judaism** and **Islam**. Each faith claims Israel as their holy land.

The Israeli Flag
The flag shows the Star of David, a traditional Jewish symbol, between two stripes. The lines represent the Jewish prayer shawl. Blue represents the sea, the sky and also God.

While the rising red mountains and deep cut gorges of this land have been here since the beginning of time, the country we call Israel is both very old and very young. Israel grew up as a nation of people over 3,000 years ago when Joshua marched into this strip of land (then called Canaan), with the 12 tribes of Israel. These 12 tribes were the descendants of Jacob, Abraham's grandson, whom God had renamed Israel. We read in the Book of Genesis: *"Your name shall no longer be Jacob, but Israel…"* (Gen.33:28). For over a thousand years, the Israelites

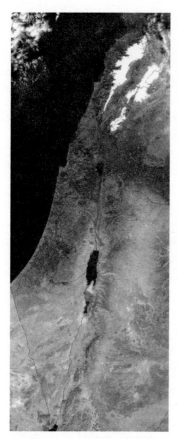

called this land home, herding flocks of sheep on the hillsides, fishing in the Sea of Galilee and harvesting wheat in the valleys. Yet a mere 70 years after the crucifixion of our Lord Jesus Christ, the conquering Romans burnt the Temple at Jerusalem, sending the Israelites fleeing to other countries of the world. The actual land had fallen into the hands of the Romans. The Jewish people no longer governed their own country of Israel. For 1,800 years, if you put your finger on a map of this part of the world, it would not have read the name Israel, but the name "Palestine." Still, in the hearts of the Jewish people scattered around the world, a flame of hope blazed for a revival of their homeland, Israel. Then, in 1948, God made a way for Jewish people dispersed all over the earth to finally return home to this land flowing with milk and honey. As He always does, God has faithfully fulfilled His promise! Nearly 2,000 years later, God has done precisely what He said He would do in the first book of the Bible: *"To your descendants I have given this land"* (Genesis 15:8). This is how Israel is a very old country — and a very young country — at the same time!

Now that you have pinpointed Israel on your map, you'll find this sliver of a country in the shape of a tilted triangle, perched on the eastern edge of the Mediterranean Sea. You probably already knew that God Himself is often symbolized as a triangle, with one tip of the triangle representing God the Father, another God the Son, and another God the Holy Spirit. Now you can remember that Israel is also in the outline of an oddly-shaped triangle!

Nearly 7 million people have made this narrow triangular country of Israel their home. From our view from space what can you determine about Israel's geography? Where do you think Israel grows nearly all the food necessary to feed its people? Does this look like the land of milk and honey? *Photo courtesy of viiibleearth.nasa.gov*

Israel is a rather small country, comparable in size to the state of New Jersey and comprising only about 1% of the land in the Middle East. You could drive right from one tip to the other tip of narrow Israel in an afternoon. Ivan, with his responsibilities of milking goats and tending to the hives can't come with us, but *we* might tour this captivating country and send home some photographs to our hard-working friend. Are you ready to discover the land of Israel and capture the wonder of its four geographical regions: the beautiful Central Hill region, the Coastal Plains, the Negev Desert region, and the Jordan Rift Valley? Focus your eyes of faith, fetch a fine map of Israel, and don't forget your camera!

Our first stop is the Central Hill region. Running like a backbone down the middle of the country, Israel has such an abundance of hills, they are divided into three sections: Galilean, Samarian and Judean. (Can you detect the raised **elevation**, or height, of these hills on a map of Israel? Often a map is shaded a progression of dark greens to indicate land that lies low, shades of browns to signify hills and shades of white or gray to mark mountains.) Israel's northern hills are the rugged, steep Galilean Hills. Wave *"Shalom"* to the shepherd girl herding her flock. As the flock clatters past, we

From the Central Hill Region, we gaze out on the farms in the Jezreel Valley that separates the Galilee Hills of the North from the Samarian Hills in the South. Jezreel means "God will sow" and we see how God has indeed created a fertile region in this valley in the Central Hills Region. *Photo courtesy of holylandphotos.org*

A wadi is a dry riverbed that only fills with water during heavy rain. In this wadi, people have created dams to capture water for irrigation and fertile soil. *Photo courtesy of holylandphotos.org*

snap a picture of the girl waving back with *"Salaam!"* (Won't Ivan appreciate this Galilean photo of goats like his? In spite of the intriguing differences in how we live in different parts of the world, we are surprised at the similarities in our stories!) While the home of shepherds and herders, these Galilean Hills are where our Savior, Jesus Christ, spent most of His life walking. Pull your sweater tight, for it gets windier the higher we climb. Some of the harsh slopes are sparsely vegetated, but fertile valleys often lie between the rolling highlands. Today, as you gaze upon the vineyards and orchards that dot this region, you can almost hear Jesus speaking: *"I am the vine; you are the branches. If a man remains in me and I in him, he will bear much fruit; apart from me you can do nothing"* (John 15:5).

Narrow, cavernous **gorges,** or **wadis,** cut up the Galilean Hills and its vineyards. A wadi is actually a dry, rocky bed for a river. During heavy rains, raging, torrential waters carve through these valleys, transforming them into a seasonal river. When the waters eventually subside, the wadi is once again a gorge with a bottom bed of sand. Line up your camera for a shot of this magnificently carved one. Notice the sandy bottom; doesn't it remind you of Jesus' parable of the foolish man building his house upon the sand—like we find at the bottom of this wadi? In the parable, roaring floodwaters flashed down, sweeping away the foolish man's house! Yet the wise man, who built his house high up on the rock, stood unmoved (Matt. 7:24-27). Jesus used the lay of the land and the geography of Israel to paint pictures of eternal truths!

Heading south now, let's photograph the Samarian Hills. Our photos reveal that the Samarian hills are actually a mountain range, and include the mountain called Mount Carmel. A **mountain,** a landform rising notably above the surrounding countryside, is generally considered to be steeper and higher than a hill. The name Carmel is derived from the Hebrew words: *"Karem El"* which means the vineyards of God. Gazing upon the lush rising slopes of Mount Carmel, we think the name is appropriate! From the Bible passage 1 Kings 18:42 we read, *"But Elijah climbed to the top of Mount Carmel; and fell to the ground and prayed"....(NLT)* for a rain cloud to blow in from the Mediterranean Sea, which you can see from Mt. Carmel's peak, to water the land of Israel. Isn't it amazing to photograph today the geography of long-ago Bible events?

Look at the amount of water rushing through this wadi. I certainly wouldn't want my house built down here! *Photo courtsy of holylandphotos.org*

Can our camera capture the brilliant palette of spring colors painted on the slopes of the third section of hills, the Judean Hills in the south? For hundreds of years, the Judean Hills, home of Jerusalem, Israel's capital city, have burst into a spring blaze of wildflower bloom. Pictures of these

Don't you think Ivan will wonder at this picture of a view out towards Mount Carmel and the Galilean Hills? ~*Photo by permission: Darko Tepert*

hills a few decades ago however, would have looked markedly different. Not so long ago, so many people picked bouquets of wildflowers off the hills each spring, they became bare and nearly colorless! Everyone knows that for a land to flow with honey, the bees need a profusion of flowers. Today Israelis abide by the signs not to pick wildflowers and buy their bouquets in the marketplaces. The Judean hills are once again plush with carpets of red poppies every spring. As we take photographs of wildflowers lightly swaying in the warm breeze, we think of Jesus asking, *"And why do you worry about clothes? See how the lilies of the field grow. They do not labor or spin"* (Matthew 6:28).

One of Jesus' disciples, Peter, wrote that, "For all flesh is as grass, and all the glory of man as the flower of grass. The grass withereth, and the flower thereof falleth away" (1 Pet. 1:24). Do you think he was speaking of a flower like this riotous mass of poppies growing wild in Israel? Actually, the hills above the Jordan River have more different kinds of plant per unit area than any on the whole planet! Israel's landscape of colorful flowers and various plants changes abruptly as we travel from one geographical region to another.

Field Notes

I am so interested in hearing what you think of this "land flowing with milk and honey" so far!

Press record and talk to me:

~ about Israel's beginnings and its peoples :

According to the Bible, how did the Jews come to live in this land? Have they always lived here? How did God keep His promise to the Jewish people? What three major religions consider Israel their Holy Land?

~ **about Israel's location and size**:   What three continents meet near Israel? What shape is the country? How big is it? How long would it take you to drive across the country?

~ **about the Galilean Hills**:   Do you remember who spent a lot of time here? Can you describe the landscape? What grows here?

~ **about wadis**: What is a wadi? What does one look like? What parable does the geography of a wadi remind us of?

~ **about the Samarian Hills**:   Are the Samaritan Hills really "hills"? What Biblical mountain will we find located here?

~ **about the Judean Hills**:   What city is located in this region?   What gives the hills their color in springtime? Can you tell me more about this?

As a young person, I had to remember that a vehicle with wings was spelled P-L-A-N-E while something rather common, like unflavored ice cream, was spelled P-L-A-I-N.   Did you know there is another P-L-A-I-N? Get ready to snap another round of photographs for Ivan at home with his goats and bees!

A plain, in geographical terms, refers to a broad flat expanse of country that lies relatively low. Such a plain is what we finding slipping down Israel's Mediterranean shore. We've arrived in the second geographical region of Israel: the western coastal plain. (**Coastal** refers to the land that runs alongside an ocean or other large body of water.)

Nine months out of the year, Israelis may bask in the warm sun on the beautiful sands of the beaches along the Mediterranean Coast. Can't you almost here the sea gulls calling? But be careful about swimming far out in the waters: unusually strong undertows along the coast can whisk away even a strong swimmer! And if you are going to sunbathe, watch out that you don't get stepped on by an Israeli playing one of their favorite sports: paddleball.

This plain is so *un*plain that it has three names. In the North of Israel, it is called The Plain of Zebulun; in the middle it is referred to as the Plain of Sharon; and in the southern section of the coast, folks call it the Plain of Judea. Did you notice more homes and families in this region than the hill region? Two out of every three people in Israel live here, basking in its inviting Mediterranean climate.   A **Mediterranean Climate** means that summers are relatively dry, winters are generally wet, and the temperature is rather mild and moderate. A large body of water like the Mediterranean Sea regulates the temperature, making it cooler in the summer, and warmer in the winter.

This tower overlooks the beautiful water near Jaffe. Long ago, Jaffe was an important harbor for Israel, but over the years, silt built up along the coastline and eliminated the natural harbor.

No wonder the majority of Israel's families live here amidst the surf-pounded cliffs and holiday resorts. Indeed, the sandy beaches that meet the Mediterranean here are among the most dramatically white and beautiful beaches in the world, certainly worthy of a picture for our farmer boy. Even the dirt of the coastal plain isn't ordinary dirt but rich, fertile soil perfect for farming orange and lemon groves and bountiful crops of wheat. Many small rivers that flow down from the Galilean, Samarian, and Judean Hills, water the coastal plain and its crops of sweet mangos, strawberries and grapefruit.

Hasn't God perfectly orchestrated the geography of Israel? The moisture-laden winds blow off the Mediterranean bringing seasonal rain, and the soil conditions are perfectly suited to growing fruits and vegetables with a distinctive delicious taste. Make sure to get a picture of the strange clear plastic tunnels we see everywhere. If you take a peek inside these light-filled tunnels, you will see flowers and vegetables growing in the warm sunshine. Since Israel experiences little rainfall in summer, these tunnels act like small atmospheric ceilings, or miniature greenhouses, trapping water vapor to fall as droplets again on the crops. Don't you think hard working Ivan would appreciate us bringing him home a juicy coastal plain strawberry?

This flat expanse of plain along the lapping waves of the Mediterranean is also one of the easiest routes for people of countries to the north and south to travel through. As such, through history, this slender coastal plain allowed for neighboring nations passing through to interact with people who knew Yahweh, the One, true Living God. When these people from other lands met those who knew God, they heard stories and saw evidence of His love for His people. This introduced them to the rich gifts of the Lord and brought more of them into God's family. God uses the geography of Israel, as well as the landscape of other countries, to influence the direction of people's lives and the very course of history!

Standing with cameras in hand, looking out at the stunning blue of the Mediterranean, we are taken with the fact that this coastline seems very straight, with relatively few curves or indentations. Because of this, Israel has only one significant natural harbor along its coast for ships to stop. A **natural harbor** is a place with land cupping around on three sides to allow ships to anchor and shelter from the weather. What causes Israel's coast to be relatively straight?

Currents in the Mediterranean Sea carry **silt**, which is a water-transported soil finer than sand. This silt washes up against Israel's coastline, filling in or "silting up" any coast line indentations. Do you recall Jonah of the Bible who, trying to run away from God, *"went down to Joppa* (called Jaffe today), *found a ship which was going to Tarshish,"* (Jonah 1:3) and sailed away? Thought to be founded by Noah's son Japheth, the 4,000 year old city of Jaffe is one of the world's oldest cities and is still a bustling center on Israel's coastline. (Can you locate it just south of Tel Aviv?) However, if Jonah showed up today at Jaffe looking for a ship to escape on, he'd find no harbor on Jaffe's shoreline but a flat little plain instead! The natural harbor that created the port city of Joppa is now entirely silted up!

If we walked north out of Jaffe, we'd walk right into its twin city, Tel Aviv.   More business deals are made here in the tall skyscrapers of Tel Aviv than anywhere else in Israel. Tel Aviv, with its white sands, warm seas and cloudless blue skies, is also the country's most exciting city with many restaurants, dozens of museums and a world-class symphony.   Let's sit for a bit in a Tel Aviv restaurant and refresh with a **felafel** sandwich—Israel's vegetarian hotdog.   Inside our falafel, a warm pita bread made with ground chick peas and spices,   let's heap cabbage, eggplant, cauliflower and **tehina. (Tehina** is a sauce of ground seeds, a bit like peanut butter both in taste and looks, that is as common in the Middle East as catsup is in North America.) Founded by exiled Jews returning home, Tel Aviv – which means "hill of spring" - finds its name from Ezekiel 3:15: *"Then I came to the exiles who lived beside the river Chebar at Tel-abib."* As we snap photographs of this bustling city we think of this "hill" on the coastal plain, "springing up" business and grand amusements for the entire country of Israel!

Our search for Israel's one natural harbor leads us north to the ancient city of Haifa, Israel's major port city. A port is an area on the water's edge built up with docks and cranes for receiving ships and transferring cargo to and from them. A clean and green city that stretches from the coastal plain shores of the sparkling blue Mediterranean up into the Galilean   slopes of Mt. Carmel, Haifa's name may come from the Hebrew word *hof yafe*, meaning "beautiful beach." Ships dock easily in Haifa, a city which grew up around a sheltered bay near the mouth of the Quishon River. Do you see the white cruise ships, the heavy-laden cargo ships, and the big gray warships crowding about the harbor? Because of this harbor and its

If we stand in Jaffe, we can look across the water to Tel Aviv, Israel's bustling, exciting city.

prominence as a port city, Haifa is one of Israel's most industrious cities with oil refineries, automobile manufacturers, steel mills and shipbuilding plants. The way God sculpts the geography of a place determines what people will make and build and work at in a region.

Interestingly, Haifa's name may also be tied to the Hebrew verb *"hafo,"* meaning "to cover or hide." When you realize that Haifa is considered by some to be where the prophet, Elijah, hid in a cave from the wrathful King Ahab, the name Haifa seems quite fitting indeed!

Don't you think it's time to sort through the photographs we've taken so far and send them home to our goat-milking, honey-collecting friend, Ivan? Which photos of these two regions of Israel do you think will catch his eye? The plastic light tunnels of the coastal plain? Or the flower painted Judean slopes? The carved wadis of the Hills region? Or the sand white beaches of the Mediterranean Coast? We find God's Word true: Israel *is* a most beautiful land. Oh, but what still lies ahead on our adventure: a camel trek across the sands, a diving exploration of a coral reef, a blizzard of white flakes in the midst of desert heat, a ride down white water rapids—and more! Are you as excited as I am about our exploration of Israel's two other interesting geographic regions?!

Don't you think Tel Aviv looks beautiful lit up at night? Israel's second largest city after Jerusalem, Tel Aviv is Israel's business and cultural center. Shall we buy tickets for an evening at the Habima National Theater or the Israel Philharmonic Orchestra?

Haifa is Israel's leading industrial city, producing such products as cement, chemicals, electronic equipment, glass, steel, and textiles. What do you think the ships out in the harbor are carrying?

Field Notes

I hope you've captured lots of good photographs for Ivan! Will you describe them to me?

Press record and talk to me:

~ **about plains**:   What does this word mean in geography? What plains did we discover in Israel? What is the weather like on Israel's coastal plains? What is grown here? Describe what it might be like to live here.

~ **about the Mediterranean coastline**: Is it straight or curvy? Why does it look this way? What is a **harbor**? What is the name of Israel's only natural harbor? What Biblical harbor has now disappeared from the coastline?

~ **about Tel Aviv**: What is the city like? Tell me about its history. What tasty Israeli food might we buy here?

~ **about Haifa**: What is a **port**? What would we find in the important port city of Haifa?

Travel Log

Using your globe or atlas, draw an outline map of Israel.

As we travel, let's make a record in our very own travel log of the places we've visited and the unusual sights we've seen! Make your map large enough to hold all of your discoveries!

Don't worry about making a perfect map, just do your best. Drawing the basic shape yourself will help you remember it better. Or use the map provided for you on the CD-ROM if you are short on time.

Map Notes: Let's record the locations of:

- *Mediterranean Sea*
- *Sea of Galilee*
- *Galilean Hills*
- *Samarian Hills*
- *Judean Hills*

- *Mount Carmel*
- *Jerusalem*

If you'd like, draw pictures or symbols on your map representing:

- *Wadis in the Galilean Hills* (perhaps a picture of a dry riverbed?)
- *Wildflowers on the Judean Hills* (be creative!)

Travel Notes: Geographers write what they've seen in order to share the adventure with others—and so they can revisit the places in their memories! **On the next page of your travel log, record three important sights you want to remember from your photos of Israel.**

~*art* ~*books* ~*food* ~*music* ~*poetry*
. . . .

Bringing It Home

Simple ideas to bring the world to your door

Art:

The Jewish culture has a long tradition of paper-cut art. Sometimes these elaborate designs are hung on a home's eastern wall to remind the family which way to pray – towards Jerusalem. This is called a ***mizrach.*.   Paper cutting is also used to make ***ketubah***, or beautiful wedding contracts which may be displayed in a new couple's home.

You can make your own simple paper-cut art by folding a piece of paper in half and drawing a design on the fold. Simply cut out the design using scissors (or a craft knife, for older children) and open the paper. Experiment with different colors of paper, layers and fancy writing or calligraphy.

The link below provides pictures and simple instructions for a paper cutting project:
http://www.hgtv.com/hgtv/cr_paper_crafts_other/article/0,1789,HGTV_3294_1382520,00.html

Learn the Hebrew Aleph bet!

 The Hebrew alphabet, called the Aleph Bet, contains 22 letters. You can learn to read, write and say them at this site:
http://www.akhlah.com/aleph_bet/aleph-bet.php

Music

Music captures so much of a land and people. Introducing your children to Israeli music is a simple way to transport yourselves around the world. Why not check out these sites while your young geographers notebook and map and let the music play while they recount their travels?

Listen to samples of music from Israeli artists:
http://worldmusic.nationalgeographic.com/worldmusic/view/page.basic/country/content.country/israel_36?fs=plasma.nationalgeographic.com
http://music.calabashmusic.com/world/israeli_folk#

One of the world's foremost violinists was born in Tel Aviv. You can most likely find recordings of Itzhak Perlman's music in your local library. For a small sample and a brief biography: http://www.geocities.com/BourbonStreet/2571/perlman.html

The Extraordinary Ordinary:
Farms in the Desert and the Healthy Dead Sea

Israel ~Part 2~

I often wake from dreams where extraordinary things seem bizarrely ordinary, dreams in which I madly run but never go anywhere, in which I can build snowmen on the beach, and in which I can walk through a torrential rainstorm but oddly, never get wet. All that may be the stuff of fantastical night adventures, but would you like to come to a real place on earth where the extraordinary *is* ordinary? A place where deserts bloom strawberries, blizzards of white blow on sizzling hot afternoons, and people find life-giving health on the shores of dead waters? Only God could make such wonders a reality. Come, you simply must see this to believe it! (Don't forget your three essentials: keen eyes, a steel-trap memory, and that vibrant faith - oh, the places we'll go!)

The Negev Desert once hosted Abraham, Isaac and Jacob and their flocks of sheep. Israel has become a world leader in the skills necessary to make the desert blossom. Mark Twain once described the Negev Desert as "a desolation that not even imagination can grace with the pomp of life and action..." but the Israelites are changing that. Would you like to someday live in the blooming, beautiful Negev Desert?

Having photographed two of Israel's geographical regions—the hills region, and the coastal plain—let's ready our camera for Israel's third geographical region: the Negev Desert. To travel into the Negev Desert, we pass through the streets of Beersheba. Once little more than a watering hole for Abraham's sheep, today we find Beersheba—a bustling modern city. Yet the Biblical past seems rather present as we stand on a street corner gazing into the stone-enclosed well said to be used by the patriarch Abraham. Do you hear the bleating of sheep there in Beersheba's famous market, just like they did in Abraham's day? Let's ask a merchant if he might loan us a camel for our trek across the desert. Before leaving the market, we purchase a hunk of *halvah* (ground sesame seeds mixed with honey), fill our canteen with cold water, and pull down the peak of our cap: we are about to embark on the hottest part of our exploration of Israel.

Shaped like a dagger, the Negev Desert of the south comprises more than half of the country of Israel. Derived from the Hebrew word *neghev*, meaning dry, the Negev Desert is indeed aptly named. A **desert** is any geographical region where it rains 10 inches [25.4 cm] or less in an entire year (umbrella rarely needed) and vegetation is sparse (no lawnmower necessary). The hardy **Bedouin** tribes, however, make their home in the Negev Desert and their camps of tents and herds of roaming sheep and goats dot the region. See the friendly Bedouins over there waving us **tourists** into the cool of their tent for a sip of sweet tea? Remember to slip off your shoes as we sit down on

47

the rugs to eat a delicious **pita**, filled with a mouth watering combination of spices and goat cheese. Goat-milking Ivan at home will be so taken with our pictures!

Heading an hour south out of Beersheba across the craggy Negev, sunlight glinting ever-changing colors from minerals in the scattered rocks, we discover a massive depression in the landscape. Stretching out in the shape of a skinny heart, this gaping 24.8 mile [40 km] long, 1 – 6 mile [2 - 10 km] wide, .3 mile [500 m.] deep cavity is Ramon Crater, the world's largest **karst crater**. A karst crater isn't formed by falling meteorites like other craters, but by massive amounts of water, (such as the **Global Flood**), wearing away at rock. Snap a photo of the striking reds and brilliant yellows of

The word Bedouin generally means "desert-dweller" and refers to any nomadic (or traveling) people groups that make the Middle Eastern deserts their home. These beautiful people travel across the sands following water and plant

the colorful, looming walls of the Ramon Crater. Focus the lens now on the exposed spiral **fossils**, some small enough to lie in the palm of your hand while others stand the size of huge tractor wheels.

Climbing up on our camel to ride further into the Negev Desert, we wonder if we see tractors and buildings off on the horizon…or is it a **mirage**? Incredibly, right in the middle of the Negev Desert where the thermometer can soar higher than 120F [49C], more than 250 farm settlements flourish. The blistering desert of hardpan gravel has shrunk by 20 percent due to the ingenious development of desert into *farmland*. The sandy desert not only produces Desert Sweet tomatoes, but sweet grapes, strawberries and melons. How have the Israelis accomplished such an astounding feat?

In the north of the Negev, God has covered the ground with a powdery yellow soil called **loess**. When watered, loess is very fertile. You may be asking where one would find water for crops in this harsh desert? Amazingly, it is right under your feet! Beneath the Negev Desert's soil lie underground pools or **aquifers** of salt water (called brackish water) which Israelis use to irrigate desert crops. In many locations throughout Israel, expensive equipment removes the salt from the underground water (a process called **desalination**) so as to make the water suitable for irrigation.

Isn't this Ramon Karst Crater spectacular? This is a geologist's delight with fossils, rock formations and volcanic wonders. The name Ramon comes from the arabic "Ruman" meaning "Romans," and is probably linked to a track that Romans built here. One wall of the Ramon Karst Crater was once entirely covered with ammonite (spiral) fossils. So many tourists took home a fossil souvenir, however, only a few remain to bear witness of the amazing march of time and history on the earth.

48

Yet in other locations, Israeli's have reversed the process: they have developed plants that only soak up the water and leave the salt behind! These processes are called **brackish-water agriculture**. Is this what the Bible means when we read in Psalms 107:35-37, *"[God] changes a [desert] into a pool of water, and a dry land into springs of water; and there He makes the hungry sow fields and plant vineyards, and gather a fruitful harvest?"* Creatively using their God-given ingenuity, Israeli farmers work throughout Israel, even in the desert, to feed the more than 6 million people who live in Israel, and still export or sell the remainder of their crops for people in other countries to eat. In a few years, this Negev Desert will be a sea of greenhouses and the main producer of vegetables for families in Europe to eat during the snowy winter months! It is just as the prophet Isaiah wrote: *"The desert and the parched land will be glad; the wilderness will rejoice and blossom. They will see the glory of the LORD, the splendor of our God"* (Isa. 35:1).

Israel's southernmost city, amazing Elat, is a popular choice for vacationing families. There are so many wonders to see! From the red mountains to the brightly colored fish and coral in the warm waters to the skies filled with migrating birds. Doesn't Elat sound like a wonderful getaway?

This journey through the stifling hot, harsh desert is worth it for what we find at the very tip of the dagger-shaped Negev. Before us, out of the desert dust, rises the resort city of Elat, an oasis of luxury on the shores of the Red Sea. Though at the very "bottom" of Israel, Elat is sometimes called Israel's first city, since it has been suggested that this is where the Israelites, led by Moses, first set foot on this land. Now tourists like you and me come through the Negev Desert to Israel's most southerly destination to see what swims in Elat's waters and flies in its skies. More different species of fish swim among Elat's breathtaking coral reefs than in any other waters in the whole wide world! Let's leave our camels at the shore and climb in this glass-bottomed boat. Focus your camera lens on a shot of that venomous lionfish or that moray eel swimming about the coral reef. A **coral reef** is a massive rock-like structure built by millions of very small marine animals called corals. **Corals** squirt **calcium carbonate** - which is the same substance that makes our bones hard—from their tiny bodies. This calcium carbonate forms a solid cup-like skeleton outside the coral's body. Over time the joined outer skeletons of thousands of corals harden into rock and form a reef. Looking down through the transparent bottom of our boat, the coral reef looks like a bustling city or community, with the buildings made of coral, and thousands of colorful, strange-looking marine creatures swimming about. In this sense, Israel's coral reef is like a metropolitan city under the sea!

Now aim your camera lens high overhead. Approximately one billion birds **migrate** through Elat's skies twice yearly, making southern Israel the site of one of the greatest concentrations of migrating birds in the world. God created Israel as a beautiful land figuratively flowing with milk and honey, but also as a land teeming with fish in its seas and swarming with birds in its skies!

Elat's Underwater Observatory is 19 feet [6 meters] below sea level. Once you get below the surface, find a spot by a glass window and watch the living coral reefs and schools of fish that surround the Observatory. Doesn't it seem as though the Creator must have had a great time making such colorful and interesting creatures? *Photo by: Henrik Reinholdson*

Field Notes

What amazing sights we've seen today. I hope our photos capture all their beauty.

Press record and tell me:

~ **about the Negev Desert**: What is it shaped like? Describe a desert. Who lives in this dry, sandy place? What is the temperature like here? Can anything grow in this desert? Why is the Negev shrinking?

~ **about the Ramon Crater**: What is it? How was it created? What colors would we see in it? What else would we find in its walls?

~ **about Elat**: Where is it located? What is it sometimes called? What would we find in the water here? Describe the coral reef. What would we see in the skies above Elat?

I try to avoid divisions and rifts, don't you? A **rift** can mean a break in friendly relations (best to avoid), or a break in the Earth's surface (best to explore). Israel's Rift is definitely unavoidable. One the most prominent natural geographical features on the entire planet, the valley can even be seen by astronauts orbiting in outer space. Winding along Israel's eastern border, the Jordan Rift Valley lies on a **fault line**, a crack in the Earth's crust where two **plates** meet. During the catastrophic world wide flood of Noah's day, it is quite likely that the two plates were ripped apart along this **strike-slip fault zone**, creating the Great Rift Valley which cuts through the Middle East and down into Eastern Africa. The deep gash of the Jordan Rift Valley is part of the larger Great Rift Valley.

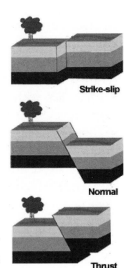

What would you expect to find slithering through the Jordan Rift Valley? How about something God used to cure Namaan miraculously, something that once stopped in its course to make way for a passing prophet, something which baptized Jesus and which eventually finds itself at a dead end? Yes, through this Jordan Rift Valley winds what some consider the holiest river in the world: the Jordan River. Deriving its name from the Hebrew word *"descender,"* the Jordan River does indeed descend down through Israel to… well, you just wait and see it where descends to!

Mt. Hermon is actually three mountains, all of similar height, clustered together. Because of its height, Mount Hermon captures a great deal of precipitation in a very dry area of the world. Its head and shoulders are covered with snow throughout spring and winter. Mount Hermon is the only place you can ski in Israel! Mount Hermon marked the northern boundary of the Promised Land (Deu. 3:8), and at its southern base, Jesus revealed to his disciples his purpose to build his Church (Matt 16:13-21).

The Jordan River is regarded as one of the most holy and famous rivers in the world. Not only is it a life-giving source of water for dry Israel and surrounding countries, but the Bible tells us this is the river where Namman was healed and Jesus was baptized. People's usage of the Jordan's waters and its tributaries has dramatically changed the ecosystem, or the community of plants and animals, of the Jordan River. Where freshwater foliage once flourished during Biblical times, today we often find saline vegetation.

All rivers begin somewhere. To find the Jordan's **tap**, or source, we look to the very northeast corner of Israel to "Gray Beard with the Eye-in-the-Sky." A majestic sight to behold, this mountain, otherwise known as Mount Hermon, is the highest peak in Israel. (Mount Hermon lies in the territory over which Israel and its neighbor, Syria, are disputing; hence, some do not feel Mount Hermon lies within Israel's borders.)   Named "Grey Beard" because of its snowy peaks, Mount Hermon is also called Israel's "Eye-in-the-Sky" since from its peak one can see far off into the lands of Israel's neighbors. Depending on the season, we may catch a glimpse of skiers snaking down Mount Hermon's snowy slopes. Snap a picture of these Israelis so excited to see Israel's only snow that they are sledding down the slopes on cookie sheets! The snow that melts on Mount Hermon's sides, coupled with bubbling springs at the mountain's base, is the headwaters of the mighty Jordan River.

As the Jordan River flows south, it waters the orchards and cotton fields of the lush valleys south of Mount Hermon. As we frame up a picture of an Israeli family picnicking under eucalyptus trees, we wonder if Lot saw a similar scene in Genesis 13:10: *"Lot lifted up his eyes and saw all the valley of the Jordan, that it was well watered everywhere like the garden of the LORD."* The most frequently mentioned river in the Bible (noted over 200 times), we recall how Elijah once walked across this Jordan River on dry ground (2 Kings 2:8,14). Today, we catch a glimpse of daring white water rafters riding the Jordan's tremendous rapids as it courses down towards Lake Kinneret.

On most of its journey, the Jordan River slowly meanders, but in some places the white water tells us the River is in a hurry to rush by!

Lake Kinneret's Hebrew name comes from the word, *kinnor*, meaning harp, so named because of the lake's harp-like shape. But the only instruments we see anyone playing with at Lake Kinneret are water skis and wind surfboards. Did you know that once a man even walked on these Lake Kinneret waters? Yes, Jesus! For Lake Kinneret is the Bible's Sea of Galilee. This "sea" is actually a large lake fed by the Jordan River. Like a giant bowl of water nestled into the Galilean hills, the surface of the Sea of Galilee is easily stirred by the winds that rush down the hillsides. Waves may billow as high as 20 feet [6 m]. Jesus, however, simply *"rebuked the wind, and said unto the sea, Peace, be still. And the wind ceased, and there was a great calm…And [the disciples] feared exceedingly, and said one to another, What manner of man is this, that even the wind and the sea obey him?"* (Mark 5:39, 41). Today our same God controls the winds and waves of the Sea of Galilee—and the whole world!

With the warm Sea of Galilee waters lapping at our toes we recall Jesus walking these shores and *"going along by the Sea of Galilee, He saw Simon and Andrew, the brother of Simon, casting a net in the sea; for they were fishermen"* (Mark 1:16). Fishing boats sail the sea today, weathered fishermen hauling in catches of silvery fish. Let's slip into one of the many restaurants that ring the shores and order a freshly caught "St. Peter's fish" as our luncheon fare, just like Jesus and his disciples once fried up on these shores.

Here you can see the beautiful Sea of Galilee (known as Lake Kinneret to Israelis) with Mt. Hermon in the distance. Israel's largest freshwater lake and one of the lowest freshwater lakes on Earth, the Sea of Galilee is only 13 miles [20.9 km] long by 7 miles [11 km] wide. Along these shores Jesus taught His disciples. Today, tourism is the most important economic activity in the region with holiday resorts dotting the landscape.

While Lake Kinneret may be a bit of a fishbowl for fisherman, it is rather like a water bottle for the country of Israel. Like a huge straw, a large pipeline called the National Water Carrier carries drinking water from this lake to families and crops all over Israel. If you only had one bottle of water on a smothering hot afternoon, you would wisely ration your consumption; so the Israelis carefully conserve the fresh waters of the Sea of Galilee. More than 20,000 Israelis recently linked hands in a ring around the Sea of Galilee, "hugging" the sea from which so much of the their water flows, and to again cheer the motto that every Israeli knows and lives by: "Don't waste a drop!"

Just as the River Jordan feeds into the north end of the Sea of Galilee, so it slides out the south end of the Sea of Galilee, carrying more of this life-giving water further down the Jordan Rift Valley. As we sweep down the current, we think of where Jesus once immersed himself in the waters of the Jordan in baptism. Standing on these banks, we try to imagine what it would have been like to hear the voice of God declare, *"This is My beloved Son, in whom I am well-pleased"* (Matt. 3:17).

Israelis, however, also know this area south of the Sea of Galilee, on the banks of the Jordan, as the location of Israel's first farming village, known as a *kibbutz*. Do your parents ask you to co-operate and share with your siblings? Well, a **kibbutz** is an Israeli farming village where everyone works co-operatively, sharing absolutely everything: all the work, all the decisions, and the profits. If you zoom in your camera's focus, you'll capture some memorable scenes of workers eating together in communal dining rooms, selecting their clothes from a community shop, and driving about in community-owned vehicles. In some co-operative villages in the past, parents did not even live with their own children, but shared them with the community! In such a kibbutz, all the children of the kibbutz lived in separate houses with their own caregivers and made daily visits to their parents. Many farms throughout the various geographic regions of Israel are still organized today much like the first farming kibbutz established along the banks of the Jordan River.

In a kibbutz, everything is shared...homes, work, fields, and food. Children spend most of their days with other children their own age, but at night most of them came home to sleep with their own families. Though not many Israelis lived in the kibbutz movement, the hard work, vision and passion of those of the kibbutz, invigorated all of Israel.

Flowing past these co-operative villages, the Jordan River makes its way to its own dead end. Look around at the jagged cliffs where the Jordan River ends in a steamy, gray lake. Does this look like the lowest place on the face of the Earth? It is! The Dead Sea—the end of the Jordan River—is indeed the very lowest place on the entire surface of the Earth. Standing on the shore of the Dead

The houses in this kibbutz are mud domes. Don't you think the mud construction will help keep their families cool in that desert heat?

Sea we are 1,300 feet [400 m] below sea level. **Sea level** is a rather complex measurement, determined in part, by averaging the ocean levels between high tide and low tide. The height of all land and mountains on Earth are measured from sea level; that is to say, sea level is considered the starting point of zero. Think of sea level as zero on a thermometer, and the Dead Sea being far below the zero, at the bottom of the red bulb. Visualize us here at the Dead Sea as being so far pocketed down in the Earth's surface that we'd have to climb 1,300 feet straight up before we'd have even reached "sea level" or the mark zero! The Dead Sea is not only a dead end for the Jordan River; it is also rather a dead end in terms of the earth's depths!

We won't be eating fish on the Dead Sea as we did at Lake Kinneret, nor will we be sipping a drink of its waters. Not unless you prefer your cup of water to be one-third salt! The Dead Sea is the saltiest body of water in the world and no life, except for brine shrimp, can live in these murky waters; hence, its apt name of "Dead" Sea. The dead end Dead Sea, with no drainage outlet, continues to increase in saltiness as the **minerals** from the cliffs are washed by **erosion** into the sea and the sun's heat **evaporates** water, leaving salt behind.

The high salt content and warm temperatures make the Dead Sea a big attraction for locals and visitors alike. There is so much salt in the water that if you took a dip, you would be able to float and read a book, just like this man - with no trouble at all.

If you'd like to cool off with a dip and a good book, by all means, dive in! You'll find it challenging because the high salt concentration causes everything to float. You may float on your back in the Dead Sea while you easily read a book with nary a page getting wet! That's a photograph farming boy Ivan will shake his head over! (But if you've skinned your knee recently, best stand on shore, and take a picture of me since that salt water will sting any open sores!)

You are also more than welcome to roll about in the Dead Sea's mud like the other tourists. The mineral-rich mud from the salty Dead Sea is considered healthy for your skin. You may look very muddy in this photograph but we'll explain to Ivan how refreshed your skin was! Many tourist resorts line these shores for this very reason and the salt from the Dead Sea is sold around the world as a life-enhancing bath salt.

The Dead Sea is a unique body of water. It is not only the lowest place on earth; it is also the saltiest and the healthiest. Doesn't it look beautiful in the sunrise? The area offers fascinating landscapes: in its southern region, we find mushroom-like hills from a mixture of minerals and sand that God has masterfully sculpted through erosion. In the northern area, we see threatening rocky cliffs with waterfalls. Describing the Dead Sea region, the biblical geographer George Adam Smith wrote: "surely there is no region of earth where Nature and History have more cruelly conspired, where so tragic a drama has obtained so awful a theater." Yes, for here Lot's wife turned into a pillar of salt and Sodom and Gomorrah was forever destroyed.

These shores are, however, the site of death and destruction for the Biblical cities of Sodom and Gomorrah which once stood overlooking the Dead Sea. You may well recall Lot's wife who looked back at the judged, burning cities and herself became a pillar of salt (Genesis 19:26). Towards the saltier south end of the Dead Sea, we clearly see salt hardened into strange, contorted formations.

Snap a picture of what appears to be a constant blizzard of snow in the midst of soaring desert heat. That flurry of white is the blowing of salt at the Dead Sea Mineral Works factory, where salt is harvested for commercial sale. In a country with few **natural resources**, the Dead Sea robustly energizes the Israeli economy with the world's largest source of **potash**, a kind of **fertilizer** to make plants grow, and plentiful magnesium bromide, magnesium chloride and of course, salt. While the Dead Sea may be a barren, desolate place, our creative Creator God has also made the Dead Sea, the lowest place on Earth, a place that fosters growth, health and life.

And there! You've explored the wondrous landscape God has wrought in Israel: its spiny hill region, its anything-but-plain coastal plain, its blooming, sweet desert, and its gaping rift that leads the Jordan River down through the Hula Valley, the Sea of Galilee and to its dead end at the Dead Sea. Look to Mount Hermon in the north boasting its snowy slopes; now turn to balmy Elat in the south, with its spectacular coral reefs and colorful, tropical fish. Lying between these two extremes we've traveled through arid Negev desert, lush oases, green Mediterranean woods, and the lowest, saltiest point on earth—the Dead Sea. Deuteronomy 26:15 reads, *"Look down, [God], from Your holy habitation, from heaven, and bless Your people Israel, and the ground which You have given us, a land flowing with milk and honey, as You swore to our fathers."* With our own keen eyes and our robust faith, we've seen God's blessings upon the land of Israel, and the memories we've netted from our journey are enduringly ours to share— with folks like farming Ivan!

Looking out at the Sea of Galilee and the rolling hills of Israel, we think of Deuteronomy 26:15, "Look down from thy holy habitation, from heaven, and bless thy people Israel, and the land which thou hast given us, as thou swarest unto our fathers, a land that floweth with milk and honey."

Field Notes

Israel is truly a miraculous place.

Press record and talk to me:

~ <u>**about the Jordan Rift Valley**</u>: What part of this valley can astronauts see from space? What runs through the valley? Where does the Jordan River begin?

~ <u>**about the Sea of Galilee**</u>: What is its other name? How does the water benefit the people of Israel? Do you remember any stories about the Sea of Galilee from the Bible?

~ <u>**about a kibbutz**</u>: What is it? What kinds of things do the families in a kibbutz share? Do you think you would like to live in a kibbutz?

~ <u>**about the Dead Sea**</u>: What makes this body of water unique? What would swimming in the Dead Sea be like? Why do people take mud-baths here? What important mineral is harvested here?

Travel Log

Using your globe or atlas, let's add the following locations to your map of Israel... We've seen things today that simply must be mapped, so that they will never be forgotten!

Map Notes: Let's record the locations of:

- *Jordan Rift Valley*
- *Jordan River*
- *Mount Hermon*
- *Sea of Galilee or Lake Kinneret*
- *Dead Sea*

If you'd like, draw pictures or symbols on your map representing:

- *Skiers on Mt. Hermon* (or sledders on cookie sheets?)
- *Fishermen on Lake Kinneret*
- *Kibbutz along the Jordan River* (perhaps a group of children playing together in their village?)
- *"swimmers" in the Dead Sea* (remember how the salt affects swimmers!)
- *Dead Sea Mineral Works factory* (a building? A giant salt shaker?)

(Challenge mapping: Add the National Water Carrier and the Hula Valley to your map.)

Travel Notes: Geographers write what they've seen in order to share the adventure with others—and so they can revisit the places in their memories! **On the next page of your travel log, record three important sights you want to remember from your photos of Israel.**

~art ~books ~food ~music ~poetry
. . . .
Bringing It Home
Simple ideas to bring the world to your door

Books

The Never-Ending Greenness *by* Neil Waldman**,**
A story of a young boy and his family escaping Nazi soldiers in Lithuania and emigrating to "eretz Yisrael" (the land of Israel) to replant a barren and empty land with trees and hope. An uplifting story, it is a most worthy tribute to the work of new settlers "greening" Israel. *Appealing to all ages.*

Three Wishes: Palestinian and Israeli Children Speak *by* Deborah Ellis,
The moving stories of 20 Jewish, Christian and Palestinian children, ages 8-18, interviewed in 2002, who speak their own stories of everyday life in a region of conflict. Offering glimmers of hope in the even the grimmest stories, the voices of these children will compel readers to further explore the issues of the Middle East and to pray with fervency. *Gr-4-8*

The Dog of Knots *by* Kathy Walden Kaplan
 Set in the turmoil of the Yom Kippur War of 1973, 9-year-old Mayim moves to Haifa, meeting a stray dog that bonds neighbors together. Offering a glimpse life in modern Israel, this is a story of loss, courage and compassion. *Gr. 4-8*

Jerusalem of Gold: Jewish Stories of the Enchanted City *by* Howard Schwartz
Eleven stories set in Jerusalem, from King David to Rabbi Nachman, are complemented with a brief historical background to further understanding of the Jewish traditions. *Gr. 4-8*

Poetry
Did you know that some of the world's most famous poetry is from Israel? The Bible is full of Jewish poems, many written by the Hebrew King David (the same David who slew Goliath!). One sample of his work from Psalm 65 is below:

8   *They who dwell in the ends of the earth*
    stand in awe of Your signs;
    You make the dawn and the sunset shout
    for joy.
9   *You visit the earth and cause it to overflow;*
    You greatly enrich it;
    The stream of God is full of water;
    You prepare their grain, for thus You
    prepare the earth.
10 *You water its furrows abundantly,*
    You settle its ridges,

    You soften it with showers,
    You bless its growth.
11 *You have crowned the year with Your*
    bounty,
    And Your paths drip with fatness.
12 *The pastures of the wilderness drip,*
    And the hills gird themselves with
    rejoicing.
13 *The meadows are clothed with flocks*
    And the valleys are covered with grain;
    They shout for joy, yes, they sing.

Howdy, Pilgrim!

Israel ~Part 3~

Come, walk the way o f the pilgrims through the Holy Land; walk old streets in Jerusalem and along the byways of the Israeli countryside. Have you experienced the lands of the Bible today?

When you think of pilgrims, does your mind's eye conjure up a scene of the Pilgrim's progress to the Celestial City, wallowing and wrestling through the miry Slough of Despond? Or do scenes of Pilgrims setting up a Thanksgiving Feast at Plymouth Rock flash through your mind? Let's close our eyes and become a different kind of pilgrim; one who journeys all the way to the Dome of the Rock in the heart of Israel's Old World.

A **pilgrim** is one who travels or pilgrimages to distant lands, or one who journeys to sacred places. We are going to do both! God's Word promises a blessing to him *"whose heart is set on pilgrimage"* (Ps. 84:5 NKJV). Let's see how God will bless us!

The early church historian, Eusebius, speaks of the first pilgrim, Alexander, (later to become the Bishop of Jerusalem), who traveled to Israel before 213 A.D. "for the purposes of prayer and investigation of the Holy places." That was a mere 200 years after the crucifixion of our Lord. For the following 1,800 years people just like you and me have been strapping on their sandals, filling their water jugs, and coming to see with their own eyes the places where Jesus was born, where He lived and taught, and where He sacrificed Himself for all the world---then staggeringly, rose from the dead! So, would *you* like to go on this pilgrimage?

Can you sing the song with me? "O Little Town of Bethlehem…" Stand here atop one of the rolling Judean Hills, looking out over the white buildings of Bethlehem, and listen to the words the prophet Micah spoke of this place, *"And you, Bethlehem, land of Judah, are by no means least among the leaders of Judah; for out of you shall come forth a ruler who will shepherd my people, Israel"* (Matt. 2:6). Ruth, from the Book of Ruth, may have lived in Bethlehem; but it was great-grandson, King David, who was both born in Bethlehem, and rose to shepherd the nation of Israel. Yet the Scripture speaks most importantly of this Bethlehem as the place where God became flesh.

Looking at the Church of the Nativity, one of the oldest Christian churches in the world, do you think it has a fortress-like exterior? As one of the most fought over Holy Places throughout the centuries, the church was once spared by Persian invaders (614 A.D.) who, having found a colorful mosaic in the church of the worshiping Magi from Persia spared the church out of respect for their ancestors.

Does this look like the house of bread? Today, we find the "little town of Bethlehem" to be a city of more than 60,000 people. Where cars now travel, the Magi once brought gold, frankincense and myrrh to a humble stable to worship God made flesh, swaddled in a manger. Rachel, the mother of the patriarch Joseph, was buried on the way to Bethlehem.

(Can you find Bethlehem on your map of Israel? From the streets of Bethlehem, we can see the buildings of Jerusalem 6 mi [10 km] to the north.) Doesn't it seem fitting that the Good Shepherd, Jesus, whose body would be like bread broken for us, would be born in the town of Bethlehem whose name means "the house of Bread?" Breathless from our hike up here, we'll never again think of Mary's donkey easily cantering down a flat road into this dusty town. Bethlehem rises up out of the steep rugged terrain in the Judean and Samarian hill country. Our pilgrim road journeys over extremely rocky hills punctuated by deep ravines and plunging gorges that make travel in central Israel a strain on both man and machine.

Past Rachel's tomb, we travel Bethlehem's main thoroughfare, Manger Street, seeking to find the exact spot where Jesus was born. Actually, no one knows the spot for certain! Centuries ago, a certain cave used as a barn for cattle was believed to be where our Lord Jesus spent His first night on Earth. But if we visit that cave today, on Manger Square, we find a white-stoned church: the Church of the Nativity. As Jesus humbled Himself by coming to earth, so we too bend low to enter the small doorway of the Church of the Nativity. Built by order of Constantine the Great (A.D. 330), and rebuilt by Emperor Justinian after its destruction during a revolt, this dimmed Church of the Nativity with its ancient stone walls, may be the oldest Christian church in the world. Inside the hushed place of worship, we step down a dark,

narrow stairway into a candle-lit space revered as perhaps the manger of Jesus' birth. Don't you marvel that He came at all? We worship too.

Stepping back out into the street and the light of day, we venture past another nearby grotto, or small cave, where during the 5th century St. Jerome is said to have spent thirty long years hunched over texts, translating the Scriptures into Latin.

When Jesus was born, Bethlehem was a Jewish town. After the time of St. Jerome, Bethlehem was a Christian town. Today Bethlehem, with a population of more than 185,000 people, is a Muslim town. There is however, still a bylaw that requires the mayor of Bethlehem to be a Christian.

Bend over to slip through the Door of Humility, the entrance of the Church of the Nativity. Some suggest that the low entrance was to prevent horsemen from just riding into the church!

We pilgrims now shake the dust off our sandals, and head north out of Bethlehem and up to the northern hills of Galilee to the city of Nazareth, the town where Jesus grew up and lived most of His 33 years. Why did Jesus live in Nazareth instead of any other town in Israel? The Bible tells us, *"This was to fulfill what was spoken through the prophets: 'He shall be called a Nazarene'"* (Matt. 2:23).

Isn't it a spectacular view looking south, down into Nazareth? That large black–roofed building is the Basilica of the Annunciation which is said to be built over the site where the angel Gabriel declared to Mary that she would bear the Messiah. Do you notice how this "center" of Nazareth is situated down "in the bottom of a bowl" with the hills rising up all around it? *Photo courtesy of holylandphotos.org*

The word Nazareth is thought to be rooted in the Hebrew word *"netser"* which means "shoot" or "branch." And do you remember these words that Isaiah prophesied about the Messiah? *"And there shall come forth a rod out of the stem of Jesse and a Branch shall grow out of his roots"* (Isa. 11:1). Jesus was that branch! How fitting it is that Jesus' hometown was Nazareth, the "branch."

Cupped as if in a basin, looming **limestone** hills rise around Nazareth. Nazareth's red roofed houses were built of the white limestone from these hills. Now where exactly did Jesus live with Joseph and Mary in Nazareth? Or can someone point the way to the carpenter shop where He hammered away? Again, we don't know for sure. We do see a sign directing us to Mary's well. Gaze down into the well's dark eye. Can't you see the boy Jesus drawing up water here for Mary's washing and cooking?

Across the modern plaza in front of Mary's well, we wave hello to Elias Shama, a Christian Arab and owner of the Cactus gift shop. While offering us a cold drink, Mr. Shama explains to us that the floor of the storage room at the back of the gift shop was always damp, so he began digging in search of the problem. Come see the startling discovery he dug up! We step down into a beautiful high-vaulted room from which Mr. Shama guides us through underfloor heating channels to a white marble floor and tile columns meeting overhead in an array of **arches**. Unbelievably, we are standing in an unearthed **Roman bathhouse**. Is it from the time of Jesus? One pilgrim wrote over 500 years ago, *"arriving the next day in Nazareth…[t]he citizens told me that there existed a hot bathhouse where the Mother of Jesus immersed herself."* Perhaps this indeed is the bathhouse of Jesus!

Saying our goodbyes to Mr. Shama, we pass children playing in the streets as we walk up the hill to the **souq**, the Arab Market. Today Nazareth is a city of more than 80,000, half of the residents Christian, while the other half are Muslim.

Leaving Nazareth behind, we follow Jesus' trail 18.6 miles [30 km] to the east of Nazareth, passing through the little village once known as Cana, now known as *Kafr Kanna*, where Jesus performed his first miracle of turning water into wine and make our way to the Sea of Galilee. In the eastern shore town of Tabgha, let's slip into the Church of the Multiplication of the Loaves and Fishes. If we look down to the design on the church

Do you think it was a day much like today when Jesus preached the Sermon on the Mount to thousands sitting here overlooking the Sea of Galilee? *Photo courtesy of holylandphotos.org*

Do you see the two fish and the four loaves in the mosaic on the floor at the Tabgha church? A real loaf of bread is placed on the altar overhead, to bring the total to the miraculous 5 loaves and 2 fishes of Mark 6:38.

floor, we see a mosaic of a basket of bread and two fishes, just like Jesus miraculously multiplied for the ravenous crowds! If you visited my home, you'd find that very same tile picture on a plate hanging on my wall, my very own two "St. Peter's Fish," from the Sea of Galilee.

Meandering south along these wave-lapped shores of the blue-green Sea of Galilee, we think of the Beatitudes Jesus spoke on these hills: *"Blessed are the poor in spirit."* If we peer through the flowers and palm trees, do you see the **octagonal** Church of Beatitudes perched there with a breathtaking view of the lake? Let's follow the other pilgrims into this beautifully domed church with its eight walls, one for each of the **Beatitudes**, and a beatitude inscribed on each of the eight windows.

Are you discovering the two very different kinds of holy sites in Israel? Some sites are churches where devoted pilgrims have worshipped down through the centuries, while other sites remain as God created them and our Lord Jesus actually saw and experienced them. Stepping out of The Church of the Beatitudes, into the glorious sunshine of the Mount of Beatitudes, we are struck with the realization that these rolling hills are the same today as when Jesus once stood here; that the water of the Sea of Galilee rocks and rolls today as when our Lord Jesus once preached here; and as Jesus once spoke truth to the crowds on these hillsides, so we too continue to listen to His words.

Let's trek south now to David's city, Jerusalem, where native Israelis mill through congested booths and shops lining narrow streets, where merchants ply their crates of oranges and nuts, and where ancient cobbled-stone streets wind down to modern highways a-blur with cars and tour buses. Valleys drop away on all sides from the perched city of Jerusalem which was the capital of Israel in the time of King David and is claimed by Israelis today as the capital of the modern country of Israel.

The Palestinian Arabs who lived here before the Jewish people returned to this land consider the eastern section of Jerusalem to be the future capital city of their state of Palestine. Thus, Jerusalem is a contested, disputed city with two nations of people claiming it as their very own capital city. In the midst of this ongoing conflict, pilgrims from three of the world's most

The octagonal Church of the Beatitudes, topped by its large copper greenish-blue dome, has a magnificent bird's-eye-view of the Sea of Galilee. Looking at the eight windows of opaque glass, we can see that each window is adorned with verses from the Sermon on the Mount. *Photo courtesy of holylandphotos.org*

What sounds and sights do we experience amidst the vendors outside the Damascus gate on the northern wall of Old Jerusalem?

recognized faiths—Judaism, Christianity and Islam—pilgrimage to this one city of Jerusalem, dressed very differently, worshiping very differently, and esteeming different locations, yet all seeking to encounter God.

Let us follow these Orthodox Jews, dressed in black suits, some with long side curls wisping out from under their black hats, to their holy site. Before a looming honey-colored stonewall, the bearded men drape themselves in a white prayer shawl with tassels and bow their heads in prayer. Why do Jews the world over make pilgrimage to this wall built with massive stones? These stones are the last remnant of the Western Wall of Herod's Temple, from the time of Jesus. Jews believe the Western Wall has greater holiness than any other place on Earth to which they are able to pilgrimage. (At the top of the Western Wall lies the area where the hallowed Solomon's Temple once stood. While it is revered as more holy, Jews do not have ready access to this area since it is under Muslim control.) Sometimes the **Western Wall** is referred to as the Wailing Wall—but neither does the wall wail, nor do Jews cry here. If we listen closely we may hear Jews praying in Hebrew for God to bless the land of Israel. As this wall was once part of God's Temple, Jews believe that to pray before the Western Wall is to pray before the ear of God.

Respectfully standing before this long, expansive Western Wall, with its clumps of grass sprouting up here and there, we are in awe of living during this time in history, when Jewish men, women and children may worship here. From the time of Romans walking around in togas, the Western Wall was not controlled by Israeli Jews but by distant, non-Jewish powers. During a short but fierce six day war in 1967 the Israelites captured the eastern section of Jerusalem and for the first time in 2,000 years, Jews once again controlled the Western Wall. Jews around the world cried tears of joy. We too tuck a scrap of paper with our prayer of thanks in with the other paper prayers stuck between the great stones of the Western Wall.

This friendly Jewish man in a Jerusalem market shows us his wares. Do you know what he is holding in his hand? Phylacteries or tefillin are leather straps with boxes carrying Biblical verses. Many Jews wear the phylacteries daily, except on the Sabbath, to live out Deu. 6:6,8, "And these words, which I command thee this day, shall be in thine heart:... And thou shalt bind them for a sign upon thine hand, and they shall be as frontlets between thine eyes." Do you recognize any of his other wares?

Doesn't the mosque of the Dome of the Rock glimmer brilliantly over the city of Jerusalem? Over 714,000 inhabitants live in Jerusalem – the most holy city in Judaism – the very city where King David once lived and reigned over Israel. Jerusalem remains the capital of modern-day Israel and is the home of the Knesset, the legislature of Israel. What a contrast to see the old southern wall of Jerusalem against the backdrop of skyscrapers!

The Western Wall is the last remnant of the last Temple where Jews from around the world come to pray. But did you know the Western Wall is much longer than the Wall we see at the Prayer Plaza? Hundreds of feet of wall continue underground beneath the streets and houses of Jerusalem. Perhaps someday you will explore the Western Wall Tunnels to see more of the Wall.

Field Notes

Howdy Pilgrim! Are you ready to take a rest and talk about your travels so far?

Press record and talk to me:

~ **about Bethlehem** : Which Biblical people were born here? Can you tell me about the journey Mary and Joseph took to get here? What is the Church of the Nativity? How do we get in? What will we see inside?

~ **about Nazareth**: Can you describe the town? Why is Nazareth an important city historically? How many people live here today?

~ **about the Sea of Galilee**:   What miracle did Jesus do at Cana?   What would we see inside the Church of the Multiplication of the Loaves and Fishes? Can you describe the Church of the Beatitudes?

~ **about Jerusalem**: Why do so many pilgrims come to Jerusalem? What is the Western Wall? Can you tell me about the people who pray there?

Just above the Western Wall with its praying Jews, do you see turbaned and veiled Muslims pilgrimage to their holy site: the Mosque of Omar? The Mosque of Omar is *not* actually a Muslim mosque (a Muslim place of worship) but a holy **shrine** (a building that houses items considered holy) and no one named Omar built the mosque, but Omar prayed here! Better known as the Dome of the Rock, don't you think its golden **dome** dazzles and glimmers brilliantly in the Middle Eastern sun? Indeed one of the most famous landmarks of Jerusalem, the dome was once covered in genuine gold, but now is an aluminum dome covered with gold leaf, a gift from a king of the nearby country of Jordan.

Take your shoes off as we step into the Dome and onto its plush carpet. Tiled **mosaics** of paradise decorate walls and ceilings, marble columns supporting artful arches. Inscribed in Arabic on the interior octagon of the shrine are the words, "O you People of the Book, overstep not bounds in your religion, and of God speak only the truth. The Messiah, Jesus, son of Mary, is only an apostle of God, and his Word which he conveyed unto Mary, and a Spirit proceeding from him. Believe therefore in God and his apostles, and say not Three. It will be better for you. God is only one God. Far be it from his glory that he should have a son."

A visitor to Jerusalem in the 10th century wrote of the Dome of the Rock, "At dawn, when the light of the sun first strikes the dome and the drum catches the rays, then is this edifice a marvelous sight to behold, and one such than in all of Islam I have not seen the equal..."

As magnificent as the shrine is architecturally, it is the rock underneath the glittering dome that makes this place holy. Named the Noble Rock, the rock under the golden dome is thought by Muslims to be the place where their founder, Mohammed, ascended up to heaven to the throne of Allah. For Muslims, this Noble Rock is the third holiest site in the world. Jews and Christians revere Noble Rock as Mount Moriah. For Jews and Christians, this Noble Rock of Mount Moriah is the place where Abraham prepared to sacrifice Isaac and where the Jewish Temple's Holy of Holies, the very dwelling place of God, once stood. Yes, Noble Rock indeed! And now we understand the name, Dome of the Rock.

Emerging from the shrine, we note the expansive area, part of the Temple Mount, between the Western Wall and the Dome of the Rock. Someday, perhaps in your lifetime, another glorious temple, the Third Temple, might once again be constructed on the Temple Mount. Then devout people the world over will make pilgrimage to that spectacular holy site, and maybe *you* will write to tell us all about it!

Shall we join in the procession down the Via Dolorosa? Each Friday at 3 p.m. priests lead pilgrims along the Way of Sorrows, beginning in the Muslim Quarter, in the northeast corner of the Old City of Jerusalem, and winding throughout the city. Stopping at the 14 Stations of the Cross to whisper prayers, pilgrims find their way to the Church of the Holy Sepulcher in the Christian Quarter.

While Christian pilgrims visit Muslim and Jewish holy sites, we also quietly walk the Way of Grief, often called by its Latin name, the **Via Dolorosa**. To walk the Via Dolorosa and its winding cobblestone streets is to follow what many believe to be the same path our bruised Lord Jesus dragged His heavy cross to the crucifixion. As our minds fill with thoughts of our Savior, we pass Israeli children running home from school and Jewish mothers, kerchiefs knotted under their chins, carrying home the groceries from the marketplace. We wonder what Jesus thought as He trod these stones and how He loved the people of this world.

Our Via Dolorosa route leads to a sprawling, domed church, the Church of the Holy **Sepulchre**. This cavernous church, its dim recesses lit only by lamps and candles, is thought to stand at the location where our Lord Jesus was nailed to the cross. Where once our Lord hung on a rugged cross, today candles glimmer and create shadows before an altar and paintings of the crucifixion. We step into the small inner building housing the place thought to be Jesus' tomb. Leaning low to look into the burial shafts of carved stone, we marvel at the miracle before our eyes: the tomb is empty! Jesus is *alive*! This explains why some Christians refer to the church not as the Church of the Holy Sepulchre, but as the Church of the Resurrection!

Five different Christian denominations share the Church of the Holy Sepulchre, robed priests sweeping this way and that. But until just a few years ago, the church had only one entrance of colossal doors. The five different Christian groups could not agree on who would step up the short ladder to the keyhole, head-height off the ground, to lock and unlock the creaking door. To keep the peace, the door's foot-long iron key was entrusted to a Muslim family, the Nuseibehs. For over eight hundred years, from the time of the Crusades, Nuseibeh grandfathers have passed the key down to their sons. In the blue light of early morning, the Nuseibeh family still comes to unlock the church's massive wooden doors, returning to lock the church door each evening at dusk. Here, at the Church of the Holy Sepulchre, Christians come to one of Christendom's most holy sites, a church shared by 5 different Christian groups, whose front door is unlocked and locked every day by a

Aren't the doors into the church of the Holy Sepulcher massive? If you'll look under the right window, do you see an old wooden ladder? The ladder was placed there in the 1800's and hasn't been moved since the various Christian communities caring for the church can't agree on its removal!

66

Muslim, to see where a Jew died for the sins of the world. Israel truly is a holy land for three different faiths.

When I was younger, I mistakenly thought Israel remained an ancient place where people today still lived just like they did in Bible times. Pilgrims of the faith may explore Israel's ancient sites, but Israelis themselves are exploring the future, areas of knowledge and education, creative innovations and ideas! Actually, the Bible land of Israel is today one of the most progressive, modern countries in the world! Israel has more scientists and engineers amongst its peoples than any other country on earth. The technology involved in the computer on which I write was first designed in the country of Israel. Computer programs such

At the time of Jesus, this site was a rocky outcropping outside of Jerusalem, with an unused stone quarry into which tombs had been cut. In the 4th century, the hillside was cut away, to allow the Church of the Holy Sepulchre to be built around the tomb. Today we find a wall of marble over the area of Jesus' tomb. *Photo courtesy of holylandphotos.org*

as Yahoo and MSN Messenger are entirely Israeli products. The scientists and engineers of Israel also invent more medical devices to help sick people than any other country. A medical test at my doctor's office has the words "Made in Israel" printed in small letters on the side. The lands of the Bible are actually very modern!

Do you know someone with a sparkling diamond ring? That diamond may well have passed through Israel! Digging in Israel's dirt will not yield you any diamonds, but more Israelis purchase rough diamonds from other places in the world than any other country on Earth. Israelis operate lasers and robots to cut these purchased rough diamonds and Israeli craftspeople, using sophisticated polishing equipment, work to manufacture many of the world's most beautiful diamonds. Touch the next diamond you see—it may have come from the hand of an Israeli diamond craftsman. And no wonder, as it said about the Israeli people in the Bible: *"For they are as the stones of a crown, Sparkling in [God's] land"* (Zech 9:16).

Israeli students in the city of Haifa attend classes at the Computer Science Faculty building at the Technion Institute for Science. What cutting-edge scientific inventions will they design for our modern world?

We've set our hearts on pilgrimage, traveling throughout Israel, and hasn't God blessed us, just as He promised? Psalm 122:4 declares that *"All...the LORD's people make their pilgrimage here. They come to give thanks to the name of the LORD"* (NLT). So do we. Yet the "Holy Land" is not only over in Israel; every place where the Spirit comes into a person's heart is holy ground. Oh, to remember: ***"The earth is the LORD'S and all...those who dwell in it"*** (Ps. 24:1). Amen!

What a view of the Church of the Holy Sepulcher we have from the tower of a nearby church. The larger dome of the church is directly over the traditional site of Jesus' tomb. The smaller, grey-white dome is thought to be built over the location of Jesus' crucifixion. Understandably, the Church of the Holy Sepulchre is considered the holiest site of Christianity. *Photo courtesy of holylandphotos.org*

Field Notes

What a rich and fascinating place Israel is. Have you enjoyed our journeys through Bible lands?

Press record and talk to me:

~ **about the Dome of the Rock** : Can you describe the Dome? What does the inside look like? What is Noble Rock? Why is the rock a holy site for Muslims? What do Christians and Jews call the rock? Why is it important to them?

~ **about the Via Dolorosa:**   What does the name mean? Who walked this way?

~ **about the Church of the Holy Sepulchre:**   What site is this church believed to be built upon? What is another name for this church? Who holds the key to the door? How is it unlocked each day?

~ **about modern-day Israel**: What kinds of things are made in Israel? Why do so many diamonds travel through Israel? Is Israel a modern place, like your own town or city? Or has it remained as it was in Bible times?

Travel Log

Using your globe or atlas, let's add the following locations to your map of Israel... We've seen things today that simply must be mapped, so that they will never be forgotten!

Map Notes: <u>Let's record the locations of:</u>

- *Bethlehem*
- *Nazareth*
- *Kafr Kanna*
- *Tabgha*

- *Sea of Galilee*
- *Jerusalem*
- *Mount Moriah*

<u>If you'd like, draw pictures or symbols on your map representing:</u>

- *The stable where Jesus was born* (perhaps a star?)
- *Jesus' home in Nazareth* (maybe a hammer to represent Joseph's work as a carpenter?)
- *Jesus' miracles* (a basket of bread and fish in Tabgha? A jug of wine in Kafr Kanna? A Man walking the Sea of Galilee?)
- *Western Wall* (a scroll of paper to represent the prayers?)
- *The Dome of the Rock* (a shining gold dome seems appropriate!)
- *Via Dolorosa* (a cross?)
- *Church of the Holy Sepulchre* (an empty tomb? A long metal key?)
- *Modern Israel* (perhaps a computer? Or a diamond ring?)

Travel Notes: Geographers write what they've seen in order to share the adventure with others—and so they can revisit the places in their memories! **On the next page of your travel log, record three important sights you want to remember from your photos of Israel.**

~art ~books ~food ~music ~poetry

Bringing It Home

Simple ideas to bring the world to your door

Food

Bagels and Lox

The bagel may have originated in Poland in the 1600s and been brought to America by immigrating Jews, but today it is customarily associated with Jewish cuisine.

Top a poppy-seed or sesame-seed bagel with cream cheese and lox (smoked salmon) and enjoy! (If you don't have smoked salmon, your store should carry salmon-flavored cream cheese.)

Hamentaschen

These triangular shaped cookies are baked and enjoyed during the feast of Purim, which celebrates the salvation of Israel through Queen Esther's heroic act. The name comes from the Hebrew words *osnei haman* (literally, Haman's Ears).

2/3 cup butter
1/2 cup sugar
1 egg
1/4 cup pulp-free orange juice
1 cup white flour

1 cup wheat flour – no substitutes
2 tsp. baking powder
Jam of your choice

Beat butter and sugar thoroughly. Add egg and mix until well combined. Add the orange juice and mix again, until well combined. Add flour, ½ c at a time, alternating white and wheat, blending thoroughly between each addition. Add baking powder with last addition of flour. Refrigerate until chilled thoroughly – a few hours or overnight.

Roll dough as thin as possible without tearing (you may want to roll it between two sheets of flour-dusted wax paper). Cut out 3-4 in [7.6 – 10 cm]circles. Put a dollop of jam in the middle of each circle and fold up sides to make a triangle, overlapping as much as possible so only a small amount of jam shows in the center. Pinch corners to seal. Bake at 350 F [176 C] for 15 – 20 minutes until golden brown.

Go into all the world...

A walk of prayer

As we've journeyed through tiny Israel we've been amazed to walk the land of the Bible and see that all the places we've read about really exist! And we've discovered that Israel is full of **boys and girls** *not so different from us at all. They were created by a God who loves them dearly—just as He loves you.*

Will you and your family join me in praying for the Israeli people?

Lord, give us Your love for the peoples of the world, and help our family to live in a way that shows our love for them.

Father, we think of this little country that is the center of so much attention, and we think of how much You love her people. We pray for **peace** and Your purposes for the nation of Israel.

~As the holy land for 3 major religions, Israel is continually being wrestled over. Lord, may the people who live within her borders live at **peace with their neighbors**. May they learn to **love each other** as You patiently love us. We pray for godly wisdom for the world's governments as decisions are made regarding this region of the world and may Your will be accomplished.

~We think of the families, mothers and fathers, children and grandparents, cousins and aunts and uncles, who must live their lives in the midst of such turmoil. **We ask that You keep families safe**. We ask that You **provide for their needs** in the middle of conflicts. May there be food for their tables and warm houses to find safety. May they find joy in You.

~We pray for the thousands of **immigrants** who leave other countries behind to embrace Israel as their homeland. Many are without jobs or homes. Please provide for their needs. May no one go hungry or live in the cold.

~We pray for the **pilgrims** who make their way to Israel each year. As they travel, may they discover You, and make their pilgrimage complete.

We love you, Lord, and the people who are living in Israel today. May the Light of our Savior dawn over all nations today. Draw us all closer to You, Father. In Jesus name, Amen.

"Joseph took the young child and his mother by night and Departed into Egypt... that it might be fulfilled by the prophet Saying 'Out of Egypt, have I called my son.'" Matthew 2:14-15

Wearing Egypt

Egypt ~Part 1~

Up in my Granny's attic bedroom, corners piled high with musty books, I sifted through tattered pictures of a time before my own time when my grandfather roamed far away lands. Slipping out of the stack, a graying photo fell to the floor. I bent over to pick it up. My bespectacled grandfather, hands on hips, posed before a mammoth pyramid of stones rearing up out of the desert. My grandfather was in Egypt! What mysterious sights had he beheld in those pyramids? Were the Egyptians he had met on his travels much like the Egyptians I read of in history books? Did he too travel up the Nile, like the dazzling pharaohs of the past? I ran my fingers over his coins and stamps from Egypt. Egypt wasn't simply an ancient, mummified civilization, contained in the yellowed pages of old history books. Egypt was alive, in rich, living color, beckoning explorers to come breathe the enchanting air of the land of the pharaohs today.

When Grandfather wore his khaki pants and shirt, green belt buckled around his waist, safari hat crowning his head, he actually looked just like the country of Egypt. As Grandfather donned his four pieces of clothing, so God clothes Egypt in 4 geographical regions. With his sandy-colored shirt and pants, Grandfather resembled the tawny sand dunes of Egypt's Western and Eastern Deserts, his belt of green like the slithering, fertile Nile, and his rust red safari hat crowned his head like the red mountains of the triangular Sinai Peninsula!

Slightly larger than the Canadian province of British Columbia, Egypt holds an interesting seat on the Earth's surface. Egypt is considered a country of the Middle East, yet nearly all of it lies in the continent of Africa. The rusty, barren peaks of Egypt's Sinai Peninsula lie in the continent of Asia. Egypt literally stretches into two continents.

Let's begin our exploration of Egypt in its Sinai Peninsula. Derived from Latin words *"paene insula"* meaning "almost island," a **peninsula** is just that: a narrow strip of land almost made into an island by the water surrounding it on three sides. Looking at the map of Egypt on the next page, can you name the bodies of water that make the Sinai a peninsula?

If a sea were called the Red Sea, what color might you envision such a body of water? Ironically, God painted the Red Sea sapphire blue. It is the red rock of the Egyptian Sinai Peninsula reflecting upon the lapping waves that give this body of water its name, the Red Sea. To me, the Red Sea seems to reach with two arms, one the Gulf of Aquaba, and the other, the Gulf of Suez, to embrace the Sinai Peninsula. (A **gulf** is a large area of ocean (or sea) that is partially enclosed by land.) Which perspective is yours? When you look at the map of this region, do you see what I see? Or do you see the Sinai

One of the greatest civilizations the world has ever known, Ancient Egypt grew up along the Nile for more than 3,000 years.
Photo: Erik Hooymans

From our seats in space, can you see how Egypt might look like Grandfather's attire? Can you name the four geographical regions with which God has clothed Egypt? *Photo courtesy of visibleearth.nasa.gov*

Peninsula and mainland Egypt wrapping around to embrace the Red Sea, forming the Gulf of Suez? It is just as Proverbs 8:29 says of our God: *"He set for the sea its boundary so that the water would not transgress His command, when He marked out the foundations of the earth."*

As the seas follow the Lord's command, so Moses followed God when He led the twelve tribes of Israel into Egypt's Sinai Peninsula over 3,500 years ago, as we read in Exodus 19:1, *"…after the sons of Israel had gone out of the land of Egypt, on that very day they came into the wilderness of the Sinai."* The origin of the name Sinai is thought to be related to the Babylonian moon god, "Sin." With more camel trails than roads through its central region, Egypt's Sinai Peninsula does in many ways, resemble a landscape as foreign and as barren as the moon. Today, simple towns of thatched roof huts fringe the Sinai Peninsula's coasts, as do luxurious vacation destinations, offering scuba and snorkeling gear for underwater explorations through coral reefs and exotic marine life.

We, however, will pass by these seaside resort towns of palm trees and pools, to follow the harsh, dusty trail into the interior of the Sinai where Moses and the Israelites may have journeyed. Our trek leads us southward to the foot of towering, rugged *Jabal Musa* - meaning Mountain of Moses - oft times referred to as Mount Sinai. Is this gnarled mountain the Mount Sinai we read of in Exodus 31:18? *"When he had finished speaking with him upon Mount Sinai, He gave Moses the two tablets of the testimony, tablets of stone, written by the finger of God."* While the events recorded in the Bible are indeed true, geographers and historians are not certain exactly where Mount Sinai of the Bible now stands. However, since the time of Helena of Constantinople, Jabal Musa has been considered the true Biblical Mount Sinai, and thousands of pilgrims travel the world over to ascend to its peak.

As dawn breaks, we sit high on our camel mounts, riding up to what may be the exact geographical location of God's awesome, blazing descent to speak the law to Moses. From Mount Sinai's summit, can you see the ruddy crest of *Jabal Katrinah* to the south, the highest point in all of Egypt, over 2642 ft [8,668 m.] high? (Observant as you are, have you figured out the Arabic word for mountain? Yes, *jabal*!)

In the warmth of morning, we join the tourists in the wearisome descent down the 3,700 rock-hewn steps from Mount Sinai's peak, eyes fixed on the craggy red mountains casting shadows all around. Did Moses, tablets of the Ten Commandments in hand, see a similar scene four thousand years ago of mountains with Israeli tents huddled about its base?

One of the two arms of the Red Sea, the Gulf of Aquaba, stretches up alongside this resort at Dahab on the Sinai Peninsula. Can you hear its waves lapping now? God marked its boundary and the waters go no farther.

Standing atop Mount Sinai, we agree with what the great traveler Edward Hull wrote in 1885, "Nothing can exceed the savage grandeur of the view from the summit of Mount Sinai. The infinite complication of jagged peaks and varied ridges, and their prevalent intensely red and greenish tints..." On a clear day, we can look across this ocean of rocky waves and see the hazy blue of the Gulf of Aquaba and the Gulf of Suez. *Photo: Ian Sewall*

Bedouin children, with their coal black hair and jet black eyes, gather around us at the rocky foot of Jabal Musa, selling trinkets and necklaces. When I wear my Mount Sinai necklace, with its watery blue heart purchased from Mount Sinai's Bedouin children, I often wonder where those nomadic Bedouins of Egypt have wandered now...and pray they too encounter God in the Sinai wilderness.

Tucked near the base of Mount Sinai stands St. Catherine's Monastery, built fifteen hundred years ago; the oldest operating church in the world today. If you'll listen, you can hear the old language—Byzantine Greek—spoken during the five services a day. It is quite a surprise as no culture has spoken Byzantine Greek in more than a thousand years! In addition to the church, St. Catherine's includes a library with the world's second largest collection of religious manuscripts. (Have you ever traveled to such a remote location to visit a library? Once the ruler of Russia borrowed a very precious manuscript from St. Catherine's library and he never bothered to return it, but sold it to a museum! The long over-due manuscript happens to be the text from which the King James Version of the Bible was translated!) Within the honey colored stone walls of the monastery, we stand stilled before a sinewy bush shading a well, considered by some to be Moses' Burning Bush. The monks of St. Catherine believe a wild raspberry bush, much like one you might find in the woods, to be the actual bush Moses encountered ---but it used to be located on the other side of the small walkway. Yes, they moved the Burning Bush! Is this the very bush out of which God's voice thundered? We'll never know for certain, but we stare at this shrub, trying to imagine what Moses might have felt when he heard the voice of the Lord speak on that unforgettable day.

North of Mount Sinai, we discover Colored Canyon gouged out of the Sinai Peninsula. A **canyon** is a narrow **chasm** or valley with steep **cliff** walls, cut into the Earth's surface by running water. Today, no water runs through this twisting canyon. Did Moses and the Israelites also squeeze through these narrow canyon walls flanking sixteen stories high on both sides? Perhaps they too ran their fingers along the rocks striped soft shades of pink, orange and yellow and praised our creative Creator God who carved these stones with torrents of water.

Located at the base of Mount Sinai, St. Catherine's Monastery was built by order of Emperor Justinian in 527 A.D. One of the oldest monasteries in the world, it is built around what is thought to be the Burning Bush. More than 4,500 illuminated manuscripts are housed here in this desert library. Would you like to go for a visit? *Photo: G. Piezinger*

After our morning of hiking and exploring the Sinai's rugged Jabal Musa and Colored Canyon, we welcome the opportunity to sit with the Bedouins and refresh with some strong herbal tea. The Bedouin have a centuries old tradition of generous hospitality---a newcomer in such isolated regions is always welcome! We sit in the *mag'ad* or 'sitting place' section of the Bedouin tent, while behind the woven curtain, known as a **ma'nad**, the women cook and receive female guests in the **maharama**, 'the place of the women.' As we bid farewell, our Bedouin friends offer us their cell-phone number. (Yes, modern-day technology even extends to such desolate places like the Sinai and to nomadic people like the Bedouin.)

A Bedouin woman and her children offer necklaces for tourists to purchase. A Bedouin woman's jewelry is a sign of her wealth. Upon her death, her jewelry will be melted down and fashioned into new adornments. Which necklace do you choose?

Bedouin comes from the Arabic word meaning 'inhabitant of the desert.' While many Bedouin still live a nomadic lifestyle in the Sinai Peninsula, many changes have affected their land and lifestyle. Bedouin have modern day conveniences, yet there is a growing appreciation for the value of the ancient Bedouin culture that exists in the Sinai and how fragile it is. Isn't it a privilege to meet this Bedouin and have tea with him?

Scuba diving off the coast of the Sinai Peninsula can't be missed! Just watch out for the barracudas, stingrays and sharks amidst the coral reefs!

Field Notes

Don't you wish you could visit Egypt for real just like my Grandfather did? Would you like to own a red safari hat like his?

Press record and talk to me:

~about the Sinai Peninsula: What is a peninsula?
What bodies of water surround the Sinai Peninsula? Is the Red Sea red? What color are its waters? What color are the rocks around it? What is the other name for *Jabal Musa*? What important Biblical event may have happened here?

~ **about St. Catherine's Monastery**: How old is the church?   What language is spoken here? Tell me about its library. What famous manuscript was "borrowed" from St. Catherine's?   What famous bush would we find within the monastery's walls?

~ **about Colored Canyon**: What is a canyon? Can you describe how God carved and colored the canyon?

To explore the next geographical region of Egypt, point your **compass** east and head out of Sinai. As Moses and the Israelites discovered, we find ourselves on a coastline, not at all surprising for a peninsula. Although we are traveling further west into Egypt, and the Israelites were headed in the opposite direction *out* of Egypt, we wonder: where exactly did God miraculously part the waters of the Red Sea so that Moses and the Israelites might cross on dry ground? If you gathered several maps charting the route of the exodus of the Israelites out of Egypt, none of the maps may agree on the route! Some chart the phenomenal crossing at the northern tip of the Gulf of Suez, while others argue that Moses led the Israelites across the entire Sinai Peninsula to cross the Gulf of Aquaba. Still other historians suggest God wondrously made a way across a swampy region north of the Gulf of Suez called the "Reed Sea."

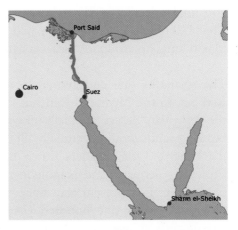

Can you trace the path of the Suez Canal across the isthmus? If it weren't for the canal, how else might you transport your ship of goods to the Mediterranean Sea?

We may not know the exact Egyptian location of the crossing but we are certain that God indeed wrought a breathtaking miracle such that thousands upon thousands of Israelites passed through walls of water into glorious freedom!

Our ship chugs down the Suez Canal, careful to stay in the single shipping lane. Ships travel this canal around the clock, in three convoys. Ships traveling south, moor to the side to allow the northbound convoy to pass. You ask if we are there yet. An average crossing through the canal takes 11-16 hours.

As no miraculous route appears to afford us a dry crossing of the Gulf of Suez, we opt for the land route, trekking through the Isthmus of Suez. An **isthmus** is a narrow strip of land connecting two larger pieces of land. The Isthmus of Suez connects the Sinai Peninsula with the rest of Egypt. But here we again meet with a waterway.

Have you ever spent an afternoon at the beach digging a channel from the water's edge then watching the water trickle up your little canal? What if your **canal**, which is a man-made river, took a span of 10 full years to dig and required the assistance of 1.5 million friends? Such is the case of the world's longest, lockless canal of water cutting across the Isthmus of Suez. Parting the desert with its ribbon of blue water, the Suez Canal is one of the world's most striking short cuts. Imagine you had a shipload of goods in the Red Sea and wanted to deliver those goods to Haifa in Israel. Haifa may not be that far geographically from the Red Sea, but the only natural way to sail a ship into Haifa's harbor is to take the long way around Africa's tip, up Africa's east coast, and ride the waves of the dazzling Mediterranean Sea into

the harbor. The Earth's geography can make travel between destinations less than direct and rather laborious. To avoid the long route around Africa, you could do what was done for hundreds of years: dock your ship on the shores of the Gulf of Suez and carry the goods across the arid desert to ships waiting in the Mediterranean Sea. Wearied by either option, you might decide to dig a shortcut canal through the desert. That 120 mile [193 km] canal would save you the 6,000 mile [9,656 km] trip around Africa—what a worthwhile short cut!

The pharaohs first endeavored to create this canal from the Red Sea to the Mediterranean but the winds whipping across the Egyptian desert gradually clogged any attempts, just as blowing sands would eventually fill in your miniature canal on the beach. Other leaders down through the ages, such as Ptolemy, Cleopatra and Napoleon tried to finish the project, but failed. The present day Suez Canal, carved out of the desert well over one hundred years ago, is supported with stone, cement and steel to prevent the canal from slowly eroding away. Truly a modern-day engineering wonder, the Suez Canal plunges to a depth of 70 ft [21 m]; that is 7 times deeper than your community pool! Do you see that special ship called a **dredger** down in the canal? With its big hoses sucking up sand and dirt from the bottom of the canal, dredgers are making the canal even deeper and wider so more

Can you see the Suez Canal from up here in space? Parting the desert with a canal allows ships to travel from Asia to Europe without circumnavigating the continent of Africa. Imagine what it would have been like to have been one of the 1.5 million workers who worked more than 10 years to dig that canal!
Photo courtesy of visibleearth.nasa.gov

ships can take advantage of this shortcut. More than 15,000 ships chug up this canal every year, an average of 50 ships per day, crossing between the Red Sea and Mediterranean Sea in less than 16 hours. (Check the tag on your shirt. Was it made in a distant country? If so, it may very well have passed through the Suez Canal before it reached your hands!) These mammoth ships we see streaming up the blue waters do not freely take the shortcut from the Indian to Atlantic Ocean, however; the bigger the ship, the higher the toll fee charged by the government of Egypt. We wave to the cargo and oil tankers being piloted down the canal by especially trained captains, and decide that instead of driving through the darkened road tunneled underneath the canal, we'll cross the Suez Canal via the world's longest swing bridge. A line of cars patiently waits on the bank as the bridge mechanically swings out of the way to allow the gigantic ships clear passage. When the bridge swings back into place, our line of cars streams across the Suez Canal into Egypt's second geographical region: the Eastern Desert.

Often called the Arabian Desert, the Eastern Desert gradually slides from jagged mountains punctuating its Red Sea coastline down to the cliffs lingering over the Nile River. Our exploration of the Eastern Desert drops us into deep **ravines**, called **wadis**, that cut through the rising, rocky hills, and over shifting golden sands, brushed with a hint of red, a reflection of the minerals in the limestone rocks. In our trek we do not, however, encounter many Egyptians or any permanent settlements. Who can grow crops or raise animals in a desert where it does not rain?

The Eastern Desert may not produce bushels of wheat, but it does produce barrels of oil. Towns spring up where the Eastern Desert meets the Red Sea since oil was discovered in this region over 100 years ago. Far out on the Red Sea and Gulf of Suez, oil rigs pump oil up from deep under the seafloor. Close to the shoreline, wells drilled into rock below the Eastern Desert produce heavy oil. That first oil well drilled by the Egyptian government into the Eastern Desert produced only 25 barrels of crude oil per day. Today, while you eat and sleep, Egyptian oil wells will fill more than 750,000 barrels of oil. Countless Egyptian families will buy food and clothes and more, based on the sale of those oil barrels. God created Egypt's geography to include a natural resource like oil underneath the desert sands. Even in this region of the world, God made a way for families to work and live and play!

With God-given resources, however, comes God-expected responsibility. While spilled milk at the dinner table may be easily wiped up, spilled oil in areas like the Red Sea may kill birds and marine life. Paying a small fee to visit one of the stunning beaches in the town of Hurghada on the Eastern Desert shoreline, we sight numerous White-eyed Gulls flying overhead. Just off the coast of Hurghada, a string of small islands is the largest breeding station for White-eyed Gulls in the world. Now, however, these black-headed gulls with a striking brush of white feathers accentuating their eyes, struggle to survive because of **polluting** oil spills on the Red Sea where the gulls feed. Adventuresome tourists such as you and I may unknowingly harm the geography of a region; our hotels destroying nesting sites, our garbage polluting the landscape, and our presence inadvertently causing the destruction of coral reefs in the Red Sea. Ps. 19:1 trumpets *The heavens declare the glory of God, and the firmament proclaims his handiwork.* God created this world to glorify Himself. Caring for God's world—its geography, animals and plants—brings glory to God. Egypt's government is diligently working toward laws and management plans to ensure the care and protection of God's creation.

Before riding our camel further westward across the rugged Eastern Desert towards Egypt's third geographical region, let's visit a Hurghada street vendor for a hearty meal of **tamiya**. Forming a handful of soft, cooked fava beans into a patty, the street side chef fries the patties up in a frying pan of sizzling hot olive oil. Offering a *"Shukran"* (thank you) to the vendor for the crispy bean cakes that will refresh us for the trip westward, we are ready to embark, like Grandfather, for the famed Nile River, and the wonders of the heart of Egypt. I can hardly wait!

Aren't the waters magnificent off the beaches of Hurghada in the Eastern Desert? How we need to be wise stewards of God's creation to preserve His beautiful world.

Field Notes

What a fascinating landscape we've come through so far! Are you enjoying the camel ride?

Press record and talk to me:

~ **about the Isthmus of Suez**: How has God created an isthmus? What does the Isthmus of Suez connect? Tell me about the Suez Canal . How does the Canal help people deliver goods? What does a dredger do? Describe the bridge that allows people to cross the canal.

~ **about the Eastern Desert**: Would we find lots of people in this area? Why or why not? What is produced in the Eastern Desert? How does this help Egyptian families? What happens if the oil spills? Why must people be careful with the geography of a region?

Travel Log

Using your globe or atlas, draw an outline map of Egypt.

As we travel, let's make record in our very own travel log of the places we've visited and the unusual sights we've seen! Make your map large enough to hold all of your discoveries!

Don't worry about making a perfect map, just do your best. Drawing the basic shape yourself will help you remember it better. Or use the map provided for you on the CD-ROM.

Map Notes: Let's record the locations of:
- *Sinai Peninsula*
- *Gulf of Aquaba*
- *Gulf of Suez*
- *Jabal Musa (or Mt. Sinai)*
- *EXTRA: Jabal Katrinah*
- *EXTRA: Red Sea*

If you'd like, draw pictures or symbols on your map representing:

- *The Ten Commandments on Mt. Sinai*
- *Bedouin children* (perhaps a blue heart?)
- *St. Catherine's Monastery* (a stack of books to represent the library? A church? Don't forget the Burning Bush!)

Travel Notes: Geographers write what they've seen in order to share the adventure with others—and so they can revisit the places in their memories! **On the next page of your travel log, record three important sights you want to remember from your camel ride through Egypt.**

~*art* ~*books* ~*food* ~*music* ~*poetry*

. . . .

Bringing It Home

Simple ideas to bring the world to your door

Art:

Make a cartouche:

A **cartouche** is an oval shaped ring enclosing the written name of ancient Egyptian pharaohs. The word *cartouche* was given to this oval-shape by Napoleon's soldiers, who thought it looked like a gun cartridge (*cartouche*). Inside the oval is the Pharoah's name written in hieroglyphs.

You can make a cartouche for your name here:
http://www.kidzone.ws/cultures/egypt/hieroglyph.htm

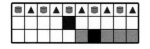

Play Senet:

Would you like to play a game that may have been played by the Pharoahs and other Egyptians? Archaeologists have discovered evidence that ancient Egyptians enjoyed board games just as you and I do. Senet is one of those discoveries. It is a simple game that involves throwing sticks and moving pieces along a board.

You can print your own senet board here:
http://www.tabula-rasa.info/JamesAdams/treasure_trove/senet/printableSenetBoard.htm

Or you can play online here:
http://www.ancientegypt.co.uk/life/activity/main.html

Music:

Music captures so much of a land and people. Introducing your children to Egyptian music is a simple way to transport yourselves around the world. Why not check out these sites while your young geographers notebook and map and let the music play while they recount their travels?

You will find a wide selection of samples here:
http://worldmusic.nationalgeographic.com/worldmusic/view/page.basic/country/content.country/egypt_39?fs=plasma.nationalgeographic.com

Some beautiful instrumental examples are here: http://www.aldokkan.com/mp3/mp3.htm

Navigating the Nile

Egypt ~Part 2~

Have you ever stood on your head so that up was down and down was up? Of course, to everyone else, your down was up and your up was down. Now that you are completely confused, come see why Egypt's up is down and down is up.

Generally, we speak of places in southern locations as being "down south." In Egypt, however, the southern region of the country is unexpectedly called, Upper Egypt. Why, you ask? Egypt's south is "up" because the Nile River flows from mountains in Southern Africa DOWN stream to the Mediterranean Sea in the North. Since southern Egypt lies upstream it is referred to as "UPPER Egypt." On the other hand, we normally refer to northern locales as "up north." But not so in Egypt: the northern region is actually named Lower Egypt since it lies downstream. Can you now explain why Egypt's up is down and down is up?

While the direction a river flows depends simply on where mountain ranges are, we tend to think all rivers flow in the same direction as the rivers we live near. If you were an Egyptian living on the north-flowing Nile River, you might think that the rest of the world was upended. One Egyptian Pharaoh, Tuthmosis I, described the great south-flowing Euphrates River as "the inverted water that goes downstream in going upstream." The poor Pharaoh sounds as confused over south flowing rivers as we may be over north flowing rivers! In Egypt, it is the mighty Nile, covering one sixth of the earth's circumference, that determines upper and lower—and all of life. Step on board for a cruise down the Nile that will change forever how you see Egypt!

In the dim before dawn, we wake early on the deck of our *felucca*, a traditional Egyptian sailboat, to watch as the Nile riverbank stirs to life. Do you hear the blaring chant of the muezzin in a hidden village mosque calling sleepy Egyptians to prayer? A kingfisher skims inches above the waters. The felucca's triangular white sail billows in a gentle gust of wind. Did you catch a glimpse of the pure white egrets standing stock still in the bulrushes clumped along the water's edge? On the riverbank, a brown humpbacked cow chews its cud under the shade of a date palm. Further down the river, fishermen in a small rowboat haul in their nets of catch. Don't you almost want to crane your ear for the baby's cry, to peer over the railing in hopes of sighting a glimpse of

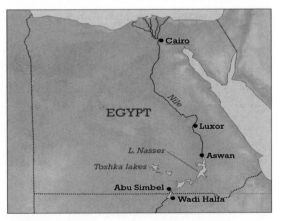

The longest river in the world, winding through 10 African countries, the Nile snakes a ribbon of fertile green growth through Egypt. More than 95% of all Egyptians live near its banks. And yet God is the One who controls this life-giving water, as He says in Ezekiel 30:12 "I will dry up the streams of the Nile." *Map: Mark Dingemanse*

a bobbing basket? For this is the same Nile River that carried baby Moses to the feet of the Pharaoh's daughter. The waters of the Nile have known Aristotle and Alexander the Great, Mark

An ancient sailboat of the Nile, our felucca is a common means of transport up and down the Nile River. It's broad triangular sail is made of canvas while the boat itself has a shallow deck. Let's sit upon its thick cotton covered pads and watch the dark waters of the Nile slide by in the hot dry desert wind.

Anthony, Cleopatra and Julius Caesar. Can you envision Joseph, second in command only to the Egyptian Pharaoh himself, floating down these same waters, past the towering pyramids? Isn't it hard to imagine this magnificent Nile running red with blood during one of God's Ten Plagues? Jesus, the Christ Child, journeyed here to Egypt and her regal river. The longest river in the world, the Nile may transport you and me back through the pages of history and the Bible, but for Egyptians today and for thousands of years of history, the Nile River has been the essence of existence, the life breath of the desert.

Coursing almost 1,000 m [1, 600 km] through the heart of Egypt, the Nile river forges a gorge of green growth 10 miles [16 km] across at its widest point. (The word Nile comes from the Greek word that means "*river valley.*") Today nearly all of Egypt's 77 million people live within a slender 12 miles[19 km] of the Nile River, only a narrow 4% slice of Egypt's land.

Through the mist rising off these waters, we see women in dark *burqa* gowns, (a loose robe worn by Muslim women, covering them from head to toe, with veiled holes for their eyes) carrying laundry from mud-brick houses with flat straw roofs down to the Nile. Sons of the *fellahin* (farmers), not much older than you, herd sheep and goats to drink Nile waters before leading them out to graze. A boatman, heading south, rows slowly against the Nile's northerly stream. Today, as in the sweep of Egyptian history, we see the waters of the Nile River as Egypt's wash tub for families, as its garden hose for thirsty crops, as its highway, carrying boatloads of tourists, sugarcane, and cotton bales across the country. Yet this magnificent river has changed with the march of time. If you will travel south, to Upper Egypt, you'll discover how.

Near the city of Aswan, (can you locate that on your map?) you can't miss seeing one of the world's most massive structures, the Aswan High **Dam**, rising 364 feet [111 m] out of the depths of the Nile. It would take three 12 story apartment buildings, stacked on end from the Nile's riverbed, to reach the height of this enormous granite wall corking the Nile! Taking ten years to construct, one billion dollars to fund, and using enough rock to build seventeen Great Pyramids, the Aswan High Dam, straddling 2.3 miles [3.7 km] across the river, is Egypt's heavy net to capture the Nile.! The **reservoir** formed by the dam is one of the world's largest man-made lakes, the 312 miles [502 km] wide Lake Nasser.

While modern civilization has changed the banks of the Nile River, much of the river still retains the same scenery today that would have been familiar to the ancient Egyptians. *Photo courtesy of visibleearth.nasa.gov*

For thousands of years, the Nile, swollen from rains in southern Africa, annually overflowed its banks, flooding the entire valley. In modern times, the Nile swamped the basements of homes in the northern city of Cairo. When the Nile ebbed away, it gifted Egyptians with four million tons [3.6

million metric tons] of rich silt spread over their fields. But the Bible records how God sometimes chose not to raise the Nile: *"He will smite the waves in the sea, and all the deeps of the [Nile] shall dry up...and the scepter of Egypt shall depart"* (Zech. 10:11). When the Nile did not flood the valley, the power of Egypt indeed departed: crops withered in the fields and tummies ached for food. Not long ago, Egyptians decided to capture the annual flood with a dam across the river and release the water steadily over the course of the year. The thunder of foaming white waters that now roars continuously through the dam, not only aids faster travel of boats down the Nile, but generates electricity used throughout the country. Without the annual flooding of the Nile, the Egyptian fellahin now plant three seasons of crops, have more fields to cultivate, and irrigation of crops such as cotton, onion, rice and potatoes is much easier. The Aswan High Dam has changed the flow of the Nile and the face of Egypt.

Can you see one of the world's largest embankment dams from our space side seats? The huge Aswan Dam captures the Nile River, creating one of the world's largest reservoirs, Lake Nasser. *Photo courtesy of visibleearth.nasa.gov*

While people may have good reasons for changing the God-given geography of a place, there are often harmful outcomes. As the Aswan High Dam inflated Lake Nasser with the Nile River, more than 90, 000 poor Egyptian peasants were forced to pack up what little they owned and move out of the way of the rising waters. The lake formed by the dam also threatened to flood some Egyptian treasures that couldn't be easily moved, such as the stone temple of Abu Simbel. Would the four 66 ft. [22 m] high statues of Ramses, (that's as high as 12 tall men standing one on top of each other!) that had guarded the entrance to the temple for thousands of years drown in the rising waters of Lake Nasser? Heroic rescuers from all over the world rushed to save Abu Simbel's great temple and the four statues, cutting each into hundreds upon hundreds of blocks, hauling the sections to the new lake shore, and reassembling the puzzle of pieces. (It took ten years to complete the rescue mission!)

The two temples at Abu Simbel were among the most impressive monuments in the world. The rescue operation to move them out of the way of the rising waters of the newly created Lake Nasser was just as impressive! This picture shows where the temple was originally built thousands of years ago, and how it was dismantled, raised over 197 ft [60 m] up a cliff, and reassembled. Did you notice that the two temples were placed in the exact same relationship to each other and the sun? And yes, they were then covered with an artificial mountain!

Some effects of the Aswan High Dam, however, cannot be altered: the rich silt God intended to fertilize the parched desert land during the annual floods now lies trapped behind the dam at the bottom of Lake Nasser. Egyptian farmers, clad in flowing **galabeas** (an ankle-length loose shirt), can be seen today spreading a million tons of artificial fertilizer on their fields as a substitute for the natural nutrients that God once deposited on the dry floodplain. Pharaoh's daughter may have bathed in the Nile, but today one warily avoids these waters. The construction of the Aswan High Dam has increased the population of a tiny **parasitic** worm that can penetrate the skin of anyone swimming in contaminated water. With no dry spells between floodings, the parasitic worms thrive, making infected children especially sick with fever. God designed the world in an intricate balance; when we alter His creation in hopes of making it better in some ways, we often inadvertently make it worse in other ways.

The massive Aswan High Dam captures floodwater during the rainy seasons and releases the water throughout the year. The dam also generates tremendous amounts of electric power for Egyptians – more than 10 billion kilowatt-hours every year. That's enough electricity to power one million color televisions for 20 years.

Across the river, children wave to us from the balcony of their cruise ship, one of the hundreds that sail the Nile River. Egyptian merchants paddle their rowboats out to the larger cruise ships, tossing up towels emblazoned with pictures of famous Egyptian monuments. The tourists barter for a deal, tossing down money in return for a keepsake from Egypt. Nearly 500 years *before* the birth of Jesus, there were tourists sailing up and down the Nile, pursuing the wonders of already ancient Egyptian civilization. A tourist named Herodotus, possibly history's earliest recorded travel writer, wrote his own field notes of his Egyptian excursion: "*Egypt is the gift of the Nile.*" Today tourism is one of Egypt's main industries. Everywhere, we see sightseers streaming from one ancient Egyptian wonder to the next. We also see armed tourist police monitoring travelers' safety and safe-guarding the all-important business of tourism.

During our northward sail down the Nile, the captain of our small felucca docks often and we slip under the dappled shade of a date palm tree. Egypt is the world's top producer of dates. In some fields, a crop of cabbages grows in the shade of the date palms.

We often see millions of harvested dates spread out like a pebbly carpet, drying in the Egyptian sun. With woven baskets at their feet, veiled Egyptian women diligently sort through the rug of dates by hand. As you bite into your next date, remember that Egyptian woman: perhaps it was she who sorted your date!

More than 4 million tourists come from all over the world to explore Egypt every year. Would you like a seat on a cruise boat such as this to experience all the sights and sounds of the majestic Nile?

On our sail towards the Egyptian city of Luxor and the Valley of the Kings, do you notice that none of the mud houses of the fellahin villages have windows of glass, but merely have open spaces in the walls? Call "*Assalaamu aleikum*" (ah-sah-LA-moo ah-LAY-koom) (Arabic for "hello") to the young girl collecting cow dung for fuel in the open hearth of her family's outdoor kitchen. While your family may cook dinner outside on the BBQ during the summer months, rural Egyptians cook dinner outside year-round!

Near Luxor, we drift past fields where electric pumps bring water to irrigate crops, and donkeys pull two wheeled carts heaped with sugar cane. Together with other tourists from around the world we line up in the Valley of the Kings to see the ancient tombs of Egypt's long dead pharaohs. Can you hear the commentary of our guide over the voices of the other German, Italian, and Spanish guides educating their own groups of explorers? Travelers come to descend the steep ramps down into the stuffy burial chambers. The walls of the pharaoh's tombs still radiate today with the original paintings from thousands of years ago!

Does this rural Egyptian house look like your house? While many houses in Egyptian cities may be similar to yours, houses in the Egyptian countryside are made of mud---and may have a camel waiting outside the front door!

Does this look like one of the world's greatest burial sites? It is! For more than a thousand years, the pharaohs of Egypt were buried here in the Valley of the Kings. Located on the west bank of the Nile River, King Tut's famous tomb was discovered in the Valley of the Kings. The archaeologist, Howard Carter, who discovered King's Tut tomb in this valley, wrote of his experience, "At first I could see nothing, the hot air escaping from the chamber causing the candle flame to flicker... details of the room within emerged slowly from the mist, strange animals, statues and gold - everywhere the glint of gold...."

To these Egyptian women, with faces unveiled, the Nile is everything: they launder clothes in it, cook with its waters, fish in it, water their animals, and use it for transportation and irrigation. Do you think they too, like Pharaoh's daughter, draw their bathwaters from the Nile's current? *Photo: Steve Evans*

Field Notes

What an exciting trip down the Nile! There are so many surprising sights along the river.
Press record and talk to me:

~ **about the Nile River**:   Which direction does the Nile flow? What direction do rivers usually flow? Can you describe the beginning of our ride on the waters? What kind of boat were we in? What kinds of animals did we see? Why do the majority of Egypt's peoples live close to the Nile?

~**about the Aswan High Dam**:   Can you describe it? What Lake is formed by the Dam? Before the Dam was built, what would happen to the Nile's rising waters? What happens now? How has that affected the land?

~**about tourism**:   Which kind of ships sail up and down the river each day? Who rides on them? Tell me about the merchants who row out to the ships. Do all these visitors help or hurt Egypt?

~**about the *fellahin* villages**:   What is a *fellahin*? What do their houses look like? How do some of the villagers prepare their food?

Don't the paintings on the walls of King Tut's tomb still glow with color? Of all the royal tombs found in the Valley of the Kings, King Tut's was the only one found with nearly all of its original treasures—all 3,500 items!

The site nearly every tourist comes to Egypt to see lies further north on the Nile, near the city of Cairo. (Can you locate Cairo on your map?) Outside of Cairo looms the world's most enormous and renowned grave markers, weathered by thousands of years of Egyptian sands. Perhaps you have visited quiet cemeteries, kneeling to run your hands across names carved in granite headstones? Nothing you have ever seen in a cemetery prepares you for this breathtaking burial site. The famous French general, Napoleon, came to these sands outside of Cairo, looked up at the towering, indescribable gravestones and declared, "From atop these pyramids, forty centuries look down upon you." If you lined each freezer-sized stone of this grave-marker end to end, the stones would pave a one-lane road stretching from San Francisco on the southwest coast of the United States to New York City on its northeast coast! These are the **Pyramids** of Giza.

Weighing more than 15 billion pounds [nearly 7 billion kg], with each side of its base measuring the length of 2 ½ football fields, the Great Pyramid is where the royal mummy of Pharaoh Khufu (Cheops) once rested in death. Camel-mounted tourist police ensure no sightseers attempt to climb the gravestones of the pharaohs. You may, however, step down the steep, tunneling ramp into the bowels of the Great Pyramid, your hand touching the massive polished limestone sides. Did an Egyptian Pharaoh, centuries ago, touch this same stone? Standing in the deathly still and bare King's Chamber where Khufu once laid, doesn't your mind return to Ecclesiastes 3:11 which reads *"[God] has also set eternity in the hearts of men"* (NIV)? This mind-boggling monument, one of the most famous structures on the whole planet and the

What would it be like to stand at the base of one of the most famous sites in the world? The Pyramids of Giza, more than three thousand years old, took more than 20,000 workers to build. And yet we remember, heaven and earth will all one day pass away, including the pyramids, and only God's Word will never pass away.

work of more than a hundred thousand ancient Egyptians, stands as a magnificent witness of how the hearts of all people beat with a God-given desire for eternal life.

What do you get when you put a head of a man with a body of a lion? A sphinx! Made of limestone bedrock, the Sphinx once also wore a beard—which can now be found on another continent, in the British Museum.

Have you ever buried your body in heavy sand with only your head and toes poking out? That is how the world's largest single-stone statue, the Great Sphinx, remained for thousands of years in front of Khufu's pyramid: the lion-like body of Sphinx hidden under the sand with only its man-like face sticking up! The tons of sand God sweeps across the Egyptian deserts have actually preserved the **Sphinx** through the centuries. Under its blanket, the soft limestone has been protected from erosion by a constant barrage of wind-blown grains of sands. **Erosion** is the movement of soil particles by water, wind, ice and general weather. Through the process of erosion, God constantly reshapes the landscape of our earth, carving soil with streaming water, sculpting shorelines with crashing waves, and sweeping sands across the desert—which bury, and protect the Sphinx!

Looking up at the Sphinx's 13 ft [4 m] wide face, you immediately notice that it is missing something important – its nose! Did the Sphinx lose its nose because of erosion? Just like we don't know who the Sphinx's face is carved to look like, when it was built, or who built it, we also do not know for certain what happened to its nose. Few believe the legend that Napoleon's French soldiers blasted the nose off with a stray cannonball, but some suggest a devout Muslim cut the nose off when he discovered Egyptian peasants worshipping the Sphinx. We do know, however, that the statue is now eroding away right before our very eyes, chips of limestone falling off under the blazing the heat of the Egyptian sun and the drifting smog of Cairo.

Welcome to Cairo, Africa's largest city! The Nile River curves through this city of ancient mosques, Coptic churches, palaces, museums and more than 15 million people. More than 2 million cars crowd the streets of Cairo. Watch out for speeding vehicles—and the odd camel or donkey cart!

If you'll shift your gaze from the 2,500,000 limestone blocks of Pharaoh Khufu's (Cheops) tomb and from the 65 ft [20 m] high Sphinx, can you see the dwarfed houses of a Cairo suburb just several hundred meters away? The children playing soccer - Egypt's favorite sport - in the shadow of the pyramids, live right over there in those houses. Cairo, Egypt's capital city spills over, nearly right to the feet of the Great Sphinx himself!

As modern-day tourists wander through the remnants of ancient Egypt, so do modern and ancient ways mingle in the city of Cairo. Here in one of the most populated cities in the world, and the largest city on the African continent, we spot camels and donkey carts sharing the clogged streets with careening cars driving "wherever they can find space." Drivers are unconcerned about traffic safety as they believe regardless of their efforts, whatever happens will be Allah's will. As with everything in Egypt—"*Inshallah*" (If it pleases Allah.) We carefully weave our way through ten widths of cars just to make it to the other side of the street.

Look at all of the apartment buildings that line the streets! Swarming Cairo has more people seeking a place to live than it has living accommodations. More than 100,000 people live in every square mile of Cairo [or 2.6 sq km], making it one of the most crowded cities in the world. Thus, valuable land is used to build apartment buildings for many families instead of a single house for only one family. With few yards to play in, children relax with their families out on balconies in the cool of the evening after dinner. And dinner is served late at 10:00 pm or even later!

In this tangle of high rises and buses, we discover some of the most valued ancient Egyptian treasures. Do you recall how all the tombs we visited were empty? That is because all of the treasures are here in the Egyptian Museum of Cairo. Take a long look; no cameras are allowed in this sprawling museum of marvels. You have only your memory to focus on the hair of Ramses' mummy or the gold funerary mask of King Tut.

In this city of opposites, mummified Egyptians lie in ancient storehouses of dazzling wealth, while across town from the museum some Egyptians make their homes on trash heaps or in amongst the grave markers of a cemetery.

Mokattam is Cairo's garbage dump where the **zabaleen** (garbage collectors) families live in the trash piles, their children playing in the rubbish heaps. But there is work to do in Garbage City, Cairo. Girls and boys sift through the 2,000 tons [1, 814 metric tons] of garbage dumped here each day, digging for materials to recycle or sell. Carved out of a nearby mountainside is a church that seats 20,000 people where city dwellers gather to praise the God who "*raiseth up the poor out of the dust*" (Ps. 113:7).

Not far from Garbage City is the City of the Dead – which is very much alive. Amongst the tombs of Egypt's past rulers, we see laundry strung up to dry, and grave markers used as desks and shelves.

Tens of thousands of Egyptians make their home in the quiet of these cemeteries since families can't find affordable places to live in crowded Cairo.

As you read these words, an Egyptian child may be playing in their backyard across from the pyramids, a fellahin boy may be bringing the goats to drink at the Nile's edge, while his sister cooks flatbread in the family's outdoor oven. While you sleep tonight, Nile waters will still roar through the Aswan High Dam on their course from Upper to Lower Egypt, just as it has for millennia, painting the Egyptian desert green with life. When you wake tomorrow morning, you may wash your face with a washcloth made in Egypt and the date in your breakfast muffins may have grown in the sunshine beside the Nile. The land of ancient

To see the treasures of Egypt, we leave behind the Valley of the Kings and the Pyramids and come here to the Egyptian Museum on Tahrir square in Cairo. More than 136,000 treasures are housed in its 107 halls. Do you want to begin here at the ground floor, gazing on the huge statues? Or shall we go to an upper floor houses to see the small statues, jewels, Tutankhamon treasures and the mummies? *Photo: Gérard Ducher*

wonders, Egypt is a land very much alive today—this very day—pulsing with the current of the Nile.

Field Notes

*Now we have seen some of Egypt's famous and ancient sights.
Were you as amazed as I was?*

Press record and talk to me:

~about the pyramids: What and who were they built for? How big are they? Could we climb to the top of one of them? Could we go inside one?

~about the Sphinx: Please describe it to me. What has been happening to the Sphinx over time? What important feature is it missing?

~about Cairo: Are the houses of Cairo far away from the ancient monuments? What might we see in the Egyptian Museum? Tell me about Mokattam. What do the *zabaleen* do there? Can you describe the City of the Dead? Why do people live in places like Mokattam or the City of the Dead?

Travel Log

Using your globe or atlas, let's add the following locations to your map of Egypt:

Map Notes: <u>Let's record the locations of:</u>
- *Nile River*
- *Aswan High Dam*
- *Lake Nasser*
- *Luxor*
- *Cairo*

<u>If you'd like, draw pictures or symbols on your map representing:</u>
- *A felucca on the Nile*
- *Aswan High Dam*
- *Date trees along the riverbanks*
- *Groups of tourists in Luxor*
- *The Pyramids of Giza*
- *The Sphinx*
- *Mokattam* (*perhaps a garbage can? Or a family with a bag of goods to recycle and sell?*)
- *City of the Dead* (*a tombstone?*)

(<u>*Challenge Mapping*</u>: *Can you point out the following on your map? Upper Egypt and Lower Egypt.*)

Travel Notes: Geographers write what they've seen in order to share the adventure with others—and so they can revisit the places in their memories! **On the next page of your travel log, record three important sights you want to remember from your photos of Egypt**

~*art* ~*books* ~*food* ~*music* ~*poetry*

Bringing It Home
Simple ideas to bring the world to your door

Books

Your local library will probably have many books available about ancient Egypt. Here are three good titles to look for. (A caution for younger children: nearly all books on this time period contain pictures of mummies in various states. Parents may want to preread for sensitive children.)

Exploring Ancient Egypt with Elaine Landau *by* Elaine Landau
An enjoyable book with cartoon figures as "guides." Elaine Landau takes children on a tour through many of Egypt's most famous archaeological discoveries. *Appealing to all ages.*

Secrets of the Sphinx *by* James Cross Giblin
A beautiful and detailed book, Giblin explores the facts, myths and strange stories surrounding the Sphinx. The book is divided into separate chapters, so parents can pick and choose what information to share with their children. *Appealing to all ages.*

The Day of Ahmed's Secret *by* Florence Parry Heide
Detailed watercolors bring the life, sounds, and smells of exotic Cairo to life in this story of Ahmed who has learned the secret of writing his name in Arabic. Young readers will experience the sense of the bustling city and its ancient past. A beautiful selection. *Gr. 1-5*

Poetry:

May I walk every day unceasingly on the banks of my water, may my soul rest on the branches of the trees which I have planted, may I refresh myself in the shadow of my sycamore.

Egyptian tomb inscription, ca. 1400 BC

"And Israel dwelt in the land of Egypt, in the country of Goshen; and they had Possessions therein, and grew and multiplied exceedingly." Genesis 47:27

Digging for Good Dirt

Egypt ~Part 3~

Like my father, his father, and his grandfather before him, I was born and raised on a farm. As far back as our family tree stretches, our family has always been dirt-lovers, growing crops to live off the land. When I grew up and ventured into the world, looking for a place of my own, I too looked for good dirt to grow crops. Dirt is what God fashioned us from, what we walk and live on, and yet we hardly even notice it under our feet. But where God formed different kinds of dirt determines not only the location and the way we live, but also the very course of history. Never belittle the value of dirt!

The family of Jacob knew the worth of good dirt. Forced by drought and famine to leave Canaan (modern-day Israel), Jacob's children - who were farmers too - came down into Egypt looking for rich soil. Their flocks of sheep and herds of cattle required lush pastures to feed on. Where does a seeking farmer find productive land in the shifting sand dunes of Egypt? One of Jacob's sons, Joseph, had a suggestion: *"[W]hen Pharaoh calls you and says, 'What is your occupation?' that you shall say, 'Your servants' occupation has been with livestock from our youth even till now, both we and also our fathers,' that you may dwell in the land of Goshen..."* (Gen 46:34 NKJ).

There's our clue: if we find Goshen, we've found fertile, Egyptian soil! Carefully scanning our map, we realize there is no longer any area named *"the land of Goshen"* in Egypt.

The name of this region is now the Nile Delta, but its soil today remains much like the rich, productive land Jacob's sheep once grazed upon. Let's explore the riches of the Nile Delta today!

In Lower Egypt, slightly down-river from crowded Cairo, the Nile River fans out into streams that flow to join the waters of the Mediterranean Sea. Just like you, every river has a mouth, and the Nile is no exception. A river's **mouth** is the last lower portion where it flows into a larger body of water. When the mouth of the Nile River meets the Mediterranean, it opens wide, leaving tons of sand and soil that has been carried from upriver. This sediment-rich area is called a **delta**.

The delta region we are looking down at from space is one of the oldest intensely cultivated or farmed areas on earth. Where do you think Jacob and his family lived? The Delta is heavily populated, with more than one thousand neighbors living in .4 sq miles [1 sq km]! Did you know that the famous Rosetta Stone, the rock that unlocked the code to ancient hieroglyphics, was found here in the Nile River Delta? *Photo courtesy of visibleearth.nasa.gov*

When I learned Greek, I daily recited the Greek alphabet; *alpha, beta, gamma, delta*. Interestingly, the wide-open river mouth that deposits silt is actually named after the Greek letter Delta since both are shaped like a triangle. Called an "arcuate (arc-shaped) delta," the Nile delta is one of the world's largest, stretching more than 150 miles [240 km] wide, from the industrial city of Port Said near the Suez Canal all along the Mediterranean coastline to the ancient city of Alexandria. Can you guess what the Nile Delta looks like from up in space? You might see the triangular shape of a spreading green palm tree in the desert sands with the Nile River Valley looking like its slender trunk or you might envision the shape of Egypt's famed lotus flower. Whichever plant-shape you see, we know the delta is a place where *many* plants grow!

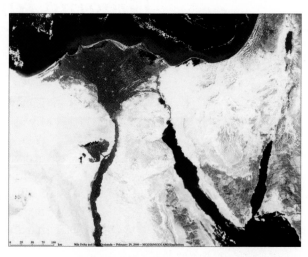

If we could have sat up in space when Joseph and his family lived in Egypt, we would have seen five tributaries of the Nile feeding the delta's marshlands with waters. Today we see that all but two of the tributaries have filled with silt; the eastern Damietta tributary and the western Rosetta. Yet just as in Joseph's time, the delta still supplies the majority of Egypt's crops today to feed Egypt's people. *Photo courtesy of visibleearth.nasa.gov*

On the farm where I live today, our corn crop grows in only about 10 inches [25 cm] of topsoil. **Topsoil** is the top layer of soil fertile enough with organic matter to sufficiently feed plants. Whereas our farm's topsoil is only inches deep, the Egyptian *fellahin* (farmers) in the Nile Delta measure their topsoil in feet—50 to 75 ft [15 - 22 m] deep of rich loamy earth! The most fertile soil in all Africa, we find Egyptian farmers growing crops such as cotton, rice, barley, wheat and maize in the 100 mile [160 km] long delta.

The Israelites didn't leave Egypt on bikes like this Egyptian boy! Perhaps you have a bike like he does? To think you and the young Egyptian are both biking around town—just on different parts of God's glorious globe!

The rich soil of the Nile Delta greatly prospered Jacob's family for hundreds of years, as we read in Genesis 47:27: *"And Israel dwelt in the land of Egypt, in the country of Goshen; and they had possessions therein, and grew and multiplied exceedingly."* Today, we see less Egyptian fellahin working the farmland of the delta region for several reasons. Firstly, there is less delta farmland due to the growth of sprawling cities. Secondly, with much silt trapped behind the Aswan High Dam, the delta region is shrinking, resulting in erosion of land along the Mediterranean coastline. Finally, the water we see irrigating the delta fields, a practice that now happens year-round instead of waiting for the annual flood, causes a build up of salt in the soil, leaving more delta land unproductive.

Yet still, the delta region is home to more than half of all Egyptians, with more than 34 million people living and working here. In the county where we live and farm, an average of 33 people lives in each square kilometer. If you visited a farm in the delta, and asked how many neighbors the Egyptian family had, they would inform you that they have 1,360 neighbors! Indeed, the Nile Delta is among the most densely populated farming areas to be found anywhere in the world.

It may look like a flying saucer but this is the new library of Alexandria on the Mediterranean coast. In past centuries, Alexandria was the home of the Pharos lighthouse, (one of the seven wonders of the ancient world), Queen Cleopatra and Julius Caesar, the Great Library of Alexandria dominating the ancient world of learning, and of St. Mark , who came to Alexandria to share the Good News of Jesus!

Although highly populated today, the delta was the region from which all the Israelites once packed their bags and left Egypt. The delta had been spared from many of the Ten Plagues that God had sent upon the country: *"Only in the land of Goshen, where the children of Israel were, was there no hail"* (Ex. 9:26). Then, in the middle of one night, the Israelites quickly gathered their belongings, and without even giving their bread time to rise, they began their Exodus out of the Nile Delta area and the land of Egypt.

The departure of the Israelites from Egypt, however, is not the end of Egypt hosting God and his people. In the first book of the New Testament we read, " *[Joseph] took the young child and his mother by night and departed into Egypt...that it might be fulfilled by the prophet saying, 'Out of Egypt, have I called my son'* " (Matt. 2:14-15). While the Christ Child Himself lived only a few short years in Egypt before returning to Israel, the Christian Church has been a part of this country for more than nineteen centuries. Mark the Evangelist, who wrote the oldest of the four gospels, traveled to Egypt to share the hope of Christ with Egyptians. He died in the Delta city of Alexandria on the Mediterranean Coast, and over his grave today stands the soaring arches of the largest cathedral not only in Egypt, but in all of Africa. Isaiah 19:19 wondrously prophesies of Mark's work in Alexandria on Egypt's northern border, *"In that day shall there be an altar to the Lord in the midst of the land of Egypt, and a pillar at the border thereof to the Lord."*

In the midst of the land of Egypt, we indeed find an altar of worship to the Lord, just as God's prophet foretold. Some of the world's first monasteries, places of worship, were built out in the lonely Egyptian desert. Today more than 8 million Egyptians, or about 1 out of every 10, are Coptic Christians. (Coptic comes from the Greek word meaning "Egypt.")

Throughout the delta, we find businesses and schools quietly closed on Fridays, as they are in all Islamic countries, as this is the weekly Muslim holy day. However, the same day finds Coptic churches full of singing children attending classes about Jesus. Yes, Coptic Christians go to Sunday School on Friday! Coptic Christians also do not celebrate Christmas on December 25th, as you may, but rather on January 7th, following the Gregorian calendar. You definitely won't find snow falling on an Egyptian Christmas, but if you peek into a Coptic Christian's home during the holidays you will find Christmas trees trimmed with flashing lights, perhaps not all that different from yours.

Would you like to visit Cairo's Coptic Museum to see artifacts of Christianity's long history in this land of the pharaohs? Today, 1 out of every 10 Egyptians is a Coptic Christian. Did you know that the Coptic language is the direct descendant of the ancient language written in Egyptian heiroglyphics? Today, the Coptic language is spoken almost solely by the priests during the Coptic church services. Do you think Joseph ever imagined that the future descendent of the heiroglyphic language would one day only be used in gatherings of God's people, praising His name?
Photo: Gérard Ducher

Field Notes

The Delta region must be an incredibly beautiful place. Would you like to visit some day?

Press record and talk to me:

~ about the Nile Delta region: What was this area called in the Bible? What is a river's mouth? What is a delta? What shape is the Nile Delta? What might it look like from space?

~about farming in the Delta region: Why do plants grow so well in here? What kind of crops do the farmers grow? How have dams and cities affected farming? What happens when the farms are irrigated regularly rather than waiting for the annual floods?

~about the people of the region: What is a *fellahin*? How many Egyptians live here? Can you tell the story of the Israelites and their exodus from Egypt? Which gospel writer died in Alexandria? What do you remember about the Coptic Christians?

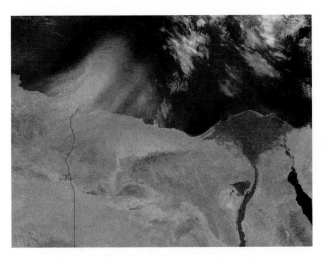

Look at that dust that is sweeping across the Western Desert and out over the Mediterranean Sea! Between March and early June, hot dry khamsin winds blow dust and sand, making it hard to see. Cover your eyes, nose, and mouth! A severe khasmsin is most unpleasant and even dangerous. *Photo courtesy of visibleearth.nasa.gov*

If we shake the dirt of the Nile Valley and Delta off our sandals, we have only the last region of Egypt left before us to explore: the vast Western Desert. Covering two thirds of Egypt, the Western Desert equals the combined size of *seven* European countries: Austria, Belgium, Denmark, Greece, Netherlands, Norway and Switzerland! Let's head west into the heat and captivating wonders of the Western Desert, one of the world's last frontiers.

Wait! Do you see that brown wall of dust blowing our way? We'll need to postpone our departure until the settling of the ***khamsin***, a hot northern wind that whips the desert into a blinding storm of sand. Pull a handkerchief over your face to ease your breathing. If your nostrils begin to fill with sand, just watch how our skilled Egyptian guide, Amr, snorts water in through his nose, then blows out to clear the sand.

With the passing of the sandstorm, we'll pack our camels with tents, food and water for a trip like no other. In sharp contrast to our exploration of the craggy red mountains of the Sinai Desert or the rocky terrain of the Eastern Desert, our camel **caravan** into the Western Desert leads us into an endless plain of sand dunes and barren plateaus.

The dirt of our farm, or any Egyptian delta farm, yields up crops. The Western Desert sand under our camel's hooves, however, will not yield any produce because it is the driest part of the larger Sahara desert that drifts across the northern part of Africa. If it rained today in the Western Desert it might not rain again in that same location for thirty years. (How old would you be the next time it rained?) The Bible declares: "*Who [but God can] cause it to rain on the earth, where no man is; on the wilderness, wherein there is no man*," (Job 38:26). Wherever and whenever rain falls anywhere in the desert, it is the work of our Omnipotent God.

Our camels can survive two weeks in the summer and up to two months in the winter without water, but we certainly can't. That is why all desert travelers journey from desert oasis to oasis. An **oasis** is an island of green vegetation growing up

People like us have been riding camels through Egypt for millennia. Joseph's brothers "sat down to eat bread: and they lifted up their eyes and looked, and, behold, a company of Ishmaelites came from Gilead with their camels bearing spicery and balm and myrrh, going to carry it down to Egypt" (Gen. 37:25). Sold into slavery, Joseph was forced to walk behind the camel caravan and down into Egypt.

around a spring of water in an ocean of sand. Occurring in lower areas or **depressions**, one finds an oasis where underground rivers coursing beneath the desert sands are close to the surface, resulting

99

in **springs**. You may ask what creates the low area or depression in the desert. Actually, it is just what we've experienced: a sandstorm. God sends roaring winds to create storms severe enough to move 100 million tons of sand and dust. That is the equivalent of loading up 2.5 million tractor trailers! Wind is the means by which God *"turneth the...dry ground into watersprings"* (Ps. 107:35), eventually sweeping the desert down to the **water table** so an oasis grows up in the desert!

Seven main depressions are scattered in different parts of the Western Desert. All but one of these lower areas are considered oases with springs of water bubbling up and Egyptian families making their home here.

What a stunning scene meets us in the Western Desert's Black Desert. A string of small hills runs from north to south, most topped by black basalt stone. Amid the hills of the Black Desert, the golden sand is littered with tiny black stones. The stones may be hard on our camel's hooves, but aren't they spectacular to your eyes!? Doesn't our Creator God take your breath away?
Photo: Michael Hoefner

Southwest of Cairo, we trek across golden sands rippling out as far as the eye can see. Under the beating sun, we think of the words of Psalm 139:17, *"How precious also are thy thoughts unto me, O God! How great is the sum of them! If I should count them, they are more in number than the sand."* Who can grasp that God's thoughts toward us are more than the countless grains of sands stretching out before us? Journeying further into dunes pebbled with spiky black shards of basalt, we quench our burning thirst with a sip of mint tea. Like natural pyramids rising up out of the desert around us, the coppery-colored sand dunes are now encased in a crumbling of black stones. This is the starkly dramatic Black Desert.

What is that you see ahead in the expanse of barren brown and blacks? There, like a green haven of life, emerges our first oasis, Bahariya, and one of its several mud brick villages. Bone-tired from our camel ride, why don't we sit down in the humble restaurant for a hearty bowl of lentil soup, with chicken, rice, beans, and zucchini in a tomato sauce? Friendly villagers sit at nearby tables, drinking tea and playing dominoes. Feeling refreshed, we wave good-bye to the oasis dwellers to head south

Thousands of palm trees meet us at Bahariya Oasis, a depression in the Western desert covering over 770 sq miles [2,000 sq. km]. Bahariya has been a major agricultural area since the days of the pharaohs and is famous for its sweet wines. Crops in the oasis include dates, olives, apricots, rice and corn. Would you like to refresh in the one of Bahariya's numerous springs? Some are actually very hot!

out of the Bahariya into a landscape of sand waves dusted in black. Riding atop our camel mount for hours, you'd almost wonder if this landscape isn't the surface of some distant planet. If you strain your eyes, what do you see ahead? Dazzling blue-white crystals, shimmering in the setting sun, spectacularly jut out from the sand around us. Amr announces that this is Crystal Mountain, where mountainous outcroppings of **quartz** stunningly push up out of the hard desert sands. Don't you want to scramble down from our camels to run your fingers over these shimmering cascades of crystals?

After hours of exploring columns of quartz crystals, we spread out our bed rolls here for a night of camping in the Western Desert. There is no sound of traffic or people anywhere; the quiet of the desert fills our ears. Amr, turban wrapped around his head, says people either love the emptiness of the desert, or are scared by its loneliness. Which are you?

The creeping cold of the desert night sets in, and Amr lights a fire to warm us. Look up at the brilliant carpet of stars blanketing the velvety black sky. We think of our God who *"telleth the number of the stars; he calleth them all by their names"* (Ps. 147:4). Doesn't your heart fill with adoration for our Creator?

When we rise in the morning, remember to shake out your shoes to make sure no scorpions or poisonous snakes have made their bed there during the night! Spellbound by dawn's light reflecting off the quartz outcroppings, we journey further south, watching as the color of the sand begins to shift and change, much like the sand dunes themselves. From a burnt toast shade to a lightly toasted tone to an almost white color, we have left the Black Desert and met the White Desert...out in the middle of the Western Desert.

Hasn't God sculpted an intriguing landform through the process of erosion? Let's be wise stewards and not remove any pieces of quartz---then later tourists too will be able to marvel at the wonders God has wrought in the Western Desert! *Photo: Michael Hoefner*

Look at the giant white chalk monoliths rising from a pure white desert floor in the White Desert! Aren't the shapes of some of the smaller outcroppings, looking like donkeys or camels, amusing? With the only sound the wind, we stand here and glorify our Creator God who made the world, even the desert, a place of beauty.

A sea of white sand now overtakes, spotted with small lumps of white **limestone** rock. It almost looks like snow has fallen in this blazing hot desert! Do you notice the chalky white rocks becoming larger? Doesn't it seem more like we are drifting with icebergs than riding a camel through the Egyptian Desert? Look over there at the bizarre rock formations! Standing like 10-15 ft [3–4.5 m] tall giant mushrooms, the limestone "stems" have eroded way from years of wind blasting its surface with sand. Like a natural art gallery, we marvel over the vast array of beautiful and bizarre rock shapes, showcases of God's handiwork with wind.

We pass half a dozen donkeys as we arrive in the oasis of Farafra, one of the most isolated places in Egypt. Riding by the mud-brick houses of the Bedouin, we can't help but notice their brilliant blue colors, with verses from the Koran, the Muslim's holy book, painted over their doorways. But why are all the houses decorated with simple wall paintings of camels and cars? As you might adorn your fridge with drawings from a special trip, Muslims consider a journey to **Mecca**, their holy city in the Middle Eastern country of Saudi Arabia, to be of such importance, that they adorn the outside of their house with scenes from the trip!

An Egyptian farmer living in this quiet oasis, Saad Ali waves to us as he walks out to the fields of trees growing produce like olives, dates, figs, oranges and apricots. At home, we run bathwater after a day of farming in the fields, but Saad Ali can take a dip in the hot springs of the oasis after his fieldwork. Not only does Saad Ali's family eat food produced in the oasis town, but his wife also handmakes her own beautifully embroidered clothes. Every daily requirement of living is harvested or crafted in the oasis instead of supplies needing to be brought hundreds of miles across the searing hot desert.

Would you ever have imagined glass in the Great Sand Sea? Found in the world's only known field of silica glass, this lustrous glass prism was discovered buried like an iceberg in the reddish sand, between two dune ridges more than 650 ft [200 m] high. Over a thousand tons [over 900 metric tons] of the glass is strewn across hundreds of kilometers of the empty Great Sand Sea, looking like shards from a giant green bottle. How do you think God created such a marvel?

After feasting on an omelet, pita bread and white cheese, we travel further south, crossing a corner of the Great Sand Sea. The size of England, the Great Sand Sea is a vast expanse of unbroken sand dunes in the southwest corner of Egypt. Do you have enough water bottles to trek out across the world's third-largest dune field? I hope so! There is not a single source of water in 150,000 square miles [390,000 sq km] of the Great Sand Sea, and certainly not one farm of good dirt. If, however, we endured the sufferingly hot journey to the southern shore of the Sand Sea, we would look down and see tiny pebbles of pale green glass scattered across reddish sand. A hundred miles from the nearest tree, we've discovered the world's only known field of **silica glass**. Some of the glass chunks, polished by ceaseless winds, weigh as much as ten pounds [4.5 kg]. The glass is a mystery. Researchers are not certain how God uniquely created it in this waterless sea of sand.

Traveling on south into Dahkla, an oasis fed by more than 600 springs and ponds, we pass farms growing rice and peanuts. Let's stop before a field of Egyptians harvesting wheat with **sickles**, the young girls collecting the **sheaves**. Boys pile the sheaves onto a wagon which a donkey will haul to the village. Doesn't it feel like we have stepped 3,000 years back in time?

Days of riding through this desert and its glaring sun, makes us feel very small and God so very, very grand. All of the fascinating dirt and sand we've traversed has been nothing short of captivating. Only God could make the ground under our feet in such creative ways! Finally loping into one of Egypt's largest oases, Kharga, we find ourselves in a modern city of 60,000 people. A railway line and bus service connect the 93 mile [150 km] long Kharga to other Western Desert oases and the rest of Egypt. Our circuit of several Western Desert oases is drawing to a close.

Traveling the paved road out of Kharga through the desert back towards the life of the Nile River Valley, we pass through the Valley of the Melons. Don't those huge, circular boulders lay scattered over the desert floor look rather curious?

In God's hand, everything is just as He intended: the craggy red ground of the Sinai Peninsula, the oil resources deep under the Eastern Desert, the winding life-line of the Nile and its fanning delta, and the strange spectacles of the Western Desert. As His Word declares, *"Who [but God] has put all the earth's dirt in one of his baskets, weighed each mountain and hill"* (Isaiah 40:12 MSG)? He is the Creator of the good dirt of our farm and of the Egyptian delta, of you reading these words and of the boy piling sheaves of wheat in the desert oasis. And He wants all our hearts to be good dirt producing an overflowing harvest of good things (Matt. 13:23) whether we live in Egypt or anywhere else on this glorious, spinning globe! No, never underestimate the value of good dirt!

Field Notes

The Western Desert is one of the most mysterious places on earth, but our camels seemed right at home, didn't they?

Press record and talk to me:

<u>~about **Western Desert:**</u> How large is the desert? What is a *khamsin*? Can you describe this desert? How often does it rain here? How do travelers survive the unending sand and heat?

<u>~about **an oasis:**</u> Can you describe one for me? How is an oasis created? Why do people build their homes around the oases?

<u>~about **the colorful sights**</u> :   Can you describe the natural pyramids of the Black Desert? What is Crystal Mountain? Where does the White Desert get its name?   Can you tell me about the white limestone rocks?

<u>~about **Farafra:**</u>   What do the houses look like? What kinds of things are made and grown here?

<u>~about **the Great Sand Sea**</u>: Why is it called this? What might we see scattered across the sand?

Travel Log

Using your globe or atlas, let's add the following locations to your map of Egypt... We've seen things today that simply must be mapped, so that they will never be forgotten!

Map Notes: Let's record the locations of:

- *Nile Delta*
- *Port Said*
- *Alexandria*
- *Western Desert*
- *Bahariya*

- *Farafra*
- *Great Sand Sea*
- *Dahkla*
- *Kharga*

If you'd like, draw pictures or symbols on your map representing:

- *Farmers working in the delta* (a plow? Some crops?)
- *Coptic monasteries in the desert* (a building? Or a cross?)
- *A khamsin* (a swirl of dust across the desert?)
- *An oasis* (a palm tree?)
- *The Black Desert* (black dots on the sand?)
- *Crystal Mountain* (make it sparkle!)
- *The White Desert* (shade it white)
- *Silica glass in the Great Sand Sea* (can you draw chunks of glass?)
- *Boulders in the Valley of the Melons* (stones like melons?)

Travel Notes: Geographers write what they've seen in order to share the adventure with others—and so they can revisit the places in their memories! **On the next page of your travel log, record three important sights you want to remember from your photos of Egypt.**

~art ~books ~food ~music ~poetry

. . . .

Bringing It Home

Simple ideas to bring the world to your door

━━━━━━━━━━━━━━━━━━━━━━━━━━━━━━━━

Food

Hummus is a dip made from chick peas (or garbanzo beans) and *tahini,* a sesame seed paste. Hummus is found in the deli section of most grocery stores, but you can make your own with this recipe. Perhaps listen to some Egyptian music and imagine being in the Land of the Pharaohs while savoring your treat!

Serve with cut up veggies, chips, or flat bread.

2 cloves garlic
¼ cup lemon juice
¼ cup water
14 oz canned chickpeas (garbanzo beans)—rinsed and drained

½ cup tahini
1 teaspoon salt

Blend together in a food processor or blender. Adjust seasonings to taste.

Fig or Date Balls (also called Tiger Nut Sweets) is an ancient recipe. Some say it dates back to 1600 B.C. A variation of this recipe was found on an ***ostraca*** (a clay tablet with writing on it). Wouldn't it be fun to eat just like the ancient Egyptians did?

- *1 cup almonds*
- *1 cup walnuts*
- *1 package of figs or dates*

- *Pinch cinnamon*
- *Pinch nutmeg*
- *Honey for dipping*

Put almonds in the blender or food processor and grind to very small pieces. Put these pieces in a small bowl and set aside. Chop walnuts in blender or processor until very small. Add figs or dates and continue blending. You may need to add a little water to help the mixture blend. Add cinnamon and nutmeg and continue blending until ingredients are combined. Roll mixture into one inch [2.54 cm] sized balls – your hands will be sticky and messy! Dip in honey and roll in the ground almonds.

Go into all the world...

a walk of prayer

*What a privilege to walk among the wonders of Egypt! Such a diverse and beautiful land is truly a gift from God. And we've discovered that Egypt is full of **boys and girls** who are much like us. They were created by a God who loves them dearly—just as He loves you.*

Will you and your family join me in praying for the Egyptian people?

Lord, give us Your love for the peoples of the world, and help our family to live in a way that shows our love for them.

Father, we think of magnificent Egypt with all its rich history, and how Egypt's ancient peoples longed for eternal life. May Your name and Your hope be known in this land of seekers.

~We pray for the great city of **Cairo** and its millions of residents. **From the richest executive to the smallest of the *zabaleen*,** You know and love them all. We pray for spiritual provision for all of Cairo's people. We particularly remember the **poor** in this massive city. May they find Your kindness day to day. Please provide food and clothing, shelter and healthy bodies for them.

~We pray for **peace between Muslims and Christians** in Egypt. Reveal Yourself to them, Lord. May they learn to walk in Your steps of peace.

~We pray for **Coptic Christians** who have a long history of faith in the land of Egypt. May their hearts be encouraged to follow after You, proclaiming the hope of Jesus in their communities.

~We pray, Father, for the millions of **tourists** every year who visit the antiquities of ancient Egypt. May their journey kindle in them a passion for eternal life in Your Son. May those who stand atop Mount Sinai reflect on Your holiness…and the hope of a Savior.

~We remember those whose lives have been affected by dramatic geographical changes over the years. We think of those who were forced to move after the **Aswan Dam** was built and who now struggle in poverty. We remember the **Nile Delta farmers** who are fighting salty soil to grow healthy crops. Even in the midst of change, You are a God who provides. We ask for Your help.

We love you, Lord, and the people who are living in Egypt today. May the Light of our Savior dawn over all nations today. Draw us all closer to You, Father. In Jesus name, Amen.

Tell-ing the Past!

Iraq ~Part 1~

Iraqi children can't wait for us to come and explore the rich history of their country!

Several times a week you drive down the road, but where on earth was the wheel invented? You are reading, carefully and well, the words on this page right now, but where on earth do these words have their roots? Many times a day you look up on the wall to tell the clock's time, but where on earth was it decided that an hour has sixty minutes? You might be surprised to discover that the introduction of the wheel, the earliest writing system, called **cuneiform,** and the very first clocks all originated from one Middle Eastern country. Did you know that much of how you live today, wherever you are in the world, has its roots in ancient Iraq?

Looking at our globe, can you find Iraq at the northern end of the Persian Gulf? (Do you remember that a gulf is a large body of water almost completely surrounded by land?) Slightly larger than the state of California, or about the size of the South American country of Paraguay, Iraq is nearly entirely landlocked, or surrounded by land, except for the mere twelve miles [19 km] of coastline along the Persian Gulf. If you were looking from space, what shape do you see in the outline of Iraq's borders? Does it look like the head of a big-eared dog, lapping up the waters of the gulf?

If you'll slip your finger up along your globe from the Persian Gulf, what two rivers do you discover meeting 100 miles [160 km] off the coast? We saw those two rivers begin in the mountains of Turkey: The Tigris and Euphrates Rivers! The Tigris River flows directly out of the snowy mountaintops of Turkey into Iraq, while the Euphrates winds out of Turkey and through the country of Syria before slithering across Iraq. The land of Iraq lies within Mesopotamia, the *"land between the rivers,"* the cradle of civilization.

Since the Tigris and Euphrates are two of the four rivers named as flowing out of the Garden of Eden, some have suggested that the Garden of Eden once blossomed in ancient Iraq. In fact, if you traveled to the dusty Iraqi town of Qurna, where the two rivers meet, you would find beside the Tigris River right next to the Garden of Eden Hotel, a gnarled old tree sometimes called *"Adam's Tree."* Welcome to what the

Trace the outline of Iraq's borders. Who are Iraq's neighbors? Where is its coastline and its rivers?

107

townspeople call *Jadan Adan*—the Garden of Eden. Is this tree, rising up out of the cracked concrete with children climbing its bare branches, the Tree of Knowledge of Good and Evil? Probably not. Because it is unlikely that today's Tigris and Euphrates Rivers are the same Biblical rivers spoken of before the Flood, no one is certain where the actual Garden of Eden once flourished, either here in Iraq, in modern Turkey, or elsewhere. We do know, however, that as early as Noah's great-grandson, Biblical events were taking place on the soil of modern Iraq. After the Ark landed on Mount Ararat in Turkey, Noah's descendants migrated south into the country. The tenth chapter of Genesis tells the story: *"And [Noah's son] Ham [begat] Cush… And Cush begat Nimrod: he began to be a mighty one in the earth…And the beginning of his kingdom was Babel and Erech and Accad and Calneh in the land of Shinar. Out of that land went forth Asshur, and builded Nineveh, and the city of Rehoboth, and Calah…"* (Genesis 10:6-10).

The green and black colors of the Iraqi flag represent Islam while the red stripe represents Arab nationalism. The three green stars symbolize *Wihda, Hurriyah, Ishtirrakiyah* (Unity, Freedom, and Socialism) while the Arabic script reads *Allahu Akbar* (Allah is Great).

You didn't read the name Iraq in those verses, did you? Actually you won't find the name Iraq in the Bible, but every time you read of Shinar, Chaldea, Babylon and Assyria, you are actually reading of places that are in the land we now call Iraq. Some even suggest that the name Iraq has its roots in one of these Genesis 10:10 cities: Erech. Those cities established by Noah's great-grandson, Nimrod, such as Babel, Accad and Calneh, were some of the very first cities in the whole world, and they grew up out of the soil of Iraq.

A city close to where I live has the most famous (and tallest) tower in the world but perhaps the tower that rose up in one of Nimrod's cities is even more famous? Do you know the name of that ancient Iraqi tower? Genesis 11 relates how the inhabitants of a city attempted to build a tower that would reach to the very heavens but God came and confused their speech. Since workers could no longer understand each other, the building ceased and *"therefore was the name of it called Babel because Jehovah did there confound the language of all the earth and from thence did Jehovah scatter them abroad upon the face of all the earth"* (Gen. 11:9). From ancient Iraq's tower of Babel the peoples of the world, now

From our seats in space, what can you see of Iraq's landscape or topography? Where might the Tigris and Euphrates rivers run?

Photo courtesy of visibleearth.nasa.gov

speaking different languages, dispersed throughout the earth. When your neighbor down the street introduces himself with, "Bonjour! Je m'appelle Monsieur Voyer!" you may remember how the beginning of different languages began in Iraq!

Did you know that the land of Iraq today can TELL us many things from thousands of years ago? Obviously the geography of Iraq cannot literally speak—but it is *tell*-ing us about long ago cities, like that of Babel. Humps of land, called **tells,** are actually mounds of rubble from destroyed, long-forgotten cities. **Archaeologists** dig in the tells in search of remains and artifacts to discover how people lived long ago in Iraq. Let's get our feet planted in Iraq and see what its land is *telling* us today!

In 1563, Pieter Brueghel's painted his rendition of the Tower of Babel, to look similar to the Roman Colosseum since Christians at that time saw it as a symbol of persecution. If you'll look carefully at Brueghel's painting, do you notice that the ultimate toppling of Brueghel's tower seems to lie in poor construction rather than in, as the Bible states, God intervening with the confusion of languages?

Our plane circles Iraq's capital city of Baghdad, on the western bank of the Tigris River, waiting for a clearing in the dust storm so we might land. Can you see through the reddish haze of dust shrouding the city? Just think of homekeepers throughout Baghdad dusting the fine film of sand off their furniture several times a day, only to have more sand sift in through cracks around windows and doors! This is a **sharqi**, a southeasterly wind (sharqi means *"easterly"* in Arabic). Blowing in from the Persian Gulf in early summer and early winter, the sharqi whips up severe sandstorms that can destroy houses, crops and uproot trees. The sharqi rages stronger than the mid-June to mid-September wind, the **shamal** that blows through Iraq nearly incessantly during the summer. Unlike the sharqi, the shamal blows in from the north, bringing blistering heat and such dry air that clouds cannot form. With no cloud cover, the summer sun beats relentlessly down on Iraq. Today, in the early winter temperatures of 52°F [11°C] we pull on our jackets, relieved that we aren't visiting Iraq on a smothering 93°F [34°C] summer day!

After finally landing in Baghdad, a city of more than 4 million inhabitants, we make our way past its ancient mosques, their intricate minarets pointing to the skies, open only to worshipping Muslims. We drive past noisy **souqs (souks)** (marketplaces) where Iraqi women in colorful scarves buy dates, jewelry, and spices of all colors, while a group of young men browse through music CDs. Wandering past the *Souk al Safafir*, Baghdad's famous copper market, we see craftsmen heating, beating and decorating copper. Did you also catch a glimpse of the crumbling fragments of the mud-brick wall that once encircled this 1,300-year-old city, making Baghdad known as the City of Peace? Driving past piles of rubble and buildings half demolished by bombs, we see that Baghdad has not known peace in its recent history but war and hardship. Mothers huddle children close, trying to escort them home safely from school; fathers search for work; but do you see workers hammering on the construction of new buildings? A revived Baghdad is rising in an era of hope.

From our plane's window seat, we see the Tigris River snaking through Baghdad. The second largest city in the Arab world after Cairo, Baghdad is the capital of Iraq. Hundreds of years ago, the city was designed as a circle, approximately 1.2 mi [2 km] in diameter. Do you think it still looks like the "Round City?"
Photo: U.S. Military Soldier

Field Notes

I've heard so much about Iraq, but not these things! Are you excited to discover the actual locations of events in the Bible?

Press record and talk to me:

~about Iraq's geography: What is Iraq surrounded by? Are any bodies of water near the country? Which two rivers slide through Iraq? What other names is Iraq called in the Bible? What famous ancient tower was built here?

~about Tells: What is a tell? What kinds of things can we learn from a tell?

~about Baghdad: Why is this city important to Iraq? What is a *sharqi*? What is a *shamal*? What might you buy in a Baghdad souk? What is the city like today?

Do these friendly Iraqi children, standing amidst the ruins of Babylon, look like Thuraya and Abdel?
Photo: U.S. Military Soldier

Under a palm tree outside Baghdad's Iraq Museum, we meet our guide, Mr. Jamal Anour, a tall man with black hair, and his son, Abdel and daughter, Thuraya. Before we set out to uncover the wonders of ancient Iraq buried in today's Iraqi soil, the Anours graciously invite us to walk home with them for lunch. Be careful as you sit down on the floor of the Anour's small living room to eat that you do not show the soles of your feet! Most Iraqis would find that disrespectful. Mrs. Anour, wearing the traditional long black cloak called an ***abaya*** over her clothes and a black scarf over her hair, asks our preference: rice and a hearty stew? Or ***kebabs*** of lamb, beef, goat or poultry? Iraqi's assent to the Muslim Koran allows for the eating of ***halal***, or lawful, meats such as these. You won't find pork in any dish however, as it is considered ***haram***, or forbidden. Even if you are left handed, you must be careful not eat with your left hand since the left hand is considered by Middle Easterners as the hand of toilet functions and thought to be unclean!

After lunch, Mr. Anour drives us south out of Baghdad across the dusty plain towards the ruins of Nimrod's city of Babylon. Known only in folklore for many years, ecstatic archaeologists discovered the actual remains of Babylon along the banks of the Euphrates, buried in the mud from floods. Do you see the walls of sun-baked bricks growing up ahead of us? Abdel pipes up to say that amongst those bricks are the ruins of the *Etemenanki ziggurat*. A **ziggurat** is a pyramid-like tower, sometimes reaching as high as 300 ft [91 m], with a temple on top, where ancient Iraqis worshipped. A

Sumerian word, Etemenanki means the "House of the platform of Heaven and Earth." While more than 30 ziggurats have been discovered in the Middle East, not much of the once massive Etemenanki remains. Thuraya explains that under Etemenanki archaeologists have found the remains of even earlier ziggurats. Is it true, as some suggest, that the buried remains of one such ziggurat in these Baylonian ruins are the actual remains of the biblical Tower of Babel? Perhaps!

Abdel calls for us to come and see the modern reconstruction of the famous *Ishtar Gate* of Babylon, brilliant blue in the Iraqi sunlight. Can't you imagine Daniel or Nebuchadnezzar once walking under its arch? (The original

Did Daniel and his Jewish friends once feel as we do, standing before this reproduction of the Ishtar Gate in Iraq? The original gate was built by Nebuchadnezzar as the 8th gate into the city of Babylon and was dedicated to the Assyrian false goddess Ishtar.

tiled panels of striding lions that decorated the first Gate have long since been excavated from the Iraqi soil and now stand in a museum in Europe, thousands of miles away from Iraq!)

The original Ishtar Gate protected Nebuchadnezzar's 700-room palace, whose walls we can still run our fingers along. Was it in this room that Daniel asked the King's steward if he might eat only vegetable and water for ten days? Daniel, Shadrach, Meshach, and Abdenego, along with the exiled Israelites, lived a term of captivity in this ancient Iraqi city. Did they too stand next to these palace walls, looking up at the thousands of trees, shrubs and flowers that once grew on the ledges of the palace walls? For here is where Nebuchadnezzar built the Hanging Gardens of Babylon, one of the Seven Wonders of the Ancient World, for his wife Amytis. (Of course, the gardens did not hang in mid air from ropes, but were overhanging from palace balconies.) Amytis longed for the mountainous landscape of northern Iraq where she had been raised as a child. To ease her homesickness, Nebuchadnezzar built these spectacular terraced gardens, resembling a mountainous, lush countryside. Like Amytis, don't you too find that the geography of where you live—hilly or

flat, rocky or fertile—becomes the landscape you most comfortably call home?

As Mr. Anour leads us through what was once Nebuchadnezzar's throne room, we pause to touch these walls, and think of King Belshazzar who, while drinking irreverently out of the golden goblets taken from the temple of God in Jerusalem, saw the "*fingers of a man's hand [that] wrote…upon the plaister of the wall of the king's palace*" (Dan. 5:5)! What a wondrous act God worked on these ancient walls of Babylon.

A reconstruction of the original bricks of the massive Ishtar Gate finds 120 lions strutting along the walls, as the lion was a symbol of the goddess Ishtar. Don't those roaring beasts remind you of Daniel in the lion's den?

As we wander through the honey-colored brick walls, don't you wonder how these walls built

From over top of the Euphrates River, we see the ruins of ancient Babylon in the background, with a hill-top palace presiding over the historical site. The historian Herodotus reports that Babylonia once sprawled across about 200 sq miles [520 sq km] on both sides of this riverbank. The flat landscape of Babylon must have indeed caused Nebuchadnezzar's wife long for her mountainous homeland. The open plain behind the ruins is thought by some to be the site of the Tower of Babel. *Photo: U.S. Military Soldier*

thousands of years ago have stood the ages so well? With thick Arabic accents, Jamal and Abdel beckon us to step close to notice that the bricks close to the bottom of the walls are Nebuchadnezzar's original bricks, stamped with praises to his name. Yellow bricks higher in the wall are not ancient but very new, laid only recently by order of an Iraqi leader named Saddam Hussein, who had begun to build a new Babylon on the remains of ancient Babylon. In these bricks, can you read the **inscription** of the words, translated from the Arabic, "This was built by Saddam Hussein, son of Nebuchadnezzar, to glorify Iraq." Standing in this place, the echo of Nebuchadnezzar's proud words ring in our hearts, *"Is not this great Babylon, that I have built for the house of the kingdom by the might of my power, and for the honor of my majesty?"* (Daniel 4:30). Don't you too await the day when we peoples no longer strive for our own renown but when *"all nations whom thou hast made shall come and worship before thee, O Lord, and shall glorify thy name"* (Ps. 86:9)?

Mr. Anour, Abdel and Thuraya are anxious to let another Iraqi tell speak to us further south in Iraq, Tell al-Muqayyar. From miles across the desert the message of the tell drifts towards us. How can you miss the massive ziggurat rising up out of the desert? Mr. Anour explains that at this ziggurat, more than 4,000 years old, ancient Iraqis worshipped the moon god, Nanna, in Sumerian mythology. But if you look around, there isn't another house in sight! It's hard to believe that about 2,000 years before the birth of our Savior, what lies under this mound of dirt may have been the world's largest city of its time: Ur with a population of 65,000 people.

Thousands of years ago, in the city whose remains are now under our feet, you could have stopped a little boy running through the narrow streets and asked him where he was from. He might have said, "I am Abram and I am from…um..er..um…yes, UR!..of the Chaldeans." In Genesis 15:7 God says to Abram: *"I am the Lord that brought thee out of Ur of the Chaldees…"* Ur was the hometown of the patriarch Abraham before he migrated north to Haran, Turkey. Did Abraham once sit here and watch with sadness as his townspeople climbed these steps to worship a false deity? Is Ur's idol worship what caused God to lead Abram away from this part of Iraq? While we may not be certain, we know God and His Word are true. Interestingly, Ur's ziggurat in southern Iraq actually attests clearly to the truth of Scripture!

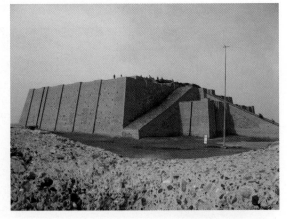

We find no town here in the barren, arid landscape of Ur, Iraq. But who can miss Ur's tremendous Great Ziggurat? Did Abraham once stand on the soil where we now stand?
Photo: U.S. Military Soldier

For many years, scholars thought Nabonidus was the last king of Babylon, and the Bible was surely wrong in naming Belshazzar last king of Babylon. However, clay cylinders found at Ur's ziggurat bore an inscription of Nabonidus closing with a prayer for his son Belshazzar—the same Belshazzar of the Bible's book of Daniel. The Bible was right! Digging about in Iraq today proved that God's Word had indeed recorded accurately the kings of ancient Iraq.

Mr. Anour and his children urge us northward across Iraq, to a mound of dirt on the east banks of the Tigris River, near the modern-day city of Mosul. (Can you locate Mosul on your map?) Thuraya can't wait to inform us of the name of this tell: Tell Nebi Yunus, which means "Prophet Jonah." Why on earth would there be a heap of dirt named "Prophet Jonah" in Iraq? That is because you are standing where legend claims the biblical Prophet Jonah was buried...and where the *"exceedingly great city"* (Jonah 3:3) of Nineveh once stood!

What do you see written on the tombs in the the Royal Cemetery of Ur, located near the wall that once surrounded Ur? Yes, that is cuneiform we find inscribed into Iraqi's ancient mud bricks!
Used with permission: Lasse Jensen

Looking across this immense area of more than 1,800 acres of ruins, can you imagine what this teeming city of more than 100,000 people may have looked like when the Prophet Jonah arrived here? We walk up the mammoth dusty ramp and under the massive arch of one of Nineveh's 15 towering gates. Don't you wonder what fainthearted Jonah thought as he passed under one of these colossal gates into the city? Wouldn't he have been a sight to behold with his hair and skin bleached white by his time in the great fish's stomach? No wonder the Ninevites believed Jonah's prophesies of God's impending wrath and chose to repent. This ancient city in Iraq is the site of the one of the most astounding spiritual revivals the world has ever seen!

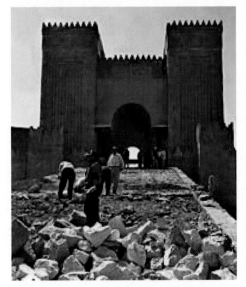

What a steep incline Jonah must have climbed up to one of Nineveh's gates! (Jonah 3:4) Built on the eastern banks of the Tigris, Nineveh is first noted in the Bible as founded by Nimrod (Gen. 10:9-12) and grew to be the capital of the Assyrian empire from 800 to 619 B.C.
Photo by Sgt 1st Class Julie Friedman

Standing here surveying the ruin-mounds of tell "Prophet Jonah," Mr. Anour tells us how, hundreds of years after Jonah's lifetime, an ancient Iraqi, Berosus, wrote the history of a fish-man named Jonah who surfaced from out of the sea to give heavenly wisdom to man. Doesn't that sound much like the story of Jonah and Nineveh that we find in our Bibles today?

As we further explore the ruins, Mr. Anour declares that one of the greatest book lovers of all time once walked where we now walk. The ancient Iraqi King Assurbanipal was the world's very first librarian. Today one can visit museums to read the more than 23,000 clay tablets of stories and writings Assurbanipal collected in the world's first library, founded in Nineveh. To think: your local library is a descendent of that long ago Iraqi library!

As we wander back to the jeep, we marvel what the Iraqi tells have told us. It is hard to fathom that the same Iraqi soil we have walked today has been the stage of many great historical events: many of the world's very first cities were founded in ancient Iraq, the birth of different languages took

place in Iraq at the Tower of Babel, and Abraham's hometown was Ur, an ancient Iraqi city. One of the world's first empires, under Nebuchadnezzar, was formed here. Ancient Israelites, like Daniel and his friends, lived here during the captivity, and God wrought the most stunning revival in history in Nineveh of ancient Iraq. Before we go, Abdel quickly adds that all the events of the book of Esther also took place in this amazing country!

Doesn't our walk through the remains of ancient Iraq whet your appetite for a tour of modern day Iraq? The tells have told the past-- Mr. Anour and his children promise us to show and tell even more wondrous sites in the next adventure of modern-day Iraq. Hold on to your hat!

Looking at this sculpture of Ashurbanipal, you are looking at the world's first librarian. Ashurbanipal gathered all the cunieform literature of that time to create a library at Nineveh. Ezra 4:10 speaks of this same Ashurbanipal: "And the rest of the nations whom the great and noble Asnapper brought over, and set in the cities of Samaria, and the rest that are on this side the river, and

Field Notes

Exploring this part of Iraq has been so exciting! Wouldn't you have loved to see Nebuchadnezzer's palace? Or his hanging gardens? **Press record and talk to me:**

~about the customs and culture of Iraq:
If we were to share a meal with an Iraqi family, what must we remember not to do when we sit down? What kind of food might we eat? What other manners must we remember? Can you describe Mrs. Anour's clothes?

~about Babylon: What is a *ziggurat*? Tell me about the Ishtar gate. What does it look like? What did it protect in ancient times? Which men from the Bible might have walked through this gate? What did Nebuchadnezzer build for his wife in Babylon?

~about Tell as-Muqayyar: Which ancient city lies beneath this mound? Who lived there?

~about Nineveh: Do you know a Bible story about Nineveh? What does the name "Nebi Yunus" mean? What would a book-lover want to know about Nineveh?

Travel Log

Using your globe or atlas, draw an outline map of Iraq.

As we travel, let's make record in our very own travel log of the places we've visited and the unusual sights we've seen! Make your map large enough to hold all of your discoveries!

Don't worry about making a perfect map, just do your best. Drawing the basic shape yourself will help you remember it better.

Map Notes: <u>Let's record the locations of:</u>

- *Persian Gulf*
- *Tigris River*
- *Euphrates River*
- *Qurna*
- *Baghdad*

<u>If you'd like, draw pictures or symbols on your map representing:</u>

- *"Adam's Tree" at the Garden of Eden Hotel* *(in Qurna)*
- *souks at Baghdad* *(perhaps some bright fabrics? CDs? Jewelry?)*
- *ziggurats at Babylon* *(pyramid-shaped towers)*
- *Ishtar Gate* *(bright blue!)*
- *Tell Nebi Yunus* *(perhaps a big fish to remind us of Jonah?)*

Travel Notes: Geographers write what they've seen in order to share the adventure with others—and so they can revisit the places in their memories! **On the next page of your travel log, record three important sights you want to remember from your photos of Iraq.**

115

~art ~books ~food ~music ~poetry

Bringing It Home
Simple ideas to bring the world to your door

Art:

Art like the picture at left was common in ancient Arab countries. It is called **bas-relief** and it is made by cutting away part of the background on a piece of clay, leaving a design or sculpture in the foreground. Would you like to make your own bas-relief sculpture?

You will need clay (Traditional clay needs firing in a kiln, or you may use self-hardening clays, or craft clays that bake in the oven, even play dough for a more temporary craft.), a rolling pin, a sculpting tool to cut the clay (such as toothpicks, knives, skewers, or actual clay tools), and a design to sculpt. (A simple shape such as a star may be best to start with.)

Begin by rolling your clay into a square or rectangle (about 6 in. x 6 in. [15 cm x 15 cm] will do), being sure to leave about an inch [2.54 cm] or more thickness for carving. Using a toothpick or knife, trace the outline of your design onto the clay. Begin to sculpt by cutting away part of the depth of the background (about ¼ - ½ inch [.6 cm – 1.2 cm]) surrounding your design. DO NOT CUT AWAY THE WHOLE BACKGROUND. You want your design to look as though it is rising out of the background, not a free-standing form. (Tip: use your finger and a tiny bit of water to smooth surfaces or to "glue" segments back together.)

Once the outline is cut away, take some time and add details to your sculpture.

Finally, you can make your background as detailed or as plain as you like. Try scoring some wavy lines into the surface, or a pattern of dots. Follow the package directions for your clay once the project is complete.

Music:

Music captures so much of a land and people. Introducing your children to Iraqi music is a simple way to transport yourselves around the world. Why not check out these sites while your young geographers' notebook and map and let the music play while they recount their travels?

You will find a wide selection of samples here:
http://worldmusic.nationalgeographic.com/worldmusic/view/page.basic/artist/content.artist/ahmed_mukhtar_46405

http://iraqimusic.com/index_maqam.htm

River Ride!

Iraq ~Part 2~

Up in the peaks of Iraq's Zagros Mountains, capped with snow, the river ride begins. Melting snows and gurgling springs flow into brooks, which flow into streams, which flow into tributaries that flow down the mountain slopes and into the Tigris River. Are you ready for a river ride?
~Photo Robin Searle

Have you ever opened a cold can of the fizzing soda, Mountain Dew? Well real mountains don't make droplets of mere dew; actual mountains make streaming, coursing *rivers*! Rivers begin their life high up in mountains, as a trickle of melting snow, or sparkling cold water bubbling from a mountain spring. The trickle becomes a stream coursing down a gully, which merges with other gully streams. Smaller streams, named **tributaries**, meet larger streams, with many tributary streams forming a river. Spilling down into valleys, the river, always restless and moving, eventually snakes its way across the breadth of a country, until it finally slips away into the sea. Iraq has mountains, mountains make rivers, rivers make life flourish…until finally the river slips out to meet the sea. Think of that grand story the next time you drink a Mountain Dew: how mountains DO make more than dew—they make rivers!

Do you see Mr. Anour, Abdel and Thuraya calling us up to the mountains of northeastern Iraq? For if we are going to go tracking the waters that flow down into the two of history's great rivers, the Tigris and Euphrates, we'll have to tie on our mountain boots and go hiking!

Like sky-high fences, Iraq's two main mountain chains define its borders with its neighboring countries. The Taurus Mountains ripple between Iraq and Turkey while the Zagros Mountains crease and crimp along Iraq's border with Iran. (Can you feel the rise of those two Iraqi mountain chains on your globe?) Abdel and Thuraya deeply breathe in the cooler air of this mountain region. Do you see the snow melting on these towering peaks? There begins the life of gurgling rivers. As these rivers birthed in the mountains grow larger, they gouge deep cuts, called **gorges**, into the rocky landscape, in their rush to join other rivers and streams, which form tributaries. Tributaries that course down out of the Zagros Mountains flow into the Tigris River. It is just as the prophet Isaiah wrote: "*On every lofty mountain and on every high hill there will be streams running with water…*" (Isa. 30:25).

The official flag of Iraqi Kurdistan, and the unofficial flag of Kurds around the world, is dominated by a blazing sun with 21 rays at its center. The number 21 is tied to the ancient religious tradition of the Kurds, called Yazdani.

Waving to two Kurdish boys, Mr. Anour calls "*Rozhbash*," meaning '*hello*' in Kurdi. The boys, jackets pulled tights as they herd their family's flock of sheep up a grassy mountainside, return our greeting with an echoing "*Bashem*!" The valleys of the north eastern mountains are dotted with the homes of the majority of Iraq's Kurdish people. The fourth-largest ethnic people group in the Middle East, 2 out of every 10 Iraqis are **Kurds**.

Did you know that the Kurds are thought to be descendants of the Medes—yes, the same Medes who, along with the Persians, had the unchangeable laws written of in the book of Daniel (Daniel 6:8)!

While the Kurdish people have always had their own language, tradition and culture, Iraqi Kurds have not had their own lands for a long, long time. The governments of the Middle Eastern countries have often treated the Kurds cruelly, refusing to acknowledge their unique community. Only recently, and after many years of struggle, have the Kurds formed the region of Iraqi Kurdistan, meaning *"the land of the Kurds,"* in northeastern Iraq. This region, while part of Iraq, is governed solely by the Kurdish people. Thuraya also points out that the first State President of Iraq, after a war that overthrew longtime leader Saddam Hussein, is a Kurd. President Talabani, the first non-Arab to lead an Arab nation, has promised that he will work co-operatively with all Iraqis—Kurds and Arabs, Muslims and Christians—to rebuild a new and strong Iraq after years of hardships.

Kurdish musician Sivan Perwer sings poetic Kurdish music accompanied by the lute or *tembur*. For many years, his music was banned in countries like Iraq because of the Kurdish lyrics. Many Kurds listened to his music secretly as it expressed their thoughts and feelings as Kurds.

Can you see one stream of water, a tributary, join the life-giving Tigris River? If you look carefully, you can see how Iraqi farmers use these waters to irrigate their crops. Can you also spot the mountains from whence the river waters rush? *Photo: U.S. Military Soldier*

While many Kurds live and work in Iraqi cities, Mr. Anour explains that some Kurds still live a semi-nomadic lifestyle, spending the harsh winters in the **foothills** of these Zagros Mountains. (Foothills, like the feet of mountains, are the hilly land between the lower slopes of mountains and an area of plain.) Come the warmth of spring, these Kurdish families move higher up the mountain slopes to their summertime dwellings called **kapras**. Their flocks of goats and sheep nibble on the lush grasses fed by melting snows and rains. These pastures are fed by the more than 40 inches of **precipitation** that falls each year in the Iraqi mountains, much of it as snow. (Forty inches is about 3 and a half feet or 1 meter—how tall are you?) This precipitation also waters crops such as wheat and barley that grow in the shelter of the valleys. The rest of Iraq receives such little rainfall, much of it is classified a desert.

Not only does more precipitation fall in this region, but the natural forests of oak trees that clothe these mountainsides are the only ones in the entire country. Many of the trees that once shaded Iraq have been cut down for use as firewood, and previous governments destroyed many mountainside forests where Kurds once hid from persecution.

Why is that Kurdish boy cutting all of the branches off that oak tree over there? Abdel tells us that Kurds have the habit of **pollarding** the oak forest, cutting nearly all of the tree's branches back to the trunk. Doesn't the Kurdish boy diligently collect the oak branches up into piles? These oak branches will be winter feed for his family's herd of hardy native cattle. Abdel assures us that new branch shoots will sprout up from this tree, it trunk growing fatter from the pollarding. Mr. Anour adds that the Kurdish villagers are careful to preserve the forests since they need the oak trees to feed their flocks when deep winter snows blanket the mountains of Iraq. Wise stewards of God's creation heed the words of Revelation 7:3, "*Do not harm the earth or the sea or the trees…*"

The city of Mosul sits on the banks of the Tigris River, its inhabitants passing over the bridge that spans these renowned waters. The name Tigris is very similar to the Kurdish word "tij" which means sharp. Don't you too think that the Tigris River courses sharp and fast?

I can recall as a child watching my white-haired Granny bend over unfolded yards of muslin to snip out shapes of Raggedy Ann and Andy dolls from the fabric. Holding the doll Granny stitched out of the muslin and untangling its red yarn hair, I never dreamed that the doll of muslin was related to a city in Iraq!

Fields of cotton and sugarcane wave in the wind as we pass by on our way to this northwestern city, on the fringe of Iraq's mountain region. Mr. Anour tells us the story of the city's name: Long ago, in the 17th century, Europeans were introduced to a closely woven, unbleached white cloth, that breathed well, perfect for wearing in hot, dry climates. The name of the material? The Europeans called it *mosulin*, after the city where they thought the material originated: Mosul, Iraq. (Do you see Mosul on your map?) Actually, **muslin** is thought to have been woven first in Asia, further to the east.

Springing up along the caravan (trade) route between Asia and Europe, the city of Mosul came to weave its own fine cotton. Now when you see sheets and curtains, dresses and dolls made from muslin, you'll always remember that the fabric is named after the Iraqi city of Mosul!

Does this area of Iraq look familiar? Yes, Mosul lies just opposite ancient Nineveh, on the west bank of the Tigris River. Isn't it intriguing that modern-day houses perch on the riverbanks opposite the remains of long ago Nineveh? The impressive remains of Mosul's ancient city walls further add to the scene's fascination. Abdel points to an unusually shaped Muslim shrine or **mashad** also towering over the Tigris River. Who can miss that white pyramid-shaped roof atop a honey-colored octagonal base? Mr. Anour tells us that the *mashad* was built nearly 800 years ago in honor of a Muslim religious leader. But Mr. Anour promises to show us an even more unusual building in this modern city with an old feel. Thuraya is the first to spot the structure in downtown Mosul: why it looks like the leaning Tower of Pisa! Called *Al-Hadba*, this soaring minaret does look like it is about to topple over! Doesn't the decorative brick pattern of the Al-Hadba remind you of an intricate carpet design? Mr. Anour then guides us down winding back streets to the *Ma Toma* (St. Thomas)

Church where the bones of St. Thomas are said to be buried. Yes, Thuraya says, Mosul is the home to more Christians than any other city in Iraq.

No, it is not you or the picture that seems a little off balance—the Al-Hadba minaret of the Ummayed Mosque in downtown Mosul truly is leaning. The mosque no longer exists, but the 800-year-old minaret still dazzles with its impressive, fanciful brickwork. The fact that the tower leans over 8 feet [2.4 m] gives it the name Al-Hadba, meaning "the humped" in Arabic. If you look on the back of the Iraqi 10,000 dinar (equivalent to $5.00 USD), you'll see a picture of the leaning Al-Hadba.

Field Notes

This part of Iraq sounds very beautiful. I would love to see the rivers gushing down from the mountains, wouldn't you?

Press record and talk to me:

~**about northeastern Iraq**: Which two mountain chains roll through Iraq? What is a gorge?

~**about the Kurds**: What is the Kurdish area called? Have the Kurds always had their own land? How many Iraqis are Kurds? What is life like for the people who live in the Zagros foothills? How much rain falls in this area? What famous Iraqi is a Kurd?

~**about Mosul**: What does the name come from? What city is across the river from Mosul? Can you describe some of the buildings we might see in town?

Thuraya declares that her stomach is growling and she would love satisfy it with **kibbeh**, small dumplings filled with minced lamb or beef, nuts, raisins and spices. **Dolma** is what Abdel is hungry for, grape leaves stuffed with rice, raisins, meat and parsley. Chuckling, Mr. Anour suggests a treat of Iraq's most famous dish: **matzgouf.** Who can resist the fish dish made of carp caught from the Tigris River? According to tradition, only men are allowed to cut the carp open, smoke it then stuff it with peppers, spices, onions and tomatoes, before grilling it over an open fire. Smacking our lips after the last bite of mazgouf, Mr. Anour offers us each a **zlabiya**, a sweet pastry that looks like a pretzel. With tummies full of such tasty fare, we are ready to explore Iraq's next geographical region: the plains.

The word "dolma" comes from the Turkish verb "to stuff." Would you like to stuff your grape leaves with rice, raisins, and meat? Delicious!

Traveling south out of Mosul towards the plains of the Tigris and Euphrates River, our curiosity is piqued over the large steel pipeline that stretches out as far as the eye can see. Did you know that liquid gold runs through these pipes? For the oil that pumps through the pipelines near Mosul and Kirkuk, (and in the country's southwest), is indeed Iraq's greatest source of wealth. One of the largest producers of oil in the whole world, Iraq's new growth is funded by the sale of millions of barrel of oil to the world community. The industries where you live quite likely use oil that came from Iraq—and thus your community is helping Iraqi families rebuild lives of hope after years of war and struggle.

Perhaps every time you go up a flight of stairs you do what I did as a child, counting each step aloud: 12, 13, 14! Did you know that Iraq has its own steppes? The geographical term '**steppe**' refers to a dry, grassy plain, usually without trees. Before us the mountains of Iraq's north give way to the rolling upper steppes, with the Tigris faithfully slipping from its mountain heights down through these hills. The Tigris (called the *Dijlis* in Arabic) and its major tributaries carve deep valleys through this grassy plain region on its slide down Iraq.

Ahead of us rises the upper plain city of *Tikrit*. (Can you locate that on your map?) Did you know that Saladin, the great Muslim general who battled against the Crusaders during the Middle Ages, was born in the Iraqi town of Tikrit? Is that the remains of his magnificent palace up there on the rise overlooking the Tigris River? Mr. Anour shakes his head. No, that is what was once the palace of a recent Iraqi leader, *Saddam Hussein Abd al-Majid al-Tikriti*. Wouldn't that be a hard name to write when you were five years old? Interestingly, Iraqis do not have a last name or surname like you or I do. For instance, Saddam was the name his mother gave him, Hussein was the first name of his father, Abd al-Majid was his grandfather's name, and can you guess where the name al-Tikiriti comes from? Yes, it means that he was born or raised in (or near) the city of Tikrit! (What might your name be if you lived in Iraq?)

You may call it the Tigris River, Kurds call it the Dijle, the Turks call it Dicle, and Daniel called it the great river (Dan. 10:4). Whatever one calls these waters, a river ride down the Tigris escorts us past some magnificent geography. Look at those hills in Iraq!
Photo: U.S. Military Soldier

Mr. Anour tells us that while the land of Iraq has been blessed with abundant natural resources like oil, natural gas and phosphates which could make the country wealthy, families like these of Tikrit live very poorly due to war and political situations. In stark contrast to some of the luxurious palatial mansions lived in by previous government officials, we drive by Iraqi children playing outside on piles of rubble in front of simple flat-roofed houses made of sun-baked bricks. Nearly half of all Iraqis experience a very low standard of living, and less than 2 out of every 100 Iraqis live as well as you or I do. Remember that tasty mazgouf we ate in Mosul? Mr. Anour shares how one out of every four Iraqi children under the age of five fall asleep with gnawing, hungry tummies.

But, Abdel interjects, most children do go to **madrasa,** or school, free of charge. Do the schools in your neighborhood have washroom facilities? Nearly half of all Iraqi students today attend a school that does not have a washroom, an effect of wars. Thuraya explains that students still go to school daily to listen intently to **Ostath's** (teacher's) lessons, with all classes divided into boys sitting on one side of the classroom and girls on the other. Children, no matter how or where they live in the world, are just like you: they too have curious questions and a thirst for learning!

The palace of Saddam Hussein Abd al-Majid al-Tikriti overlooks the Tigris River in Tikrit. Would you like to have a name that includes where you were born and raised?

I have slept in a barn, in a tree house, on a beach and in a tent, but I have never slept on the roof of a house. As Mr. Anour drives us farther south into the lower plain region, Thuraya explains that many Iraqis sleep outside on their flat roofs on hot summer evenings. Abdel chimes in that Iraqi children often stay up until midnight or later to enjoy the cool—but that is because they often take a nap in the heat of the afternoon. Would you like that?

Mr. Anour has led us south of the old ruins of Babylon, to the city of Najaf on the banks of the Euphrates River. Do you notice that the Tigris and Euphrates Rivers continue to follow us on our travel south through Iraq? The Rivers fall endlessly, even now as you read these words, down Iraq's slope towards the Persian Gulf. I am sure you haven't missed the fact that nearly all of Iraq's people congregate in cities on the banks of the life-giving Tigris and Euphrates Rivers.

How does this street in Tikrit look similar or dissimilar to a street in your hometown? Do you see any flat roofs to sleep on in hot summer nights? *Photo: U.S. Military Soldier*

Look at that vast desert plain on the outskirts of Najaf with domes and tombs stretching out for mile upon mile ahead of us! Actually, it stretches for 6 miles [10 km], informs Mr. Anour. This is *Wadi al Salaam*, the Valley of Peace, the largest graveyard in the whole world. While Najaf maybe one of Iraq's biggest cities, population nearly 600,000, its hallowed cemetery, nearly 1,400 years old, is the resting place of millions. Why does Najaf have the world's largest cemetery? Mr. Anour says it is not unusual to see minibuses traveling to Najaf from all over the Middle East and Asia with stretchers on the roof rack, often draping the deceased in the national flag. Devout Shiite Muslims the world over pray that their family will one day bear them to Najaf for burial.

One of the holiest cities in Shia Islam, al-Najaf is home to the Imam Ali Mosque. Glittering in gold, the mosque is the burial site of Muhammad's close relative. One of the world's largest cemeteries, Wadi al-Salam, lies close by. Do you think these Muslim men and women are coming to the shrine or passing to the cemetery?

Iraqi Muslims are either *Shiite* Muslims or *Sunni* Muslims, two groups that arose after Muhammad's death. Sunni Muslims thought future leaders should be chosen from Muhammad's followers while Shiites believed that the leaders should be descendants of Muhammad's cousin, Ali.

Najaf is the site of Ali's tomb, the first leader of the Shiites. Ali requested that, when he died, he be buried in Najaf because Muslim tradition claimed that Abraham had once visited the area and declared that all who were buried there would enter paradise. We watch crowds of Shiite Muslims, men draped in **throbes**, an ankle length robe with long sleeves, women covered in black abayas, making their pilgrimage from all over the world to Ali's Mosque, its golden dome glittering brilliantly in the sunshine.

Do you know the other famous ancient visitor that Muslim tradition claims walked the soil of Najaf? According to their lore, one of Noah's sons refused to board the Ark, but instead chose to perch himself atop a mountain that covered modern-day Najaf. But, so the story goes, the mountain crumbled, the son drowned in the flood, and the river that appeared in place where the mountain once stood eventually dried up. Hence, the meaning of the name of Najaf: dry river.

We laugh with the Anours over the irony of the name 'dry river' for a city on the banks of the great Euphrates! Hasn't this Iraqi exploration with the Anours been a river ride? From the mountainous beginnings of the Tigris' tributaries, to trickling and gurgling and winding our way down the gradual descent of Iraq's steppes and upper plains into its lower plains. Yes, *"by the rivers of Babylon, there we [have] sat down"* (Ps. 137:1) to praise our great God who has *"caused waters to run down like rivers"* (Ps. 78:16) and one day, *"He shall have dominion also from sea to sea and from the river unto the ends of the earth"* (Ps. 72:8). While we give God all the glory, make sure you hold your place on those Iraqi rivers—they have more unforgettable places to sweep us off to!

Hasn't this been a captivating river ride through Iraq? The Tigris and Euphrates Rivers join in southern Iraq to form the Shatt-al-Arab River. These Iraqis paddle the Shatt-al-Arab, on their own river ride. What sights they see---look at the banks lined with palm trees!

Field Notes

It is so important to learn about the lives of other people around the world. I think I would like to visit an Iraqi family and share some of their delicious-sounding food! Would you and your family like to join me?

Press record and talk to me:

~**about Iraqi food**: What is *dolma*? How might someone fix *matzgouf* for us? When would be the best time to eat *zlabiya*?

~**about Tikrit**: Whose palace stands in Tikrit? Have you ever heard of Saddam Hussein? What is life like for most of the Iraqis in this area? Tell me about the schools. Where do some people sleep during the hot summers?

~**about Najaf**: What is Wadi al Salaam? Which famous Shiite Muslim is buried in Najaf? Can you explain the difference between Sunni and Shiite Muslims? What does the name Najaf mean? How does the name fit the city?

Travel Log

Using your globe or atlas, let's add the following locations to your map of Iraq... We've seen things today that simply must be mapped, never to be forgotten!

Map Notes: <u>Let's record the locations of:</u>

- *Taurus Mountains*
- *Zagros Mountains*
- *Kurdistan*
- *Mosul*

- *Kirkuk*
- *Tikrit*
- *Najaf*

<u>If you'd like, draw pictures or symbols on your map representing:</u>

- *Kurdish flag over Kurdistan* (red, white, green striped with yellow sun in center)
- *Goats and sheep in the Zagros foothills*
- *Al-Hadba* (remember the Tower of Pisa?)
- *Oil pipelines outside of Mosul*
- *Life in Tikrit* (a hot sun and kids on roofs? A school building?)
- *Ali's Mosque* (a glittering golden dome?)

Travel Notes: Geographers write what they've seen in order to share the adventure with others—and so they can revisit the places in their memories! **On the next page of your travel log, record three important sights you want to remember from your photos of Iraq.**

~*art* ~*books* ~*food* ~*music* ~*poetry*
. . . .
Bringing It Home
Simple ideas to bring the world to your door

Books

New books are being written about Iraq all the time, so be sure to check your local library for new titles. Here are a couple to get you started:

The Librarian of Basra: A True Story from Iraq *by* Jeanette Winter
 Tells the true story of Alia Muhammad Baker, an Iraqi librarian who tries to save as many books as she can before her country is destroyed by war. *Grades 2-4*

Alia's Mission: Saving the Books of Iraq *by* Mark Alan Stamaty
Another version of the story above for older readers. This graphic novel is packed with intricate black, white and grey illustrations. *Older readers: grades 5 +*

Kiss the Dust *by* Elizabeth Laird
An historical novel set in Iraq, this book tells the story of a Kurdish refugee family trying to escape from Saddam Hussein's regime. ***Older readers 10 +*

Poetry:

The people of Iraq love poetry! If you and I were to walk down an Iraqi street together we might hear people spontaneously creating poems just for fun.   One man tells of spending the evening with a Bedouin man who recited thousands of lines of ancient poetry from memory!

Blessed is the one who said
I know the road which leads to it;
Blessed is the one whose lips uttered the four letters:
"Iraq, Iraq, nothing but Iraq." ~Saadi Youssef (2004)

Mixing Water and Oil?

Iraq ~Part 3~

Do you think these Iraqi children have engineered sandbox lakes with miniature houses on sandy islands? Perhaps they have seen such real-life scenes in their own country!

When I was a kid, my brother and I spent many leisurely summer afternoons under the leafy umbrella of our Manitoba maple digging canals, shoring up islands, and floating boats in our sandbox lakes. The garden hose fed our maze of water channels and our imagination fed adventures of miniature boats and villagers. When our Mother called from the back step, we'd break down the dams, let the waters flood our island towns, and run across the lawn for dinner.

Do you know that some Iraqis live in real life what my brother and I only imagined? We've seen fascinating sights in our explorations of the mountains of northeastern Iraq, and the rolling steppes of the upper plains of the Tigris-Euphrates River Valley. But wait until you see the places the Anour family will show us today!

Leaving Najaf (Do you recall the sights we saw in Najaf?), we watch the flat, unchanging landscape flash past our window. These lower plains of the Tigris and Euphrates River, says Mr. Anour, cover almost one third of Iraq. Abdel asks if we know how these plains were built up? From the same rivers that have sustained life here for thousands of years. While the Tigris and Euphrates have brought drinking water and waters to irrigate crops, sometimes they carried tremendous amounts of water—and mud. Melting snows high up in the mountain tops combined with heavy spring rains have caused the Tigris to rise more than 1 ft [30 cm] per hour, flooding areas of the plain more than 33 ft [10 m] deep. (That means if six tall men stood one atop the shoulders of each other, the last man would barely have his nose above the rising flood waters!) Centuries of the Tigris and Euphrates rivers flooding, depositing clay, sand, rocks, and silt in the region, have created this extremely flat alluvial plain. **Alluvial** means deposited by running water—and that is the creative way our God has shaped this plain!

Look out your window at the robed farmers working these fertile fields of heavy alluvial soils. We don't see any Iraqi farmers scanning the horizon for rain clouds. Because Iraq's weather systems bring little rainfall from the sky, farmers know they must irrigate their fields with river waters. Centuries of Iraqi families irrigating this way have caused 2 out of every 3 fields to have **soil salinity**, a serious condition where soil contains too much salt to grow crops. Thus, there are fewer farmers today working the

With a bird's eye view across the plains of Iraq, we can see how flat God has made this region of the country!
Photo: U.S. Military Soldier

127

Looking out across the fields of these Iraqi farmers, we do not see any rain clouds on the horizon. We do, however, see irrigation water in the fields, greening up these crops.
Photo: U.S. Military Soldier

fields of Iraq than once toiled here a few decades ago. Much like the ancient era, however, we still spot Iraqis forming bricks out of the alluvial soil and using it for constructing their homes and buildings.

Traveling further into southern Iraq, the barren plain ebbs away before us and a shimmering plain of *water* appears! How incredible that God would create a water landscape in the middle of desert plains! This, Abdel announces, is the Marshlands of Iraq. From reeds growing up out of the clear waters here, it is easy to understand that **marshes** are a type of wetland, but different than swamps since no trees grow here. How did God create such a marshland in the desert? Thuraya offers an explanation: since the lower plains are so flat, both the Tigris and Euphrates meandered in sinuous loops, eventually dividing into distributaries. Occurring mainly in a delta, a **distributary** is a river that branches off from a major river before it meets the sea. Far from the Persian Gulf, just south of Al Nasiriyah, the Euphrates River did indeed split and weave into a braided pattern. As farmers use the rivers' waters to irrigate their fields, the reduced water flow contributed to the rivers splitting into an array of shallow waters in its final stretch towards the Persian Gulf. Thus the Marshlands emerged where the rivers splinter off into many branches, stretching from Samawah on the Euphrates and Kut on the Tigris all the way south to Basrah. (Can you locate those cities when you look at a map of Iraq?)

Mr. Anour tell us of the Marshes in a long ago summer, not unlike the summer my brother and I flooded the sandbox, when he visited his uncle Hassan in these marshlands south of Qurna (the same town boasting "Adam's Garden"). Uncle Hassan would help him into the ***mashuf,*** the long, flat bottomed boat made out of reeds, and together they would pole along winding narrow canals, like water highways through the 15 ft [4.5 m] high reeds. Every bend in the water canal offered a new sight: the splash of the smooth-coated otter, a herd of black water buffalos, or several wild boars on the run. A flock of pelicans, powerful wings thumping, would take flight overhead. The sun would set crimson to the song of croaking frogs. Another curve in the canal would bring him home to a young cousin sitting in front of his house made of reeds, fishing for ***bunni,*** a carp-like freshwater fish. What would it be like to sit on the front step of your house and fish for your dinner?

Yes, a marshland with canals of water in a country of desert! The distributaries of the Tigris and Euphrates Rivers formed a marshland where the Iraqi Ma'dan people lived in what was the largest wetland in the Middle East. *Photo courtesy of UNEP*

128

Uncle Hassan and his family were **Ma'dans**, a semi-nomadic Iraqi people who have lived in the marsh for thousands of years—some say since the time of the Garden of Eden. The Ma'dan, residing in one the lushest environments on earth, are a living link between today's Iraqis and ancient Mesopotamians.

The warm smile of this young Ma'dan invites our friendly wave! The long pole is used for both paddling through the water canals and for herding the cattle along. Also called the Marsh Arabs, the Ma'dan have lived in the marshes for centuries, earning a living through fishing, raising water buffalo, making mats and furniture from reeds, and, in some areas, cultivating rice.
Photo courtesy of UNEP

Have you ever heard the saying that 'No man is an island?' Each Ma'dan family, however, lived on their own island, much grander versions of the islands I made as a child in our sandbox. To build his house, Uncle Hassan would enclose an area of the marsh, and fill it with hand-woven reed matting and mud until the surface was above water and dry—an island of their own! Every year he would add more layers of reeds to strengthen the platform's foundation. Some older islands might protrude six feet [2 m] above the water.

As Uncle Hassan's young visitor, Mr. Anour was received at the cathedral-like guesthouse called the **mudhif**. Made from the few building supplies the marshes have to offer: reeds, mud and buffalo dung, the mudhif's fantastic vaulted arches housed Marsh tribal gatherings. Uncle Hassan paid a kind of tax to the **sheik**, or leader, of his Ma'dan tribe, to care and maintain the mudhif. With lacy windows woven into the reed mat walls for sunlight to softly filter through, Mr. Anour sat in the cool, carpeted mudhif, eating yogurt mixed with rice and dates while he visited.

Inside the cool air of the mudhif, we sit on rich carpets, and enjoy the stories and hospitality of the Ma'dan. Built as a gathering place for travelers and visitors like us, the graceful, arching lines of the mudhif are made by fine reed mats woven by women and children. Isn't it exquisite?
Photo courtesy of UNEP

Looking out across the plain of water today, we certainly do not see the vast marshes of the extent of Mr. Anour's childhood memories. Over there are the ruins of a village, abandoned like a shipwreck, beached on cracked, salt-caked soil. Where did all of the waters of the marshlands go?

For various reasons, Mr. Anour answers, past governments built massive engineering works, dams and dikes that diverted the flow of the Euphrates and drained away the life of the Marshes. The heron and ibis flew away. The goitered gazelle and the striped hyena wandered away, never to return. Thousands upon thousands of Ma'dan families gathered their few belongings and set out to make their life elsewhere, many leaving the country of Iraq altogether. The relatively few Ma'dan families who remained learned how to "dry farm." But where will Iraqis throughout the country find fish for their tables? One of the world's greatest wetlands, and a way of life thousands of year old, had been drained away by man's own hand.

No family is an island but is connected to other Ma'dan families by watery "streets." Each family makes their own "island" from a mixture of earth and reeds pressed down to form the foundation of the hut. As many as half a million Iraqis recently lived in the marshes. Today, as the marshes are replenished with water, many Iraqis are returning to this unique lifestyle.
Photo courtesy of UNEP

But, consoles Thurayra, there are flickers of hope for the Marshes and the Mad'an. The marshlands we see today, 20% the size of what the marshes once were, are the result of new Iraqi leaders opening the dams and waters, once again flooding portions of the marshlands. Abdel says there are still questions: Is the water too salty for reeds to grow? Have the dams in countries to the north, like Turkey, restricted the flow of the rivers so that there simply isn't sufficient water to revive the marshes? Do the Ma'dan families desire to return to their life upon the water and reeds? These are questions that only time will answer. Some things we can already know with certainty: we can destroy the home God created for us much faster than we can repair it. We've also come to realize that the complex balances our all-wise Creator God established in the various regions throughout His world cannot be easily recreated by human beings.

Field Notes

Can you imagine living on your very own island? What a wonderful world God has created for us to discover!
Press record and talk to me:

~**about the Iraqi plains:** What happens to the landscape when the Tigris fills with melting snows? Does this area receive much rainfall?

~about the Marshes: Can you tell me how marshlands are created in this desert? What is a mashuf? What sights would we have seen if we had taken a mashuf ride? Tell me about the Ma'dan. What are their homes like? How do they build them? Do the Ma'dan still live in the marshes? Why not? What new skills are the Ma'dan trying to learn today?

Have you watched a DVD this week? Walked on carpet? Carried a plastic jug? Held a toothbrush, wrote with plastic pen, ridden in a car? If you have, you may thank God for how He created Iraq. Each of the products involved in those activities are derived from oil. Your every day life, wherever you live in the world, is greatly impacted by what the Anour family will show us next!

Driving across the flat-panned desert south of **Basrah**, there are no houses or trees as far as the eye can see. All that rises on the landscape are rusted tanks, like rotting teeth, scattered here and there. Large pipes shoot like thick snakes straight across this barren landscape. Mr. Anour explains that in this southeastern border region that Iraq shares with Kuwait is one of the most productive oil fields in the world. But why the rusting tanks, you ask? The abandoned, hole-riddled tanks, says Abdel, testify to the fact that nations have marched into this land with armies to wrangle and wrestle over what lies under the ground. What lies trapped far below our feet in this barren, empty land are some of the world's richest resources: oil. What an astounding feat of God that oil exists deep down in our Earth at all!

Iraq has been riddled by war and its dire effects for many years. We pray for a new era of peace. *Photo: Christiaan Briggs*

As a child, I used to dig deep in our sandbox for just the right texture of mud for a double batch of mudcakes. While the following may sound like an interesting recipe, it's actually a simple explanation of how God created **oil**: Take tons of tiny animals and plants, place them near a hot fire, cover them and then let them sit. However easy that may sound, only God could orchestrate such a series of events. First of all, God allowed mud to bury tiny animals and plants faster than they could decay. (Might this have happened during the Flood?) Then God designed it such that these **sediments** were at just the right depth—7,500 to 15,000 feet [2,286 m—4,572 m]—for heat and pressure to slow-cook the **organic** material into oil. Next, God collected the oil in a rock with many pores in which to hold the oil, much like a sponge holds water. (A **pore** is a small open space in the rock.) To ensure that the oil didn't leak away, God capped the stone with an impermeable roof of shale or salt. Isn't our God breathtaking in His creative chain of events to cook up oil in the deep depths of the earth? And, interestingly, He chose to create the world's oil primarily in the Middle East.

In the oil fields of southern Iraq, and in those we saw earlier in the northern region near Mosul, Iraqis have drilled down into the porous rock and are pumping out over 2.5 million barrels of heavy black oil every day. That is a tremendous amount of oil for a country the size of the state of

California to pump out of the earth every 24 hours! Only the Middle Eastern country of Saudi Arabia pumps full more barrels of oil in a day than Iraq. Yet our world consumes mind-boggling amounts of oil every day. Thuraya tells us that if you poured the 20 million barrels of oil that the United States of America alone consumes in one *day* into 1 gallon [3.7 liter] cans, the line of cans would encircle the earth at the equator almost 6 times. That is nearly 147,000 miles [236, 573 km] of oil cans, every single day!

The waters of the Tigris and Euphrates River mingle in the Shatt-al Arab river where the city of Basrah thrives. How do oil and water mix in Iraq?

To help provide oil to meet the world's demand, Iraqis are looking for more oil under their feet, (including in the drained marshes). As people cannot create more water, neither can they create cost-effective oil. And as important as oil is to driving cars to work and operating tractors to grow food, Mr. Anour suggests that future armies may not wrestle over the control of oil in the Middle East, but over another limited resource that only God can make, and even more necessary for living: water.

Have you ever tried to mix oil with water? The two do not mix very well, do they? But Mr. Anour takes us to Iraqi waters where oil and water meet!

Palm trees sway in the breezes, cars stream past. Buildings with arched windows line the streets. This, says Abdel, is the southern city of Al-Basrah. One of Iraq's largest cities, Basrah, congregates on the shores of the river, Shatt-al Arab, a river formed by the joining of the Tigris and Euphrates rivers. (Can you find Al Basrah on the Shatt-Al Arab on your map?) We wave to the boy biking past the towering chimney stacks of a Basrah oil refinery, puffing clouds of grey. The size of a large village, mazes of pipes connecting tanks and towers, the oil refinery turns the oil pumped from under the Iraqi soil into gasoline for vehicles all over the world. Some ocean-going vessels chug their way up the Shatt-al Arab, docking in Basrah, Iraq's only port city, to fill their hulls with oil. If we will come south of Basrah near the mouth of Shatt-al Arab, we see monstrous tankers saddling alongside platforms arching out of the blue gulf waters. While we watch the tankers load, other ships lining up for their turn, Thuraya tells us that two huge pipelines run underneath the waters, connecting the platforms to oil pipelines on the mainland. This is where oil meets water. When these two offshore platforms are operating at full capacity, declares Abdel, they load as much oil as the country of France uses in one day!

Shall we hop on one of the tankers, wave goodbye to Mr. Anour, Thuraya and Abdel, and the country of Iraq and head for home? We landed in Iraq's capital city of Baghdad and we would leave on an oil tanker south of Basrah. We have our memories of the gracious Anour family touring us through sites of long ago Babylon, Ur, and Nineveh. We hiked into Iraq's northern mountains to follow the Tigris and Euphrates Rivers as they spilled down through the highlands,

From our seats in space, can you peer down to see where the Tigris and Euphrates Rivers join to form the Shatt al-Arab River? How are the waters of the Persian Gulf affected by the rivers? *Photo courtesy of visibleearth.nasa.gov*

streamed through the sloping plains, branched out through the delta, to here, at the Persian Gulf, where oil meets water. If you're returning to North America, an ocean voyage of 41 days on the waves, sailing around the Horn of Africa, would dock you back in the southern United States. A few days later might find Iraq's oil at the gas station right around the corner from your house. Amazing as it is, it may be that the next tank of gas that fuels your vehicle may have just made that very journey from distant Iraq!

With its oil and water, ancient Biblical sites and modern-day cities, highlands and lowlands, Iraq may be a country of interesting opposites in the far away mystery of the Middle East, but it too is a country in the very middle of the Bible, in the middle of the world's industries and economies and perhaps, in the middle of your heart. The Anour family certainly hopes so!

Field Notes

Isn't it amazing that God hid such resources under the ground of Iraq?

Press record and talk to me:

<u>~about oil:</u> What "recipe" does God use to make oil? How much oil does Iraq pump each day? How much oil does the US use each day? What things in your own home might have been made with Iraqi oil?

<u>~about al-Basrah:</u> What does the maze of pipes, tanks, and towers we see produce? Why do ships gather in the waters of this port city? How does the oil get from the land to the ships? Where do the ships go after they are loaded?

Travel Log

Using your globe or atlas, let's add the following locations to your map of Iraq... We've seen things today that simply *must* be mapped, never to be forgotten!

Map Notes: <u>Let's record the locations of:</u>

- *Al Nasiriyah*
- *Al-Basrah*

- *Shatt-al Arab*

<u>If you'd like, draw pictures or symbols on your map representing:</u>

- *Marshes (perhaps some island homes for the Ma'dans? Or a mashuf among some reeds?)*
- *A maze of pipes and tanks to pump oil in the desert near Basrah*
- *Ocean-going tankers in the port of Basrah*

<u>*Challenge mapping:*</u> *Can you chart your trip home from Iraq on the tanker? If you are returning to North America, make sure you travel around the Horn of Africa!*

Travel Notes: Geographers write what they've seen in order to share the adventure with others—and so they can revisit the places in their memories! **On the next page of your travel log, record three important sights you want to remember from your photos of Iraq.**

~art ~books ~food ~music ~poetry
. . . .

Bringing It Home

Simple ideas to bring the world to your door

Food

Hospitality is very important to Iraqis. If you were a guest in an Iraqi home your host would make sure you had plenty to eat. Happily, the way to show proper appreciation for your hosts' hospitality is by overeating! Perhaps you might like to make a big pot of *Ma'mounia* – a dessert that has been around since the 9th century – and invite some guests over to practice your own hospitality.

Ma'mounia

3 cups water
1 cup sugar
1 tsp lemon juice
½ cup sweet butter
1 cup semolina (cream of wheat or you may use wheat flour)
whipped cream
1 tsp ground cinnamon

Put sugar and water in a large saucepan over low heat, and stir constantly until sugar dissolves.
Bring mixture to a boil while adding lemon juice. After syrup boils, reduce heat and let simmer until syrup thickens slightly (about 10 minutes).

In another saucepan, melt butter and add semolina. Stir until semolina is lightly fried, then add the syrup from the other pan, and let the mixture simmer another 10 minutes, stirring constantly.
Remove from heat and let cool 20 minutes. Spoon ma'mounia into individual serving bowls, top with whipped cream, and sprinkle with cinnamon. Serves 4.

The Iraqi landscape is full of **date** palm trees, which means plenty of yummy dates to enjoy. Here are some simple ways to try dates at home:

First, try eating them plain. You might find you like the sticky sweetness! Chop some and mix with different nuts and chopped bananas for a snack. Or try cutting them up and using them in place of chocolate chips or raisins in cookie recipes.

Go into all the world...

a walk of prayer

We hear so much about Iraq on the news – and now we have had a glimpse of Iraq for ourselves! I am so glad we have taken time to journey to this land. We've found that Iraq is full of boys and girls who are much like us. They were created by a God who loves them dearly—just as He loves you.

Will you and your family join me in praying for the Iraqi people?

Lord, give us Your love for the peoples of the world, and help our family to live in a way that shows our love for them. Father, we hear about Iraq all the time, but now we have learned of its beauty and history for ourselves. May our hearts be full of love for Iraq, as Your heart is.

~We pray for **peace. May the conflicts and war that have torn Iraq apart end**. We pray for new hope for the Iraqi people. We ask that one day soon Iraqi families would wake to peaceful and prosperous days.

~We pray for **the Iraqi leaders who are making decisions about the future**. May they have wisdom as they build a new country. May they have foresight and strength to make the right choices. May the **citizens** who follow them have courage to do what is best for their nation.

~We pray for **the young people** who are being raised even today, **young men and women who will decide the future course of Iraq**. May they be filled with Your wisdom and go in the direction You desire for them.

~ We pray for **Iraqi Christians**, bringing the hope of Jesus to war-torn communities and weary people. Show them how to best reach out, in Your love, to meet the needs of their neighbors. Strengthen these brothers and sisters in Christ to be brilliant beacons of the gospel of Grace.

~We ask for **safety and health for the families** who live in Iraq. May their needs be met and may Your protection surround them.

We love you, Lord, and the people who are living in Iraq today. May the Light of our Savior dawn over all nations today. Draw us all closer to You, Father. In Jesus name, Amen.

Migrations, Mecca and Mosques

Saudi Arabia ~Part 1~

This Saudi man is on the move. Let's follow him and see why millions of people flock to Saudi Arabia each year. *Photo: Galen Fry*

Every autumn the skies over my house fill with the flapping of wings and the honking of geese as they fly south in V's. I've never counted them all, but I suppose their numbers are untold.

Did you know that every year millions, yes, *millions*, of people migrate to one spot on earth, remain for as long as twelve days, and then disperse back to their homes throughout the world? Are your eyes keen, your memory sharp and your faith strong? Let's see where this endless swarm of people travels!

If you'll look on your map, you'll find we've landed in Jeddah, Saudi Arabia. The Kingdom of Saudi Arabia (for yes, it is ruled by a King) occupies nearly all of the Arabian Peninsula in the Middle East. Looking at your atlas, you will see that Saudi Arabia is bordered by the Red Sea on the west, and by the Persian Gulf on the east. What shape do you see in Saudi Arabia's borders: perhaps the head of a wolf, its nose set towards the Persian Gulf? Actually, the border that outlines the tip of the wolf's nose is undefined. Saudi Arabia is one of a very few countries in the world in which it has not been determined where some of its borders end and where neighboring countries begin.

Can you see what is missing on your map of Saudi Arabia? There are no pools or snaking lines of blue, and very little green! God created Saudi Arabia with no lakes, no permanent rivers and no expanse of forests. Nearly one quarter the size of the United States of America, Saudi Arabia is thought to be the driest large country on the face of the earth.

While we won't find many families with permanent homes in the vast, dry interior of Saudi Arabia, did you know that one out of every six people on this planet - more than one billion people scattered around the world - consider Saudi Arabia to be their *spiritual* homeland? Since Mecca, Saudi Arabia is the birthplace of the Islamic prophet Mohammed, Muslims worldwide regard this region of the world as their home. Every year during the Islamic month of *dhu al-Hijjah* millions of Muslims from over 70 countries, in the largest annual gathering at one place in the world, make pilgrimage or **hajj** to Saudi Arabia. Once having the most restrictive travel rules in the world, visitors like you and I are now permitted to visit the country - but only if we have a tour guide. Our tour guide, Saleh, meets us at the airport, wearing his white robe, called a **throbe,** and a flowing head covering of red and white checks called a **gutra**. His gutra is held in place by a black cord called an **egal,** traditionally used to tie camels.

Comprising most of the Arabian Peninsula, Saudi Arabia's borders form what shape in your mind? Who are Saudi Arabia's neighbors? And what bodies of waters surround the peninsula?

"Marhaba!" greets Saleh, "Welcome to Jeddah, Bride of the Red Sea and the gateway city to the land of the Holy Mosques."

Today, the mass of Muslim pilgrims crush by us and into the world's second largest airport terminal used only once a year during the annual pilgrimage. Look at the sweeping roof of the terminal. Doesn't it look like the draping tents of the desert Bedouin tribes? But no, says Saleh, Jeddah's airport terminal roof is not actually a tent, it is made of a fiberglass fabric and is said to be the largest roof in the world. But we don't feel hot under its cover, do we? Designed to be like a shady forest in the middle of glaring hot desert, the white roof reflects most of the sun's heat. Mankind often copies how God created the home of Earth when constructing buildings of our own.

Saleh waves for us to follow him through the crowd of pilgrims and out into the palm-lined streets of Jeddah. Eight lane highways whisk us past tall skyscrapers and modern hotels, flat-roofed homes built of coral, and mosques with slender minarets pointing into the desert sky. Fountains, some of the highest in the world, spray plumes of water that can be seen far off in the distance. Every traffic round-about seems to uplift a work of art: giant sunflowers, a block of concrete with several cars poking out of it at unusual angles, a marble sculpture of Arabic words. Saleh tells us that the city of Jeddah is thought to be the largest outdoor art gallery in

Jeddah's airport may be one of the most modern in the world, but Old Jeddah's buildings are very old and architecturally unusual. Built of coral limestone, they are tall and graceful. The intricate wooden facades, known as *rawasheen* (singular *roshan*), were designed to disperse the sun's glare yet also to allow the cooling sea breezes to drift in while shielding residents from view. *Photo: John Pint*

the world. But you'll notice that none of the sculptures are of people in this Islamic city. This is known as **aniconism**, the Muslim law forbidding representation of living creatures in art work. Muslims fear that such art might become idolized.

Aren't these the largest 'sunflowers' you've ever seen? The Saudi Arabian city of Jeddah is considered the largest outdoor art gallery in the world. *Photo: John Pint*

The Islamic religion is an all-encompassing way of life in Saudi Arabia, Saleh explains. The country's flag, flapping there in the wind, declares the Muslim faith: *"There is no god but Allah; Mohammad is the messenger of Allah."* Saleh points to an older man with a red-dyed beard walking down the street with camel whip. He is one of the religious police, the **mutawa**, who make sure that all women have their arms covered and their skirts fall to their ankles—otherwise they may receive a whipping on bare skin. Saudis practice strict Islam. While your mother may wear clothing of her choice when she goes shopping, all Saudi women must wear the billowing black abaya in public, which covers them from head to ankle. Many Saudi women further cover themselves by veiling their face so only their eyes may be seen. Face veils were worn traditionally by desert

women to protect their faces from windblown sand and the harsh sun, but Saudi women now cover themselves for modesty.

Do you hear the melodious song of the muezzin through the loudspeakers of the minaret, calling the country to prayer? It's a sight we've not likely seen near our homes: rows of men outside the supermarket or wherever they are, bowing towards the city of Mecca in prayer. Do you see the sign hanging there in a shop window, "Sorry, Closed for Prayer?" Saleh tells us that all Saudi Arabian offices and shop close for up to 30 minutes during the daily prayer times. As the caretakers of Islam's two holy mosques, Saudis pride themselves in carefully following all of these Islamic teachings.

In the creeping traffic of cars and yellow buses, we make our way south on the modern multi-lane highway from Jeddah towards Mecca, where the pilgrims are journeying. Looking out our windows at the mountainous landscape, Saleh informs us that Jeddah and Mecca lie in the geographical area known as the Hijaz. Hijaz means "barrier," an apt name for the rugged mountains God has sculpted in the northern half of Saudi Arabia's west coast. The mountains of the Hijaz, running parallel to the Red Sea, act as a jagged barrier between the great northern central plateau of Saudi Arabia and the Red Sea coast. The Hijaz also contains the slip of low lying coastal plain known as the Tihamah, where the port of Jeddah is located.

All Saudi women are required to wear an abaya in public, and often veil their faces. In public, there are separate areas for Saudi Arabian women to eat, pray, and work, apart from men. Saudi Arabian homes may also have separate women's quarters.
Photo: John Pint

Field Notes

Did you ever imagine such a migration of PEOPLE? I want to hear about everything you've seen so far.

Press record and talk to me:

~about the geography of Saudi Arabia: Which peninsula does Saudi Arabia cover? Which bodies of water border Saudi Arabia?

~about the migration of people to Mecca:
What is the *hajj*? How many people travel to Mecca each year? Why are they traveling to Saudi Arabia? Can you describe the airport?

~about Jeddah: Is Jeddah a modern city? Can you describe some of the buildings? Tell me about the art work.

~religion in Saudi Arabia: What is the religion of the Saudi people called? What are the religious police, or *mutawa*, watching for? What do Muslim women wear? What does the *muzzein's* call mean?

When I was a kid, the neighborhood boys had a clubhouse. All the community kids knew the rules: "No Girls Allowed!" Their boys-only rule was not meant to be offensive to girls but to allow a safe, special gathering place for the boys. Saleh explains how the entire city of Mecca is considered so holy that non-Muslims are strictly forbidden to enter it. Since Mecca was once a city where Muslims were driven out, when Mohammed reclaimed the city he declared it a place for every Muslim to feel safe. Can you see the special highway over there that diverts non-Muslims around the city?

A man we meet on the streets of Jeddah wears a white throbe. Hajj pilgrims also wear white, but their covering is unsewn.
Photo: Galen Fry

When we reach the archway to Mecca, shaped like the large book of Koran, Islam's sacred book, we non-Muslims can go no farther. Saleh must simply describe the hajj to us. For more than 1,300 years Muslims, no matter where they live in the world, have been fulfilling the requirements of Islam by making the pilgrimage to this city in Saudi Arabia. To try and picture how many pilgrims migrate today to Mecca, can you imagine the crowd packed into a stadium for a Super Bowl football game? Now think of twenty of those stadiums full of people all in one place!

Millions of Muslims from around the globe journey to Mecca, to the Grand Mosque, to encircle the K'abah and its Black Stone. Can you imagine the sights and sounds of such a migration of people? *Photo: Ali Mansuri*

Before entering the city, male pilgrims change into **ihram** clothing: a white, unsewn sheet with unsewn sandals; Saleh tells us that this is to show that all Muslims are equal before Allah. Women simply cover their heads. Can you imagine seeing thousands upon hundreds of thousands of men all dressed alike? Next, the pilgrims enter the city of Mecca where it is strictly forbidden to hurt people,

A Muslim pilgrim fulfills his obligatory pilgrimage to Mecca. Do you see the towering minarets of the Grand Mosque of Mecca? *Photo: Ali Mansuri*

animals or plants. Yes, says Saleh, Muslims are not even allowed to kill a stinging mosquito during hajj!

What draws Muslims to Mecca? In the center of the city sits a mosque, in the center of the mosque sits a stone cube-shaped structure, and in the foundation of the cube building sits the Black Stone, which is the center of the religion of Islam. With 48 entrance gates, and 9 towering minarets pointing to the clouds, Mecca's Grand Mosque is not only a masterpiece of Islamic design, but nearly a million people can stand within its beauty at one time! "*Labbayka Allahumma Labbayak,*" ("Here I am at your service, O Allah, here I am.") the sea of pilgrims chants over and over again as they arrive at the Grand Mosque. Here in the center of this magnificent marble mosque, we will find the cube-shaped building draped in a black silk cloth. Saleh explains that Muslims believe that the cube, called the **Ka'abah**, was built by Abraham and his son Ishmael more than 4,000 years ago. To Muslims, the Ka'abah, also known as the House of Allah, is the holiest place on Earth. Saleh explains that the mass of pilgrims march around the Ka'abah seven times, stopping to kiss one of the cornerstones of the Black Stone. Is it true that the Black Stone is a **meteorite**? We'll never know. But we understand that the Ka'abah is the geographic and spiritual center of the Muslim world. No matter where a Muslim lives on the planet throughout his lifetime, he must always face towards the Ka'abah during the five daily prayers.

Have you ever had a special time of reflection at a grave of someone you care about? Many of the hajj pilgrims next travel north to Medina to visit the tomb of the Prophet Mohammed. Passing by the slopes of the mountains near Medina, the pilgrims will look out upon dry wadis carved out by long ago rivers, and see herds of grazing camels. But their eyes will be set upon the site of the sole green dome of the Prophet's Mosque, under which lies Mohammed's resting place. Known as the land of the two holy mosques, Saudi Arabia's Prophet's Mosque, magnificent with its marble, minarets, and 24 white domes, is the second most holy site in Islam after the Grand Mosque in Mecca. As non-Muslims, we can only envision the colorful tiles and small pillars of the older part of the Prophet's Mosque, and the gleaming white marble of the newer section.

The Arabic words of Saudi Arabia's flag read: "There is no god but Allah; Mohammad is the messenger of Allah." The sword on the flag represents the victories of the king's family, the House of Saud.

On a farm close to where I live, most summer afternoons would find a cow quietly chewing cud in a clover pasture and bees humming from flower to flower. The next day, however, a look at the same pasture might find it transformed into a vast tented city, thousands of people perusing the wares of each tent. Perhaps something similar happens in a field near your home when the fair comes to town?

In the fields near Mina, a town three miles [4 km] south of Mecca, a similar tent city sprouts during the hajj. The deluge of pilgrims streams in from Medina and Mecca to stay the night in the blanket of white tents, explains Saleh. Leaving the massive tent city at dawn's first light, the massive sea of pilgrims swarm east to the Plains of Arafat. Some 820 feet [250 meters] above sea level, surrounded by mountains on all sides, these plains are where Muslims believe Mohammed gave his last sermon. During the Hajj the plains fill with pilgrims praying under the hot sun, asking Allah to forgive them. Thousands of sprinklers atop poles spray a cool mist on the

A sea of Muslim pilgrims flood the Grand Mosque and the Ka'abah during the Hajj. Only Muslims are permitted entry to the city of Mecca.

weary pilgrims. After sunset, each pilgrim gathers at least fifty pebbles the size of chickpeas at the base of nearby mountains. Saleh tells us that the pilgrims then carry their handful of stones to Mina, a city just east of Mecca, to hurl them at three walls. Being careful not to be trampled by the mass of people, or to accidentally hit a fellow pilgrim in the head with the pebbles, each pilgrim believes that the pelting of their pebbles is the 'stoning of the devil,' as Muslims believe that Abraham pelted a tempting Satan at this site.

The final act of the pilgrims' hajj is to again encircle the Ka'abah of Mecca's Grand Mosque seven times. Can you imagine the colors, the smell, the languages of millions of people from all over the earth gathered in this one place in Saudi Arabia? Can you hear the chanting in heavy Turkish accents? Do you see the African women kneeling? Or the group of Asians, wrapped in their white outfits, singing, their feet shuffling to the rhythm? The Hajj pilgrimage to Saudi Arabia, the land of the two holy mosques, may be the world's largest annual migration of people - but did you know that someday there will be a far larger gathering? Someday, *"all nations whom Thou hast made shall come and worship before thee, O Lord; and they shall glorify Thy name"* (Ps. 86:8). Think of that gathering! Where *"at the name of Jesus every knee shall bow, of those who are in heaven, and on earth, and under the earth, and that every tongue shall confess that Jesus Christ is Lord, to the glory of God the Father"* (Phil. 2:10)! While Saleh could only describe the Muslim hajj to us, I can hardly wait to actually be one of the *"[m]any peoples [who] will come and say, 'Come, let us go up to the mountain of the Lord, to the house of the God of Jacob'"* (Isa. 2:3). Can you?

Field Notes

It was fascinating to walk through Mecca with the Muslim pilgrims, don't you think? I look forward to the day when you and I will meet before Jesus' throne!

Press record and talk to me:

~about Mecca: Who is allowed inside? How do non-Muslims get around the city? What is the Hajj? What kind of clothing must the men wear inside the city? the women? What would you do if a mosquito landed on you inside Mecca?

~about the Grand Mosque: How many gates does it have? How many people can fit inside? What is in the center? What do the pilgrims do inside the mosque?

~about Medina: Whose tomb is here? What does the Prophet's Mosque look like?

~about Mina: Why does the town fill with tents each year? Where are the pilgrims going from here? What do the pilgrims gather on the Plains of Arafat? What do they do with the things they collect? Why?

~about the end of the pilgrimage: What is the last thing pilgrims do? Can you describe the gathering in the Bible that is even bigger than the Hajj?

Travel Log

Using your globe or atlas, draw an outline map of Saudi Arabia.

As we travel, let's make record in our very own travel log of the places we've visited and the unusual sights we've seen! Make your map large enough to hold all of your discoveries!

Don't worry about making a perfect map, just do your best. Drawing the basic shape yourself will help you remember it better. Or use the map provided on the CD-ROM.

Map Notes: <u>Let's record the locations of:</u>

- *Red Sea*
- *Persian Gulf*
- *Jeddah*

- *Mecca*
- *Medina*
- *Mina*

<u>If you'd like, draw pictures or symbols on your map representing:</u>

- *Airport (a striped tent?)*
- *Black Stone at Mecca*
- *Prophet's Mosque at Medina (a green dome?)*
- *White tents at Mina*

Travel Notes: Geographers write what they've seen in order to share the adventure with others—and so they can revisit the places in their memories! **On the next page of your travel log, record three important sights you want to remember from your photos of Saudi Arabia.**

~*art* ~*books* ~*food* ~*music* ~*poetry*

. . . .

Bringing It Home

Simple ideas to bring the world to your door

Art:

Calligraphy is an important art form in most Arab countries. Artists are amazingly creative in their use of calligraphy and their work is extremely intricate. One interesting style is *zoomorphic calligraphy*. An artist uses letters and words to "draw" the image of an animal – some believe this art form originated because Islam prohibits images of living beings, and this was one way of depicting animals without breaking the prohibition. In the illustration at left, the calligrapher has used Arabic letters to form a lion. Let's see if we can't use their ideas to make our own art!

First, on a piece of paper, write the name of an animal you'd like to draw, and a list of words describing or related to that animal. (For example: Zebra: black, white, stripe, four legs, swishing tail, run fast, lion escape, graze, grass, etc.)

Now draw a simple outline of your animal on a different piece of paper and begin to fill in the outline with the words you have listed. Make your letters big or small, wide or narrow, stretch them out or separate the letters, write them in a curvy line, and repeat them; whatever you need to do to fill the outline of your animal. (Perhaps the words "black" and "white" could become the stripes on the zebra's fur, etc.)

Once you have a little practice, maybe you could use the letters in your animal's name to draw the outline of the animal! (Could the "Z" in zebra become a couple of ears? Or legs?) What happens if you use wide markers? Or thin markers? Colored pencils? Or calligraphy pens?

The possibilities are endless!

Music:

Music captures so much of a land and people. Introducing your children to Saudi music is a simple way to transport yourselves around the world. Why not check out these sites while your young geographers notebook and map and let the music play while they recount their travels?

http://music.calabashmusic.com/world/middle_east/saudi_arabia#

There will come a day when… *"At the name of Jesus, every knee shall bow, of those who are in heaven, and on earth, and under the earth, and that every tongue confess that Jesus Christ is Lord, to the glory of God the Father."* (Philippians 2:10)

Treasures of a Hidden Kingdom

Saudi Arabia ~Part 2~

When I was kid, I glued together a construction paper crown, draped a bathrobe over my shoulder and waving a measuring-stick scepter, became the queen of a vast kingdom. At the heart of every kingdom lies hidden jewels, guarded secrets, and wonders untold. You may envision Saudi Arabia as a kingdom of wiry camels roaming across wind-blown sands, and in the distance, a mirage of gurgling water; but don't open your eyes quite yet. Envision troops of baboons, wild flowers carpeting valley floors, apricot orchards sweet with blossoms and a very surprising ancient palace. Could this be the desert kingdom of Saudi Arabia? Now open your eyes and come discover the treasures of the hidden kingdom!

A young Saudi Arabian boy invites us to come dig into the jewels of his country. (Do you like burgers too?) *Photo: Galen Fry*

Saleh, robed and bearded with his **gutra** flapping in the wind, guides us south from Mecca where a gap in the mountains marks the end of the Hijaz region and the beginning of the steep, rugged geographical region known as the Asir. Looking at these jagged mountains, Saleh tells us of an Asir farming community, called the Hanging Village of Habalah, connected to the outside world for centuries only by a single rope. Meaning "rope ladder" in Arabic, Habalah was a tiny stone village clinging to the side of a sheer cliff, home to more than sixty families. The only way for families to travel the impossibly steep slopes of the Asir Mountains was to be lowered on ropes attached to iron posts that had been driven into the edge of the cliff. Saleh explains that since the government couldn't offer schools and medical care for the families at the bottom of the 600 ft [183 m] gorge, the Saudi Arabian king recently built the residents a new village.

Traveling southward along the steep **precipices** that rise out of the narrow plain, we find the cooler air a reprieve from Saudi Arabia's desert temperatures. Saleh notes that the Asir highlands are not only a popular vacation retreat for heat-weary Saudis, but are one of the most populated regions of the kingdom. Gazing out our window, the reason is apparent: an ocean of mountain **pinnacles** with valleys grayish-blue in the distance, and sharp-eyed **kestrels** hovering in the cool, clear air. This fertile, mountainous region of Saudi Arabia begs the question, *"Who covereth the heavens with clouds, who prepareth rain for the earth, who maketh grass to grow on the mountains?"* (Ps. 147:8). Why, our glorious creator God, of course!

How has God created such a lush green region in a desert country? By sending rains to fall generously on this southwest corner of Saudi Arabia. Whereas the Hijaz region of the west coast is dry, the

We are captivated by these Saudis wearing colorful izars. Do you see the garlands of flowers that crown their heads? Najran Saudis are often beekeepers and go to the market in Abha to sell their white and gold honey. The bees of Asir feed on the unique flowers God has planted in this part of the kingdom to produce honeys, rich and aromatic, used by local women in the cooking of their meals. *Photo: Galen Fry*

Asir highlands lie just within the range of the southwest monsoon rains from the Arabian Sea and India. A **monsoon** is a very heavy, yet nourishing rain that sweeps in from the south. 12-20 inches [30-50 cm] of rain falls in the Asir during the summer, more than anywhere else in the kingdom, and any winter snows that descend melt immediately. Standing on this mountain ridge with a handful of flowers, we can't help but think that these breathtaking mountain peak views, a surprising selection of plants, and the roaming of animals like baboons, hyraxes, and the rare leopard, make the Asir region an unexpected jewel in Saudi Arabia's crown.

Back in our vehicle, we watch farmhouses cluster on **terraces** which are giant fields like steps up the mountainsides. Amazed to see these farms stepping up the mountain slopes, especially in a land known for its deserts, Saleh informs us that the farmers of the Asir grow crops such as wheat, apricots, pears, tangerines, grapes and pomegranates. From these terraces fashioned from soil and rock, Asir farmers have been growing and exporting coffee for more than 300 years!

The thick walls of the farm houses are made of stone and mud, dotted with small window openings and painted a pristine white. The rooftops, doors and windows are painted vibrant colors and patterns. Traditionally, Saudi women made paints naturally, boiling indigo plants for dark blues and squeezing the juice of pomegranates for flaming reds. Everywhere we travel we see firsthand how geography influences homes, and how the resources God has given in that place sustains and enriches people's lives.

Dir'iyah, located in the center of Najd and near the capital city if Riyadh, is the ancient hometown of the House of Saud, the family of Saudi Arabia's king. Once the largest city in the Arabian Peninsula, it faded in importance after its capture by Turks, when the royal family moved to Riyadh. Bedouins inhabited the city until recently. *Photo: Galen Fry*

Before departing this region of the Kingdom, Saleh says we must experience the famous souqs of Asir. Open in a different town each day of the week, and named accordingly, we visit Abha's *Suq al-Thaluth* or "Tuesday Market." Amongst the vendors selling brightly painted clay **incense** burners, silver Bedouin jewelry, and perfumes like frankincense, jasmine and musk, we find the Najran Saudis wearing bright colored *izars*, (a garment tied to the waist and covering the lower half of the body), topped with black embroidered jackets. The Najranis live south of Abha in mud towers up to 11 stories tall with tiny windows high on the **ramparts**. With a forest of **turrets,** their fort-like homes are like an impenetrable hidden kingdom in the far southwest corner of the Kingdom of Saudi Arabia! Will you remember how God uses geography to create groups of people with different and interesting homes, clothes and foods?

Driving northwest now, we see that the mountains of the Asir and Hijaz taper off in the east to a vast irregular plateau. Does this harsh landscape look like the home of a king? Across the central heartland of Saudi Arabia, we travel endlessly over barren sands, passing clusters of mountains and yet see no towns or villages. Of course, says Saleh, for only a hardy few could live in this sandswept region of Saudi Arabia. Yet the tribe of the first King of modern Saudi Arabia, the House of Saud, called this Najd region home. Najd means "highland" in Arabic, which perfectly describes this rocky desert sloping away from the coastal mountains. (This region can also be described as an elevated plateau.) Saleh tells us that a number of wadis cross the Najd from west to east.

Dir'iyah, the hometown of Saudi Arabia's king, was built on an **escarpment** overlooking a wadi. Looking like the sand castles I used to build at the beach, Dir'iyah is a maze of towers, walls, mosques and palaces made of mud and straw. Who ever heard of a king living in a palace of mud? Saleh tells us that the columns around the king's courtyard were actually trunks of palm trees and the roofs of the palace were of mud spread on palm branches. These old Dir'iyah palaces we've discovered are another guarded jewel in Saudi's kingdom!

You may be wondering where Saudi Arabia's king lives now? We'll find the King in the capital city of Riyadh. Meaning "a place of gardens and trees" in Arabic ("*rawdah*"), Riyadh is an oasis city and was founded at the meeting of many wadis. As we look out at these bustling streets and the Kingdom Center, a graceful skyscraper and the tallest building in Saudi Arabia, it's hard to believe Riyadh, one of the fastest growing cities in the world, began as a tiny mud village not so very long ago.

Saleh next points out Masmak Castle in Riyadh, the ancient mud-brick fort where the king's family lived long ago. Beyond the fort is a spacious tiled area called as-Sa'ah Square where locals gather in the evening to talk and drink tea. Come Friday morning, however, as-Sa'ah Square becomes Chop Chop Square. With one of the highest execution rates in the world, the Saudi Arabian government beheads an average of 2 people a week for crimes such as robbery, murder…or the crime of being a Christian. Saleh tells us that in Saudi Arabia passing out Bibles is a crime punishable by death. We've haven't seen any churches in our exploration of Saudi Arabia, have we? That is because one of the King's spokesman recently declared that "there are no

Welcome to Masmak Castle in Riyadh! 'Masmak' means strong, thick, fortified. Aren't these mud walls just that? This is the ancient fort of the Royal Saud family. The castle is open for you to view the city from its four watchtowers, but be sure to come on the right day because in Saudi's segregated society, boys' schools cannot come on the same day to visit as girls' schools. *Photo: Galen Fry*

churches [in Saudi Arabia], not in the past, the present, or future." We call the king of Saudi Arabia 'king,' but Saudis call him "The Custodian of the Two Holy Mosques." As the caretaker of Islam's two holiest sites, Saudi's King believes he is keeping his country pure by prohibiting all other religions in the kingdom.

There is a strange mix of past, present and future in Saudi Arabia, isn't there? Camel markets in the same city as skyscrapers, mud-houses alongside shopping malls, long-robed kings and princes living among fast cars, neon signs, and young Saudis talking on cell phones. Before leaving Riyadh, Saleh asks some of us if we'd like to actually go visit Saudi Arabia's king. Any man can! The king holds a regular ***majlis*** or court where any male in the entire kingdom may come before the king with a personal appeal or request. If you could go before Saudi Arabia's king, would you be nervous? It might help you to remember our Heavenly King and know "*there is none like unto thee, O LORD; thou art great, and thy name is great in might. Who would not fear thee, O King of nations?*" (Jer. 10:6-7).

Field Notes

Isn't Saudi Arabia an amazing, diverse land? I love to learn about her people.

Press record and talk to me:

~about the Asir region: Tell me about Habalah. What are the Asir highlands like? What is a monsoon? What are terraces? What kinds of produce are grown in this region? What animals might we see?

~about the village farmhouses: What are they made of? How are the houses decorated? Where does the paint come from?

~about the souqs: What kinds of things are sold there? Tell me about the Najranis: their houses and their clothes. What are they selling at the souq?

~about the Najd region: How do we describe the geography? Tell me about Dir'iyah. Can you describe the palace?

~about Riyadh: Tell us what important person lives here and what you know of him. What is as-Sa'ah Square? Tell us what you know of churches in Saudi Arabia?

Have you ever gone a whole day with nothing to drink? How about an entire week? Doesn't just thinking about it make your tongue stick to the roof of your mouth and your throat feel parched? Don't you feel desperate for a cold glass of God's life-giving water? Go ahead. Saleh and I'll wait here until you go quench your thirst. Saleh has deep, dry, dangerous places to take us to next. Whatever you do, don't forget your water bottle. Your life will depend upon it!

Leaving Riyadh, we drive northeast across the desert towards Dammam. Is that a train of camels we see trekking across the desert off in the distance? No, says Saleh, that is actually a train of iron! Yes, says Saleh, presently Saudi Arabia's only railway tracks across the sands between Riaydh and the Gulf Port city of Dammam. The King and his government have recently planned the railway to snake farther west across Saudi Arabia's dry dunes, through a gap between the Hijaz and Asir mountains to Jeddah on the opposite side of the country. Instead of cargo ships rocking the waves of the seas for 5-7 days around the Arabian Peninsula, freight trains will carry the goods from the Red Sea to the Persian Gulf in 18 hours, less than one full day. Who needs a water-conserving camel when one can take a train that requires no water at all?

Saudi Arabia may have scant water resources, but it produces *rivers* of fuel! Saleh points to the tower stretching like a crane out of the sands near Dammam. Is it a windmill pumping water? No, it's an **oil rig** pumping up streams of black oil from underneath Saudi Arabia's sands. God tucked more than one quarter of the world's known supply of oil under the Saudi Arabian desert. Pumping out more than 10 million barrels of oil per day, the Saudis then heat the oil so that nearly half of it becomes refined and changes into gasoline. Saudi Arabia sells its "black gold," to other countries all over the world, and with that tremendous wealth, Saudis have built a flourishing economy.

Do you see the shifting sands threatening to bury the oasis of Al Hasa, like it does the rest of Saudi Arabia? But you also likely see the protective tree barriers planted to keep the ocean of sand at bay. The barriers remind me of the windbreaks of trees near my home, holding back not sands but winter snows! *Courtesy of the T.C. Barger Collection*

Saleh waves us towards the eastern coastal plain to find the most flourishing, verdant greens, an island of growth in the sea of desert sands. There ahead of us—have you ever seen so many date palm trees in your life? This is the Al-Hasa Oasis, home to more than half a million people and not only the largest oasis in Saudi Arabia but one of the largest in the world. (If you find the city of Al-Hufuf on your atlas, you've found the principal city of the Al-Hasa oasis.) Actually, the eastern, coastal plain, the fourth region of Saudi Arabia, (do you remember the other three: Hijaz, Asir, and Najd?) is sometimes called the Al Hasa after the great oasis. While some of the world's largest oil fields can be found in the sands around the oasis, the Al Hasa produces a different kind of desert wealth: food! Over 3 million palm trees find water for their roots from the sixty springs of water that bubble up here. Everywhere we look in Al Hasa, a name meaning "drinking" in Arabic, we see water courses carrying water to farms of rice, corn and citrus fruits. Did you know that more than 100 million eggs a year are produced on poultry farms here in the oasis? In a country of sand with an average rainfall of only 4-5 inches [10–12 cm] per year, lush Al Hasa produces food eaten by Saudis all over the country.

A shaft of light follows us we climb down into the dahl or cave at **Ain Hin** towards the dark blue underground waters of the aquifer. To think that not so long ago the water level was once at the cave's entrance! *Photo: John Pint*

When I was a little child, I once went exploring in a cave. Inky black, pierced only by a shaft of sunlight, the cave was full of unknown mysteries. My father laughed that bears lurked ahead, my brother suggested snakes, and I wondered if it was time to go home! Do you think its time to explore some more

In a sea of desert sands, the oasis of Al-Hasa produces millions of eggs for the country of Saudi Arabia. Can you hear the clucking of all those hens? *Courtesy of the T.C. Barger Collection*

of Saudi Arabia's mysterious treasures? Nodding, Saleh smiles and drives us south west.

Driving to Al Kharj, south of Ridayh, (check your map!) we watch as circles of green dot the rocky desert. Saleh reports that large irrigation systems, much like your lawn sprinkler, rotate to water huge circular fields of alfalfa. Why all that alfalfa in the desert? Saleh laughs and says we are driving on what locals call "Milk Road." Do you see all the cows under special awnings, shaded from the intense desert sun? Saleh tells us that a dairy farm near Al-Kharj holds the title of the world's largest integrated dairy, milking more than 30,000 cows and producing enough milk to give a city of 100,000 people more than a gallon [3.78 liter] jug of milk everyday! But where does the water necessary for the crops and cooling the cows come from? That is part of the mystery says Saleh.

Underneath the Saudi sands God created **aquifers** of water. Farmers near Al-Kharj have dug thousands of wells, some as deep as a mile [1.6 km] into the earth, to pump out water so hot it is close to the boiling point! The water is cooled in ponds before being sprinkled on cows or crops.

Saleh asks if we would like to go diving in the desert to explore these aquifers of water. Diving into underground water in the desert? Yes, says Saleh, come!

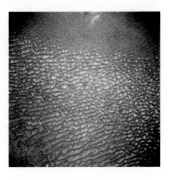

Ahead of us a massive rocky cliff rises out of the desert, a huge black slit at its base beckoning us to come explore below. This is a **dahl,** which is the Arabic word for "cave," a sinkhole in the sand. Named Ain Hit, "*ain*" meaning spring, this is one of the most famous dahls in the kingdom. Watch the sharp limestone boulders that cover the cave's floor. Notice that the walls of the cave's entrance are a grey-blue rock called **anhydrite.** Carefully scramble down the crumbly slope through a small opening—such blackness! Turn on your flashlight: ah, there is the water. Isn't it the clearest, stillest water you have ever seen? The bottom of the underground lake shimmers light green around a black hole, the entrance to an underwater cave. Saleh tells us that in earlier times, the clear waters of Ain Hit were just below the surface, making it a watering hole for thirsty camel caravans. The irrigation of farms like those on Milk Road has caused the **water table** to dramatically decline, with Ain Hit's water level now dropping far into the darkest reaches of the cave. We have no scuba diving equipment with oxygen tanks so instead of diving we settle for simply dipping our feet in the cool water. On our way out of the dahl, we wave hello to a Saudi family with three children coming to explore the underground waters of the sinkhole. Their father beckons them to come further down into the cave. But they only cling

Even from way up in space, we can see how unique these Empty Quarter sand dunes are! If the Empty Quarter was perfectly flat, if God sent wind only from one direction, and there was a limited amount of sand, all sand dunes would be barchan dunes, in a crescent shape. As God blows more sand about, these barchan dunes move and migrate across the desert, connecting to each other, forming ridges. If the barchan ridges are fairly straight, they are called tranverse dunes. Long, rolling sand dunes veining across the desert are longitudinal dunes or seif dunes, extending parallel to the prevailing winds. Some seif dunes can snake as long as 200 mi [300 km.] The Empty Quarter may *seem* empty, but this landscape is actually moving and dancing to the rhythm of God's winds and ways!

~*NASA*

One of the largest desert reptiles, this young toothless dahb eats only plants but will grow up to 3.5 ft. [more than 1 m.] His fat, spikey tail, a force to reckon with, is considered a Bedouin delicacy when roasted to perfection. *Photo: John Pint*

tighter to their veiled mother's black abaya. Children in Saudi Arabia feel just like I did about caves as a child!

Driving east, we watch the landscape grow increasingly barren, and the sand dunes grow higher, like towering mountains! Saleh informs us that sand dunes in this region of Saudi Arabi may peak as high as 1,083 feet [330 meters] high (that is about 30 times taller than your house!) Doesn't this fifth region of Saudi Arabia look different than the regions we've visited before? This is the Rub al Khali, literally meaning "the quarter of emptiness," one of earth's harshest regions. Saleh says Saudis simply refer to this area as the Sands, the largest expanse of sand in the whole world! The countries of Spain, Belgium and the Netherlands would fit into this Empty Quarter and there still would be room to spare. Almost entirely uninhabited, even the Bedouins only skirt the edges of this forbidding territory because its summer heat is too extreme.

The smothering heat of the Empty Quarter makes it hard to breathe. There is no way to escape the scorching heat; no shade to find cool relief. Quench your dry throat with a long drink from your water bottle. Too bad we aren't dhabs, Saleh mutters. A **dahb** is a bulky lizard up to 25.5 inches [65 cm] long. The dahbs of the Saudi Arabian Peninsula live their entire lives without drinking even a single drop of water! All the water they require is supplied by the dry, salty plants they eat on the edges of the deserts. Saleh suggests that perhaps we should be like a dhab and dig ourselves a tunnel 7 feet [2.2 meters] down into the sand to escape the relentless rays of the sun! Actually, God designed dahbs to become the same temperature as their environment with their skin color acting a bit like a thermometer: dark grey at night, beige as the day warms, and bright yellow when it is so hot that only a dahb would trot across the sands. Saleh tells us that the nomadic Bedouins of Saudi Arabia eat the dhab as desert delicacy which tastes much like chicken!

Does the Empty Quarter at Ghawar look empty to you? Underneath these vast sands, God has created millions of barrels of oil that will be pumped up by oil rigs such as this one. *Courtesy of the T.C. Barger Collection*

Saleh squints about. It is so easy to lose direction in the Empty Quarter with nothing to serve as landmarks. But we can't afford to get lost with such a scant water supply. A tribe of Bedouin nomads are riding a long string of camels off in the distance, and due to the extreme heat, they look as if they are walking on air. As we approach, we see that the Bedouins are setting up camp for a meal. With smiles, they wave us into their tent, out of the sun's 131 F [55 C] noonday temperatures. A circle of tribal women, entirely cloaked in black, faces hidden behind veils, sit on pillows and rugs off to the side, away from the men. An elderly Bedouin presents us with a big white bowl filled with frothy warm milk—camel's milk! Doesn't it taste rich, creamy and slightly sweet?

153

Do you see the stick in this Saudi's mouth? That is his miswak, or toothbrush—no need to squeeze a tube or vigorously brush! The miswak is a root from the *arak* tree, commonly known as the "toothbrush tree," which grows in Saudi Arabia. Amazingly, God created the miswak with 19 natural substances that are beneficial to healthy teeth. With a smile like that, who can help but smile back at Saudis?! *Photo: Galen Fry*

As we travel eastward into the late afternoon, the wind—"*hawa*"— sweeps in. Over the howl of the gusting wind, Saleh tells us that yes, uninhabited Empty Quarter sands lie before us, but what lies below that is the largest oil field on the entire planet: the Ghawar. Ghawar stretches one hundred and fifty miles [240 km] long and twenty-five miles [40 km] wide across desolate desert. Thousands of meters below these dunes lies more than 70 billion barrels of oil patiently waiting to be pumped out of the 3,400 wells punched down into it. Saudi geologists came in search of oil here because of that anhydrite rock discovered at Ain Hit—and indeed found, far below the barren landscape, an excellent anhydrite seal over immense lakes of thick, rich oil. The Empty Quarter is not empty at all!

As the sun sets, Saleh smiles that brilliant smile of his. He's given us the grand tour of Saudi Arabia. From Jeddah as the gateway city to the Hijaz's Mecca, up through the cooling heights of the terraced Asir mountains, across the rocky, gravelly central plain of Najd, slipping along the eastern region of the Al-Hasa with its lush oasis, and down into the Empty Quarter. What jewels we've discovered in this kingdom and such fascinating people we've met! What has been your favorite gem? Oh, look up! Do you see the twinkling diamonds God has sprinkled across the Saudi Arabian skies? Maybe these starry heavens on a hushed night in the Empty Quarter are the most memorable sight of all?

"Praise ye him, sun and moon: praise him, all ye stars of light…Kings of the earth, and all people, princes…and children: Let them praise the name of the Lord" (Ps. 148:3, 11-13).

Field Notes

It's hard to imagine a more different world than our own, isn't it? Let's talk about all you've seen today.

Press record and talk to me:

~about Dammam: Tell me about the railway. How does the government hope the railroad will help goods reach Saudi Arabia? What does the train replace? What liquid will we find in abundance under Dammam? What is it used for?

~ about Al Hasa: What is an oasis? What trees grow here? What bubbles up from the ground? What food is harvested? What else is produced here?

~about Al Kharj: What is "Milk Road"? What familiar animals live here? Tell me about the water these animals drink.

~about Ain Hit: What is a dahl? How do we find the water at Ain Hit? What color are the cave's walls?

~about Rub al Khali: What does the name mean? What do Saudis call it? Why? How big is it? Do many people live there? Why or why not? What is a dhab? How does a dhab tell us the temperature? Whom might we meet in this Empty Quarter?

~about the Ghawar: What lies below the expanse of sand? How is it brought to the surface?

Travel Log

Using your globe or atlas, let's add the following locations to your map of Saudi Arabia... We've seen things today that simply must be mapped, so that they will never be forgotten!

Map Notes: <u>Let's record the locations of:</u>

- *Asir region*
- *Abha*
- *Najd region*
- *Dir'iyah*
- *Riyadh*
- *Dammam*

- *Al Hasa*
- *Al Kharj*
- *Ain Hit*
- *Rub al Khali*
- *Ghawar*

<u>If you'd like, draw pictures or symbols on your map representing:</u>

- *A rope ladder for the Hanging Village of Habalah*
- *Monsoons in the Asir highlands*
- *A market at Abha*
- *A mud castle in Dir'iyah*
- *Skyscrapers in Riyadh*
- *A train winding through the desert*

- *Palm trees at Al Hasa (and eggs?)*
- *Cows at Al Kharj*
- *Caves at Ain Hit (a black hole? scuba gear?)*
- *The Empty Quarter (dahbs? a Bedouin tent? camels?)*

Travel Notes: Geographers write what they've seen in order to share the adventure with others—and so they can revisit the places in their memories! **On the next page of your travel log, record three important sights you want to remember from your photos of Saudi Arabia.**

Bringing It Home

Simple ideas to bring the world to your door

Books:

Traveling Man: The Journey of Ibn Battuta 1325-1354 by James Rumford

A beautifully written work that will kindle further exploration, this book follows the travels of 14th century Muslim Ibn Battuta from Morocco, through Arabia, to China and back, including a pilgrimage to Mecca. Eloquent text: *"Traveling it leaves you speechless, then turns you into a storyteller."* *"Traveling it had captured my heart, and now my heart was calling me home."*   Grades 1-6

Ali and the Golden Eagle *by* Wayne Grover

Fiction. Grover uses his experience living in Saudi Arabia to write this story of an American who befriends a Saudi boy. Together they raise a baby eagle and train it to compete in a falconry contest. ****older readers: *Grade 4+*

The Children's Encyclopedia of Arabia *by* Mary Beardwood

Recommended as a beautifully illustrated book for a wide range of ages. This book covers history, culture, plants, animals and people of the region. What lives in the largest sand desert in the world? Which architectural structure breaks all world records? How long can a camel live without water? A gorgeous, thorough presentation that is most worthwhile. *All ages.*

Poetry:

I sing a happy song —
happier than the sunrise
on another shore;
happier than the smile
a birthday-child smiles   ~Ghazi A. Algosaibi

Born in Eastern Saudi Arabia, Ghazi A. Algosaibi, a widely known Saudi poet, is the Saudi Arabian ambassador to the nearby country of Bahrain, while writing of a simple Arab life.

~*art* ~*books* ~*food* ~*music* ~*poetry*

Bringing It Home

Simple ideas to bring the world to your door

Food:

I hope you like coffee! Saudis consider the ritual of preparing and serving coffee the first rule of hospitality. In the past, each time coffee was served, men would roast the beans over a fire on a long-handled spoon and then grind them with a mortar and pestle. Once prepared, the coffee is poured in small cups without handles and filled half-way. To be polite to our hosts, we must restrict ourselves to three servings and shake the cup with a quick movement of our wrists to let them know when we are finished. (In case you don't like coffee, we've included a recipe for mint tea also!)

Arabic Coffee

2 cups cold water
6 teaspoons ground coffee

6 cardamom pods (crushed) or ¼ - ½ tsp ground cardamom
Cloves
A few strands of saffron

Put the coffee, cardamom seeds, cloves and saffron into saucepan with the water, bring to a boil and allow to simmer for about 30 minutes. Allow coffee to settle for a minute or two, and then pour a small amount into coffee cups.

Mint Tea

1- 2 tea bags (or loose leaf tea if you have it)
2 tablespoons fresh mint leaves

4 cups boiling water
Sugar cubes

Place the teabags (or loose tea) and mint into the bottom of a saucepan, crushing the mint against the bottom. Fill the pan with boiling water and allow to stand for a few minutes. This tea is usually drunk very sweet, so add plenty of sugar cubes!

Now that we have our tea or coffee ready, let's cook up some ***Lahooh Bel Loaz* (Almond Pancakes).**

4 cups flour
1 cup milk
2 eggs
3 tablespoons oil
1 teaspoon baking powder

½ teaspoon yeast
water
1 cup confectioner's sugar
1 tablespoon ground cardamom

Put the flour in a bowl and add milk, eggs, baking powder, yeast and water and mix thoroughly. Set batter aside to rise.

Grease frying pan or griddle with a little oil, pour half a ladle of batter into the pan. Spread the batter quickly into a thin pancake and fry over medium heat until the top bubbles, then flip and brown the other side. Repeat using all batter. Mix together the sugar, cardamom and almonds. Stuff each pancake with the mixture and roll the pancakes into cylinders. Arrange on a serving dish and sprinkle with more ground almonds. 10-12 servings.

Go into all the world...

a walk of prayer

We were astounded when we took a peek inside Saudi Arabia. We not only found a land full of ancient wonders, we found that Saudi Arabia is full of boys and girls who are much like us. They were created by a God who loves them dearly—just as He loves you.

Will you and your family join me in praying for the Saudi people?

Lord, give us Your love for the peoples of the world, and help our family to live in a way that shows our love for them.

Father, Saudi Arabia is a land that is completely foreign to most of us, but You understand and know her very well. May Your will be done in Saudi Arabia.

~We pray for **the pilgrims** who come from every corner of the globe to worship in Saudi Arabia. May Your light shine on them and may their hearts hear Your voice.

~In a country of vast oil **wealth**, we remember those who do not benefit from the natural resources You supplied this nation. While there are many rich in Saudi Arabia, there are also many **poor**. We remember those who have less. Please be their provision.

~We pray for **Christians living in Saudi Arabia.** Lord, it is a crime to worship You in that nation. May Your people have boldness to serve You and courage to walk the way of Christ. May they be protected and sheltered under Your wings. Please keep them from harm and help them to honor Your name.

~We ask for **strength** for those who are persecuted in Saudi Arabia. May they not grow weary, but may they have joy and peace even in the midst of suffering. We ask that You would move on the hearts of the government and religious leaders to allow **freedom of religion** in Saudi Arabia.

~We pray that **the peoples of Saudi Arabia** may taste the goodness and grace of You, Father. Kindle a passion for You in their hearts. Rain down Your love, mercy, and hope on that land.

We love you, Lord, and the people who are living in Saudi Arabia today. May the Light of our Savior dawn over all nations today. Draw us all closer to You, Father. In Jesus name, Amen.

T.E. Lawrence wrote of his passage through the Wadi Rum, "Our little caravan grew self-conscious, and fell dead quiet, afraid and ashamed to flaunt its smallness in the presence of the stupendous hills." As we watch the sunrise over these rocks, we think of our own smallness and the stunning magnificence of our God: *"The LORD liveth; and blessed be my rock; and let the God of my salvation be exalted"* Ps. 18:46.

Photo: David Bjorgen

The Highway Men Came Riding

Jordan ~Part 1~

As a farm girl, I have lived my whole life on gravel country-roads with potholes and puddles. Yet a few times a year, my family would drive down what was called the "401 Corridor," a hallway of highways, winding through metropolitan cities and tangles of traffic, carrying us out to Grandmother's raspberry pies and Grandfather's knee-slapping tall tales. Whenever my brother and I would drive through imaginary worlds, it was always on the 401 Highway.

Did you know that there is a highway in the Bible? Numbers 20:17 records the words of Moses, *"Let us pass, I pray thee, through thy country: we will not pass through field, or through the vineyards...we will go by the king's highway."* Where might we find this biblical highway? If you will, gently spin your globe again to the Middle East and find Israel's Jordan River Valley. Now stand on its western bank and look over to its eastern bank: there is the country of Jordan...where one of the oldest communication routes in the world, the King's Highway, twists and turns through rocky highlands and barren desert. Are your eyes of faith focused, your memory strong, and your faith ready to see evidence of God down every road we travel? Jordan awaits!

Young Jordanian schoolboys welcome us to Jordan, the middle country in the Middle East!
Photo: Brian McMorrow

The Kingdom of Jordan (for it is governed by a king) is the middle country in the Middle East. Approximately the size of the American state of Kentucky or the European country of Hungary, Jordan has the longest border (of 148 miles or 238 km) with Israel of any other Middle Eastern country. Tracing Jordan's borders, can you make out the shape of a duck's head, opening its mouth wide to the east to snap up something tasty for lunch? Actually, some call the "v" shaped jolt in the southeastern border between Saudi Arabia and Jordan "Winston's Hiccup" since the British leader who was assisting in drawing up boundary lines had just had more than a satisfactory lunch. While the story is a myth, perhaps you'll remember that Jordan's boundaries are about opening wide for lunch...and then hiccup!

Geographically, God has created the landscape of Jordan as mostly harsh arid desert with few natural resources. **Natural resources** are raw materials that God has created in nature that are essential and useful to people, such as minerals, oil, fishing and forestry. While not rich in natural resources, Jordan is, however, positioned like a bridge of land, connecting Africa with Europe and Asia. Following the precious resource of freshwater from the Jordan River, trade caravans, wandering peoples, and marching armies have used Jordan as a highway through the desert throughout the centuries.

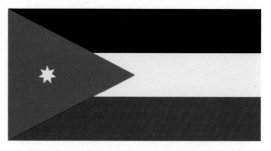

The horizontal stripes of Jordan's flag represent three esteemed Muslim leaders, the red triangle symbolizes Arab patriotism, while the seven pointed star represents the seven hills of Jordan's capital city, Amman.

Like the landscape outside my passenger window changed as we rolled along the highway to my grandparent's, so the highway through Jordan is one of diverse scenes. Jordan's geography can be divided into three main regions: the western Jordan Valley, the northern Highlands and the Desert, called the Badia region in the east and Rum Desert in the south.

Can you point to the "beak" of Jordan's outline? Jordan's eastern desert fills the duck's "beak." Tracing our finger down the western border, we find the Jordan River running like water off the duck's back. Don't you think it quite apt that open-wide-for-lunch Jordan has a River Valley called its "food bowl"? This valley, known as the *Ghor* in Arabic, with its warm, year-round agricultural climate, fertile soil, winter rainfall and summer irrigation, produces much of Jordan's food. The Jordan River Valley is a small food bowl, however, comprising only 6% of Jordan's land.

Can you make out the outline of Jordan? Where is the hiccup? And the "beak?" Can you identify Jordan's neighbors? Where is the water running off the duck's back?

Right in the middle, between the eastern desert and the Jordan River valley, we find Jordan's Highlands. This narrow high plateau is the home of Jordan's three largest cities, including its capital, Amman, situated about where the duck's eye would be. Let's land in Amman!

Can you hear the sounds of Amman? Does the call to prayer echo through the streets? And what color is every building we see? One of the city's bylaws states that all building must be faced with white stone.

Doesn't Jordan's capital city indeed look like the "White City?" Can you see the Jordanian flag flapping in the wind? Named Rabbah Amman in the Bible, Amman was selected as Jordan's capital in 1921. As there was initially no palace in Amman in which the King could live, he ruled from a train car! Today Amman is a bustling city, drawing families from all over the Middle East. *Photo: David Bjorgen*

Peering out on this city perched on the hillside, we immediately understand why Amman is often times referred to as the 'white city.' A canvas of outstanding whites, beiges and ochres, Amman's buildings are constructed from the whites stone found in Jordan. Do you notice that we are looking at nearly all apartment buildings or condominiums? Amman has few homes where only one family lives; only members of the royal family and a few high ranking officials live in large, single-family

Do you hear the Jordanian men speaking Arabic in the later afternoon sun? Few Jordanian have hobbies but prefer to spend free time visiting and socializing with family and friends.
Photo: Brian McMorrow

dwellings. Originally built on seven hills, just like Rome, Amman now blankets 19 hillsides as the city grows with families leaving other Middle Eastern areas of conflict. The sounds of car horns in the crowded streets give way to the Muslim call to prayer echoing from stately minarets gracing Amman's skyline. With each neighborhood named after the *jabal* or mountain upon which it sits, we wind our way through the district east of Jabal Amman, through kebab stalls with roasting meat, spice shops, the air thick with strong aromas and cafes with men sipping rich Arabian coffee in the warm sunshine. In a typical gesture of Jordanian curiosity, an older man wearing a **keffiyeh**, the checkered head piece of Jordanian men, asks us where we live and our plans for the day. In Arabic custom, he embraces us with a flourish, introducing himself as Malek. Might he show us the wonders of Jordan? Malek doesn't consider this an intrusion of privacy for in his Arabic language the closest word for privacy is "lonely." Malek doesn't want us to be lonely! Let's explore Jordan with our Jordanian friend.

Our newfound guide invites us to stop for some sweet pastries and to watch the locals play a game of backgammon. Why are all those Jordanian men sucking on long wooden pipes with hoses connected to an ornately decorated stand? Malek explains, in his thick Arabic accent, that many Jordanian men smoke the **argeeleh** or "hubble bubble" after eating out, sucking up a sweet-smelling smoke which causes a bubbling sound, hence the name.

Leaving behind the hub-bub and hubble bubble of Jebel Amman, Malek leads us to the top of the L-shaped hillside of Jebel al-Qala'a, to Amman's ancient acropolis. Aren't the wadis that surround this hill deep and steep to climb? In ancient times, families fled to this hill for protection, drinking water from the strong spring bubbling there, the source of the Jabbok River. 2 Sam. 12:26-27 reads, *"And Joab fought against Rabbah of the children of Ammon, and took the royal city. And Joab sent messengers to David, and said, I have fought against Rabbah, and have taken the city of waters."* Do you know you are standing in the same place of that Biblical event, where the spring gurgled up? The Bible's name for Amman is Rabbah Ammon and every time you read of the Ammonites in Scripture, you are reading of the ancient inhabitants of Ammon. Some think that it was here on this hill in Ammon that Uriah was killed by David's order (2 Sam. 11:16-17).

What fixes our attention from this hilltop, however, was built long after David's time. Malek points to the massive Roman theater made of stone at the foot of the hill, which seats over 6,000 spectators. Perhaps you are instead gazing upon the remains of the Temple of Hercules? Built by the Romans nearly 200 years after Jesus' time, these remnants and ruins of ancient people stand amidst the homes of Amman today where children

An ancient Roman theater sits alongside modern buildings in Amman. We cannot see it, but a long hidden tunnel connects the theater to the hilltop of Jebel al-Qala'a. The theater is still in use today for theatrical productions. Get a seat at the front!

are playing in the streets. Malek beckons us to wander south out of Amman on the ancient King's Highway. What historical sites, geographical landscapes and friendly people might this 5,000-year-old King's Highway take us to?

If you'll trace your finger along the King's Highway on your map, can you see that many of Jordan's towns and cities sprung up along this ancient trading route? Passing wheat fields that have been cultivated since the ancient biblical kingdom of the Ammonites, we arrive in the first city south of Amman, Madaba. Named Medeba in Scripture, meaning *"waters of quiet,"* this modern city is rebuilt on the Biblical Moabite town (Num. 21:30), which was given to the tribe of Rueben (Josh. 13:16). I have a tattered map of my local countryside that has been torn into a few pieces but taped back together. Madaba, however, has a map that was made of 2 million little pieces—and not of paper, but of vividly colored local stone!

Examining the Mosaic Map of Madaba, can you see the tiled picture of fish swimming up the Jordan River, away from the salty Dead Sea? The map originally covered a staggering 51 [15 m] by 16 [5 m] feet. Only one third of the map remains today. *Photo: Holy Land Photos*

Come, step into the Greek Orthodox Church in Madaba's city center. Isn't what we find on the church's floor captivating? The floor is tiled with pictures of plains, hills, valleys, and a smattering of villages stretching from Jordan in the north, to Egypt in the south. The famous Mosaic Map of Madaba, designed during the reign of Justinian, around 570 A.D., is the oldest surviving map of the Holy Land in the world. Can you see the huge fish swimming down the tiles of the Nile River? We are looking at one of the best topographical representation, or best picture maps of the features of the lands of the Bible. Perhaps earlier pilgrims, making their way through the Holy Land, wandered into this church to look at this map also?

I once pulled up the old linoleum flooring in my house to the delightful discovery of a pumpkin gold hardwood floor underneath. But that was nothing compared to what Madaba's residents have uncovered! Madaba may look like any other East Bank Jordanian town with flat roofed, stone houses, except for what is hiding under its floors: dazzling Byzantine mosaics!

Field Notes

Wouldn't you like to travel the King's Highway?

Press record and talk to me:

~**about the geography of Jordan**: What shape does the country resemble from above? What is "Winston's Hiccup"? What is the landscape of Jordan like? Does Jordan have many natural resources?

~**about the "food bowl"**: Which area of Jordan is named the "food bowl?" What is produced here?

~**about the Highlands**: Which important city is on this plateau? Why is Amman called the "white city"? Do most of Jordan's families live in houses or apartments? Describe some of the sights we might see in Amman. What food might we eat? What smells are in the air? What are the people wearing? What games are they playing?

~**about Madaba**: What is on the floor of the Greek Orthodox Church? When was this map made?

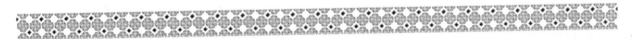

This structure of honey-colored stones protects the excavated remains of an ancient church atop Mount Nebo, Jordan. Can you hear the crunch of stones as a Jordanian couple wander down the path, footsteps where Moses may have once walked?
Photo: David Bjorgen

Perhaps your eyes of faith would like to behold the panoramic view of the actual Holy Land today, instead of an artful mosaic? Driving 10 minutes west of Madaba, we pass a few black sheep peppering a flock grazing in the rolling countryside. Can you see the Bedouin tent, there in the distance? Although very few Jordanians now live in tents, Malek tells us that Bedouin women weave strips of goat's wool on outdoor looms, then sew the strips together to make these goat-hair houses. Malek describes how the floor of the tent will be covered with large carpets, while smaller carpets, also woven of sheep, goat or camel wool, will be used as prayer rugs. A shape of an arrow, woven into the rug's end, points towards Mecca as the Muslim Bedouin says his daily prayers, no matter where his tent may be. Would you like to live in a goat-hair house?

The Bedouin camp fading behind us, we coil our way up the lonely, windswept Mount Nebo. Standing atop this highest peak in the Moabite mountain range, we read from Deuteronomy 34:1-7: *"Then Moses went up from the plains of Moab unto the mountain of Nebo… and the Lord shewed him all the land of Gilead, unto Dan, and all Naphtali, and the land of Ephraim, and Manasseh, and the land of Judah, unto the utmost sea, and the south, and the plain of the valley of Jericho, the city of the palm trees, unto Zoar. And the Lord said unto him, This is the land which I sware unto Abraham…So Moses the servant of the Lord died there."* Our feet now stand where Moses' once did. From right where you are, God showed Moses the Promised Land that he himself would never enter (Do you remember why? Numbers 20:12-14). Malek sweeps his hand across the breathtaking view of the Jordan Valley out to the Dead Sea. What God has created is far more magnificent than the mosaic map of this scene! Can you make out the rooftops of Jericho, the spires of the churches in Jerusalem and the hills of Bethlehem on the horizon?

Did the clouds dapple the hilltops with shadows like this the day God showed Moses this scene from the top of Mount Nebo? The magnificent vista from the heights of Mount Nebo provides a panorama of the Holy Land God was giving to His people. To the North of Mount Nebo, one can see out to the valley of the Jordan River. On a clear day, we can see the West Bank city of Jericho in Israel and its capital city of Jerusalem. Isn't God's landscape beautiful?

We can hardly comprehend that, close to where we now stand, God Himself buried Moses. The Holy Scriptures of Deuteronomy 34:6 are true: *"but no man knoweth of [Moses'] sepulcher unto this day."* We may not know exactly where God trod on this soil when he buried Moses, but we see evidence of Him everywhere: the sight of earth and sky meeting at the horizon, the smells of soil and growth in the spring breeze, the foreign languages of friendly tongues that fill our ears. The same God that showed Moses this land from atop Mount Nebo is the same God who meets with us to show us His world today.

Malek turns our attention to the sculpture of the Brazen Serpent. While the geographical location of the event lies further south in Jordan (Num. 21:4-10), this bronze serpent monument atop Mount Nebo reminds us of God healing those who, bitten by poisonous snakes, looked upon the bronze snake that Moses erected. The sculpture also reminds us that when we look upon the Cross of Christ, we too find healing and wholeness.

Isn't your birthday one of the happiest days of the year? Did you know one of the saddest birthday parties in history happened in Jordan? Just a few miles southwest of Mount Nebo, the King's Highway winds us up the stark slopes to the palace of Marchaerus, overlooking the waters of the Dead Sea. Looking down this steep hillside, we can easily appreciate how the geography of the land was used to best advantage: the deep wadis on three sides of the hill were a natural defense, protecting the fortress from attack. Malek asks if we can see the caves and cisterns halfway down the

eastern hillside. While the cisterns held life-sustaining water for the fortress, the caves are believed to have been about death: a prison for captives.

Looking out where King Herod's lonely fortress crowned this imposing mountain, we can envision Herod's delighted face as his daughter danced for his birthday. Imagine his horrified visage when, upon offering his daughter anything her heart desired, she responded with "*I will that thou give me by and by in a charger the head of John the Baptist*" (Mk. 6:25). Brought from one of the caves, John the Baptist was executed here at Machaerus. Malek tells us that the Arabic name for Machaerus is Al Mashnaqah, or "The Gallows."

As we take one last magnificent look out to the Dead Sea, Malek explains that just south of the Dead Sea lies the hot, dry Wadi Araba, a spectacular valley known for its sheer, barren mountains. Here Jordanian families support themselves with the mining of potash. Malek explains that Jordan's economy largely centers around the mining of such natural resources as phosphates (a kind of salt) and potash (used as a fertilizer). Jordanians then sell or export these resources to countries all over the world. An **economy** is the organizing of people as consumers, workers, business owners to generate wealth for a community. Isn't it interesting that we call this area the Dead Sea region but God created natural resources here and throughout barren Jordan to serve as the very life of Jordan's economy?

While this serpentine cross sculpture atop Mount Nebo symbolizes the bronze serpent erected by Moses in the wilderness (Numbers 21:4-9), it also represents the cross upon which Jesus was crucified (John 3:14).
Photo: David Bjorgen

As Malek tours us yet further south on the King's Highway, he tells us how this Highland region, separating the Jordan Valley from the plains of the eastern desert, receives more rainfall than other areas of Jordan, sprouting green growth after the rains. The rains may come down through wadis, all of which intersect this highland plateau.

The view out our window stills our tongues. Creasing sandstone hills, brushed with muted hues, loom, crest and roll away. This is Wadi Mujib, Malek announces, one of Jordan's most magnificent sights and often called the Grand Canyon of the Middle East. Since creation, God has scoured Wadi Mujib's sandstone deeper and deeper with coursing water, forming a spectacular, gnarled gorge. We read of this very place in Numbers 21:13, "*Arnon…is in the wilderness that cometh out of the coasts of the Amorites: for Arnon is the border of Moab, between Moab and the Amorites.*" The Bible's name for Wadi Mujib is the Arnon River, north of which the Israelite tribes of Rueben and Gad once settled.

Today we find Wadi Mujib as the lowest nature reserve (or park) in the whole world, some 1,345 ft. [410 meters] below sea level. Malek tells us that if we look carefully up on the sandstone cliffs, perhaps we'll catch a glimpse of an **ibex**, one of the most graceful of mountain goats, or perhaps a prowling **caracal**, a medium-sized cat graced with

Can you see where Herod's Machaerus fortress once stood atop this stark peak? If you look carefully, do you see the exhilarating view of the Dead Sea off in the distance? While Herod took advantage of this key geographical location for a position of defense, Machaerus lacked a natural water supply. Herod ordered a waterworks be constructed and improved roads connecting Machaerus to the Dead Sea. Today we can see their tracks and walk where John the Baptist may have once trod. *holylandphotos.org*

unique black and white ear tufts. Do you see any caracals in the rocky valley of Mujib, leaping with amazing skill to catch airborne prey?

Hasn't the King's Highway led us to the most intriguing places? Which was your favorite thus far? You should see what marvels Malek is eager to show us further down this winding road through Jordan. Traveling the high way of the King promises treasures untold—in more ways than one!

Can you find the King's Highway that snakes more than 1 300 ft [396 meters] down through Wadi Mujib, slips across the dam and then coils its way out of the canyon? The dam has created a large lake, the waters of which are largely used for irrigation purposes. Can you find irrigated areas in this scene? Looking upon such a vista, we agree with Romans 1:20 (NLT) "Through everything God made, [people] can clearly see his invisible qualities—his eternal power and divine nature." Don't you see evidence of Him everywhere?
Photo: Brian McMorrow

Field Notes

It would be amazing to stand on the top of Mount Nebo where Moses stood, don't you think?

Press record and talk to me:

~**about the Bedouin camps**: What are the houses made of? What covers the floors?

~**about Mt. Nebo**:   Why is this mountain mentioned in the Bible? What sculpture stands atop the mountain? What does it represent? What can be seen from the top?

~**about Marchaerus**: Which King built a fortress here?   What were the caves used for? What famous prisoner died at Marchaerus?

~**about wadi Mujib**: What is this wadi often called? How was it formed? How low is the park? What animals might we find here?

Travel Log

Using your globe or atlas, draw an outline map of Jordan.

As we travel, let's make record in our very own travel log of the places we've visited and the unusual sights we've seen! Make your map large enough to hold all of your discoveries!

Don't worry about making a perfect map, just do your best. Drawing the basic shape yourself will help you remember it better. Or use the map provided for you on the CD-ROM in the back of your book.

Map Notes: <u>Let's record the locations of:</u>

- *Jordan River*
- *Ghor Valley*
- *Amman*
- *Madaba*

- *Mt. Nebo*
- *Marchaerus*
- *Wadi Mujib*

<u>If you'd like, draw pictures or symbols on your map representing:</u>

- *"Winston's hiccup"* (a sandwich?)
- *Veggies and fruit in the "food bowl"*
- *White buildings in Amman*
- *Roman Theater in Amman in the district of Jebel al-Qala'a* (maybe a costumed character? Or a pair of theater curtains?)
- *Mosaic map at Madaba* (a scattering of tiles?)
- *Serpentine cross on Mt. Nebo*
- *An ibex and caracal in wadi Mujib*

Travel Notes: Geographers write what they've seen in order to share the adventure with others—and so they can revisit the places in their memories! **On the next page of your travel log, record three important sights you want to remember from your photos of Jordan.**

~art ~books ~food ~music ~poetry

. . . .

Bringing It Home

Simple ideas to bring the world to your door

Art:

Would you like to make your own **mosaic** art like the Mosaic Map of Madaba?

Choose a number of different colors of paper – plain, wrapping paper, magazine pages, foil, textured papers, whatever you have on hand. (You also might want to draw and color on a plain piece of paper for an interesting effect.)

Cut your papers into strips ½ inch [1.2 cm] wide and then cut the strips into small squares.

Lightly draw a design on a piece of background paper (such as construction paper). (Perhaps you want to draw a map of your town?)

The fun part comes next! Lay your mosaic pieces on your design and glue them in place on the background paper. (A simple method is to use spray mount glue which allows you to reposition your pieces as much as you want. If you use regular glue be sure to plan your design carefully!) If you'd like, laminate your finished project and preserve it for a long time. (It probably won't last as long as the Mosaic Map of Madaba though!)

Music

Music captures so much of a land and people. Introducing your children to Jordanian music is a simple way to transport yourselves around the world. Why not check out these sites while your young geographers' notebook and map and let the music play while they recount their travels?

Listen to samples of music from Jordanian artists:
http://worldmusic.nationalgeographic.com/worldmusic/view/page.basic/country/content.country/jordan_817?fs=www3.nationalgeographic.com

With singing:
http://worldmusic.nationalgeographic.com/worldmusic/view/page.basic/artist/content.artist/bedouism_5322

Rock of Ages

Jordan ~Part 2~

Two friendly Jordanian Bedouin girls at Petra invite us to come see the rocks of Jordan. Look at the colors of the stone behind them! Let's go exploring!
With Permission: Jeffery Scott Tynes

As a farmer's daughter, I have grunted and groaned over thousands and thousands of rocks in my lifetime, hauling off sparkly-flecked granites and chalky, powdery limestone. There is something exceptional about each stone; how God crafted its shape, its color, its feel. You too have likely paused on an afternoon jaunt to bend over and claim as special little stone as your own? The land of Jordan has stones of its own… breathtaking, stupendous stones, unlike anything you've ever seen or imagined. Focus your eyes of faith, and sharpen your attentive memory—this is one adventure you won't want to miss!

The window rolled down on this average summer day of 89 F [32 C], Malek's *keffiyeh* blows in the breeze as he winds and weaves us further south along Jordan's King's Highway. As we gaze out on the rolling Jordanian hills, Malek tells us that Jordan has a Mediterranean climate with a long, hot, dry summer and a wet cool winter from November to April. If you checked the closets of Jordanians living in the northwestern highlands (such as in Amman), you'd definitely find winter coats: white snowflakes blanket the ground several times during the winter and frost is fairly common. Yet the month before and after the blistering, parched summer finds Jordanians choking in great clouds of sand and dust, stirred by the gale force winds that they call the **khamsin**.

What is that we see rising ahead of us, Malek? Like a massive ship sailing the crest of a steep hill over deep, plunging valleys, a castle rides high on the skyline above a city. Even higher mountains rise above the imposing city. With a great flourish, Malek announces that we have arrived in Karak. (Arabs are well known for their grand gestures and body language.) A modern city of 200,000 people, Karak is built on a triangular plateau with the towering Karak Castle on the brow of the narrow southern tip. The dark, roughly shaped stones of the castle walls we now look upon date back to the 12th century and knightly Crusaders, when the castle's lord grew rich from charging road-tolls on the travelers of the King's Highway. Yet a fortress has dominated this landscape since biblical times. If you open your Bible you'll read of this place as Kiharaseth, meaning brick fortress, one of the strongholds of the Moabites.

From the King's Highway far below, we look up at the dramatic Karak Castle, the second largest castle in the Middle East. A stronghold since Biblical times, the city of Karak was the ancient capital of Moab. How do you think geography influenced the history of this place?
Photo: Brian McMorrow

2 Kings 3:25 tells us that the King of Israel, Jehoram, ravaged Moab and besieged its king, Meshua, in a fortress in this place: "*And they beat down the cities...only in Kirharaseth left they the stones thereof.*" The trapped Moabite king then "*took his eldest son...and offered him for a burnt offering upon the wall...So Israel departed from him and returned to their own land*" (2 Kings 3:27). Our God, full of compassion, says "*...mine heart shall mourn for the men of Kirheres*" (or Karak) (Jer. 48:31). Isaiah 16:7 reads, "*Lament and grieve for the men* (or, using a play on words, "raisin cakes") *of Kir Hareseth.*" (Was this play on words used since raisin cakes were a local specialty to Karak in Biblical times?) Exploring the tunnels

Remember to use your right hand as you eat mansaf, Jordan's national dish, and for which Karak is famous. Doesn't it taste delicious?

and passages of the castle's depths with our flashlights, we touch these cold stone walls and know that the just as God loved the people of ancient Karak, so He loves the people of this place today.

Eating in the rest house next to the stone castle, Malek doesn't order us raisin cakes but Jordan's national dish, **mansaf**, for which Karak is famous. A steaming platter of rice atop thin bread covered with lamb meat and dried goat's milk and a crowning sprinkle of pine nuts is set before us and we heartily eat from the communal dish with our hands. (But we don't dig in to Jordan's national dish with both hands—remember that Arabs only eat with their right hand!) True to Arab hospitality, Malek ensures we are overfed before we continue down the King's Highway.

From high upon the wall of Karak Castle, we can look out at a patchwork of fields, orchards and greenhouses across the valley. Can you determine which land is irrigated and which isn't? *Photo: Jeffery Scott Tynes*

Traveling south out of Karak, Malek points out greenhouses covering acres of precious Jordanian farmland. Do you recall how the outline of Jordan's boundaries looks like a duck opening its mouth wide? Think of the thirsting duck looking for water! One of the ten most water-deprived countries in the world, most of Jordan receives less than 7.8 inches or 200 millimeters of rain per year. In such an arid country, Jordan's farmers harvest something that doesn't grow up from the soil, but falls from the sky: water! Malek explains that farmers harvest rainwater by collecting runoff rain from roofs and ground surfaces, or building dams across wadis to collect water from sporadic torrential rainfall. Malek tells us that farmers harvest rain so that they may grow, irrigate and harvest other crops such as wheat, barley, tomatoes, melons, cabbage, bananas and potatoes.

Do you see the Bedouin tents camped there near the King's Highway? Malek tells us that while very few Jordanians now live like those Bedouin, a nomadic lifestyle of tents and herding, Bedouin culture lives on in every day Jordanian life. While dinnertime around your family table finds both males and females eating and talking together, a meal with a Bedouin family separates females and males. Activities between males and females are generally segregated in Jordan. As most marriages are arranged in Bedouin tribes, so most Jordanian weddings are arranged also.

Traveling down Jordan's modern King's Highway, we spot a Bedouin camp, reminders of an ancient, enduring lifestyle. **What might be the advantages and disadvantages of both a Bedouin lifestyle and a modern Jordanian lifestyle?** *Photo: Brian McMorrow*

Do you ever imagine your wedding day? What will you wear? You likely have no idea who you will marry. If you lived in Jordan, you might imagine wearing a black dress you sewed yourself and marrying your first cousin! First cousins are considered the best pairing, and the traditional wedding dress is black, handmade by the bride over the course of a year! Malek explains that it takes that long to carefully handstitch the elaborate embroidery—but only on the left side of the dress. The right side of the dress has coarse simple designs, since babies are traditionally carried on the right arm.

Small towns stream by our window, the towering minarets of each mosque punctuating the sky. Can you read the road signs along the King's Highway? English place names and directions are written under the Arabic words in their elegant script. While you may read the sign from left to right, Malek reads the signs the opposite way, right to left. Malek smiles as he informs us that he also begins a book from what we would call the back. Arabic has no capital letters and modern standard Arabic, the style of Arabic of Malek's newspaper, does not use the marks that indicate vowels with short sounds. That is like you reading your English newspaper without any of the short vowels printed: "hat," "hit," "hot," and "hut" would all be spelled "ht"!

We do not need to read any sign to know that the scenery outside our window truly is a sculpted landscape of brilliant magnificence! Just north of Shobak on the King's Highway, Malek announces we are driving through the Dana Nature Reserve. Can you see the ancient village of Dana nestled quietly amidst these craggy colored mountains? Strikingly different than most Jordanian villages of cement blocks, the stone village of Dana was slowly being abandoned by villagers for lack of water. Malek tells us that a new spring has revitalized the ancient village and steeply terraced gardens now grow lush in the warm sunshine. After hiking trails of the Dana Reserve's stunning sandstone structures and taking in the memorable views of the canyon-like wadi, let's slip into the village for some of their renowned apricot jam.

Do you lose keys, socks, and a shoe every now and then? I have heard of lost snakes, lost boats…and even, the worst, a teary-eyed lost child. But a lost city? How could a whole city disappear and no one know where it went?

The spectacular Dana Nature Reserve's red rock canyon seems to blush in response to our accolades over such beauty. **More than 25 different endangered or vulnerable animal species live within the reserve, along with nearly 700 plants, 3 of which are new to science.** *Photo: Robin Searle*

The dark looming walls of the Siq frames a truly unforgettable glimpse of the 'lost city' of Petra. 'Petra' means Rock in Greek, an appropriate name for these magnificent buildings and dwellings hewn out of stone by the Nabateans. The Hebrew name for this place is Sela, which also means "Rock," and can be found in the Bible in reference to the simple stone dwellings of the Edomites. What might you have first thought if you had rediscovered this city? *Photo: David Bjorgen*

As it is always best to retrace one's step to the beginning when looking for something lost, let's go back to what we know of this lost city. This southern region of Jordan was once Edom, inhabited by Edomites, descendants of Isaac's son, Esau. Moses stood in this "Red Land" and asked the King of Edom, *"Let us pass, I pray thee through thy country…We will go by the king's highway…And if I and my cattle drink thy water, then I will pay for it"* (Num. 20:17-19). The King of Edom came out from his rock dwelling and said, *"Thou shalt not go through."* Makel tells us that the Biblical Mount Hor is nearby, where it is believed that Aaron died and was buried (Num. 20:23-29), and the area's main water source is named Ain Mousa (Spring of Moses) as some think it is here that Moses smote the rock to quench the thirst of the parched Israelites.

The prophet Obadiah declares, *"Thus saith the Lord GOD concerning Edom…The pride of your heart has deceived you, you dweller in the refuges of the rock [Petra, Edom's Capital], whose habitation is high…"* (Oba. 1:3 Amplified Bible). From Biblical times, the Edomites were known to live in the clefts of these rust red rocks. Eventually, the Edomites were displaced by a people called the Nabateans who, creating more sophisticated rock dwellings, grew wealthy from caravans bringing incense, myrrh, and precious stones from Asia and the Arabian Peninsula to be traded in the west. Some believe that the three kings who came with gifts to worship Jesus may well have stayed in this rock city. By the 7th century after the time of Jesus, the Nabateans experienced a massive earthquake in their rock homes and moved away. Slowly, the outside world forgot about these rock dwellings. Yet the local Bedouin tribes always knew of the rock city, keeping it a closely guarded secret, just as you may keep the location of a special hideout a mystery. Until one day in 1812, a young explorer from Switzerland heard locals speaking of a hidden "lost city" in the mountains of the Wadi Mousa, the Valley of Moses. Malek beckons us to come see what sights the speechless explorer (re)discovered.

Field Notes

How I wish I could see the amazing rocks of Jordan for myself! Would you like to come with me?

Press record and talk to me:

~about Jordan's climate: What are the summers like? And the winters? Would a Jordanian ever need a winter coat? Do you remember what a *khamsin* is?

~about Karak: When was Karak castle built? What Biblical nation was Karak the capital of? What is *mansaf*? How is it made?

~about water in Jordan: What important resource do Jordan's farmers harvest? How do they collect the rainwater? For what purpose?

~about Jordanian culture: Describe meal time in a Bedouin family. Why might a Jordanian woman wear a black dress? Whom might she marry? Tell me about reading in Arabic. How is it different from reading in English?

~about the "Lost City":   Who were the Edomites? The Nabateans? When was the city re-discovered by non-Jordanian people? Who discovered it?

Malek leads us through the dark shadows of a long gorge called the Siq whose towering stone sides almost entirely block out the sun. Malek tells us that the Siq, meaning "shaft," is so narrow—less than six feet in places—that the Nabateans could easily defend their rock dwellings. Suddenly the gorge breaks open and, framed in a narrow sunlit slit in the cliffs, we catch a glimpse of not a simple cave house but the most spectacular intricately carved masterpiece, the *Khasneh*, (the treasury of the Nabateans), glowing in the late afternoon sun. Like all visitors, we stop short here with a gasp: the lost city of Petra is strikingly worth finding!

Hidden behind a barrier of rugged mountains, the rock hewn city of Petra is a breathtaking wonder of

Watching the sunset in Petra, we try to imagine what it might have been like for the Biblical Edomites to live in these rocks, followed by the architectural genius of the Nabateans, and then the recent Bedouin tribes. *Photo: Robin Searle*

Do you see this Jordanian man fingering the black and red stones of his worry beads?
Photo: Brian McMorrow

the world. The traveler and poet Dean Burgon offered an oft-quoted description of Petra, "*Match me such a marvel save in Eastern clime, a rose-red city half as old as time.*" Ancient Petra may still be called the "Rose-Red City" but, looking at the God-brushed color of these stones, we may well call it the "rose, blueberry, curry, slate and chocolate city!" Such hues! Exploring the city's carved building, hundreds of tombs, and canyon locations, we hardly know what is more remarkable: the obscure location? the narrow entrance through the gorge? the monumental architecture? the ingenious network of channels that carried life-giving water to this secluded place, allowing the city to thrive? Perhaps what is most mind-boggling is not that this entire city was carved out of rock by hands just like yours, but that the same Hand that chose the color of your eyes, is the Hand of God who painted this canyon such a staggering array of colors.

Would you like to live in this hidden rock city, glowing like molten copper when lit by the fiery sun? Until recently, local Bedouin families lived in Petra, but the Jordanian government has moved them now to live in nearby modern housing.

As Malek tours us further south on the descending King's Highway, past cement block villages dotting worn hillsides, he reaches into his pocket to finger a string of little stones. While your father may reach for an aspirin when feeling stress, Muslim men throughout the Middle East click along what they call "worry beads," 33 beads of mother-of-pearl, coral, date pits, ivory, or amber, one for each of their names for Allah. A practice that dates back to the 9th century, Malek says that many Muslim men feel undressed without their worry beads!

Yet watching the landscape change outside our window, we have no worries—simply awe! Mammoth rocks rise up from the desert floor. Malek tell us that this is Wadi Rum, the most dramatic desertscape in Jordan...perhaps in the world! Don't you think the scene looks a bit like streets of sand through a city of monolithic, window-less buildings of rock? Yet there are no skyscrapers, stores or houses lining paved streets through Wadi Rum. Some visitors refer to this majestic region of Jordan, with its massive cliffs and reddish sands, as the Valley of the Moon. T.E. Lawrence, the renowned British soldier and adventurer, explored Wadi Rum and wrote, "*We entered Rum at last, while the crimson sunset burned on its stupendous cliffs and slanted ladders of hazy fire down the walled avenue.*"

Do you think the Wadi Rum looks like the Valley of the Moon? You may see as many tracks of four wheel drive vehicles through these desert sands as of camels. Many explorers, however, choose to drift over this unusual landscape in a hot air balloon—and maybe the Rum looks a tad reminiscent of the moon when viewed from up in the clouds!
Photo: David Bjorgen

Wadi Rum is a place of paradox, hinted at even its name. While wadi means "valley" in Arabic, iram means "high point." Is Wadi Rum a highpoint valley? It would be more accurate to think of Wadi Rum as a high tableland plateau, with immense pillars of massive granite and sandstone rock formations breaking up through the sands.

Driving through clouds of reddish sands whipped across the desert in the hot winds, Malek escorts us to the sole inhabitants of Wadi Rum, the Bedouin. Living a semi-nomadic lifestyle, the Bedouins of the Wadi Rum graze their flocks of nibbling sheep and goats for months at a time in one vast location before moving on to greener pastures. While we see camels wandering around the encampment, we also spot expensive four wheel drive vehicles and convenient cell phones. Malek explains that the money generated from guiding tourists from around this world through this remarkable scenery has influenced the Bedouin way of life. These modern conveniences, however, do little to change the ancient tradition of generous hospitality.

Nasser, a Jordanian Bedouin, lights a fire for us in Wadi Rum. Will you have tea or coffee?

A Bedouin man named Nasser, dressed in traditional garb, warmly greets us with embraces and welcomes us into one of the black tents, *bayt ash-sha'ar,* literally meaning 'houses of hair.' Shall we have some mint tea or cardamom-flavored coffee? Malek informs us that a traditional serving of Bedouin coffee involves 3 cups of the brew; one for the soul, one for the sword and one because you are a guest. Don't ask for a fourth, or you'll be considered greedy!

Sitting next to the Bedouin campfire, we are struck by the overwhelming quiet of the Wadi Rum. Who can resist sleeping out under the stars in this place? The Bedouin serenade the night's first twinkling lights with traditional Arabic music. While Bedouin women sit in rows facing each other, singing lyrics back and forth, Malek explains that the tradition instruments of the Bedouin are the **shabbaba,** a sort of flute made out of a metal pipe, and the **rababa,** a one-string violin. Yet the most beautiful instrument of all is the voices of the women, their lilting poetry echoing off the towering rocks.

Have you ever seen a natural bridge of stone towering high overhead? God creates such wonders! Considered one of the highest natural arches in the world, the Burdah Rock Bridge, 115 ft high [35 meters], is one of God's masterpieces in Wadi Rum. Care to walk across?

Photo: David Bjorgen

Come morning, Malek promises memorable explorations of the rocks of Wadi Rum, including one of the world's highest natural arches, Burdah Rock Bridge. Are you adventuresome enough to scale the 1800 ft [550 m] sheer walls of the Rum's sandstone crags? Some mountaineers climb Wadi Rum's Jabal Rum, the highest peak in all of Jordan at 5,689 ft. [1, 734 m] If you would prefer to hike instead of climb, Nasser offers to guide us down trails where water trickles out of rocks like a crack in a big clay jar. Like leeches clinging to their host, roots of wild fig trees stretch along the rock in search of drops of water. Rare rains in the Rum can germinate

177

seeds that have lain dormant for years, carpeting the wadi in a profusion of flowers. Nasser's description of tranquil "hanging gardens" and desert blooms in the midst of the dry Wadi Rum whets our appetite to perhaps explore trails with him tomorrow. Whether we chose trails across the Rum's sands or scaling its cliffs standing like sentinels, Malek assures us that we'll bring several jugs of pure water with us, drawn directly from the great aquifer of underground water that lies under the Wadi Rum, and supplies much water to Jordan.

Smiling, Malek and Nasser express how pleased they are that a young person such as yourself came to explore Jordan. Do you know that Jordanians view children as so important that mothers and father traditionally change their names after the birth of their first child? (If your name was Mahmoun, upon your birth, your Jordanian father would become "Abu Mahmoun" [literally, 'father of Mahmoun'] and your mother become "Umm Mahmoun" [literally, 'mother of Mahmoun'].) Smiling back at our Jordanian friends, we will remember Jordan as the country that has warmly welcomed young and old alike down through the centuries, its rocks declaring the wonder of the Rock of Ages.

"The LORD is my rock, and my fortress, and my deliverer; my God, my strength, in whom I will trust; my buckler, and the horn of my salvation, and my high tower." ~Ps. 18:2

Field Notes

What a marvelous country! Petra, the Siq, the Wadi and its Stone Bridge...what an amazing country God has created.

Press record and talk to me:

~**about Petra**:   Describe a trip through the Siq. What other name is Petra called? Why? Can you share some of the history of Petra? What do you find most amazing about the "Lost City?"

~**about Wadi Rum**:   What interesting geography prompts some to call this area the "Valley of the Moon?" What surprising modern conveniences do the Bedouin of Wadi Rum have? How many cups of Bedouin coffee might our friendly hosts share with us? What are *shabbaba* and *rababa*? Would you like to cross the Burdah Rock Bridge? Why or why not? What lies hidden under the ground of Wadi Rum?

How I love adventures. Don't you? Perhaps you too feel sweet sadness when a journey draws to a close. Our travels through the Holy Lands have led us to such wonders. Haven't we seen evidence of God's glory everywhere? And the people we have met! How God loves them. May you take His love on all your future travels.

May the peace of the Lord Christ go with you,
wherever He may send you.
May He guide you through the wilderness,
protect you through the storm.
May He bring you home rejoicing
at the wonders He has shown you.
May He bring you home rejoicing
once again into our doors.

~Celtic Prayer

Travel Log

Using your globe or atlas, let's add the following locations to your map of Jordan...

Map Notes: Let's record the locations of:

- *Karak*
- *Shobak*
- *Petra*

- *Wadi Rum*
- *Jabal Rum*

If you'd like, draw pictures or symbols on your map representing:

- *Karak Castle*
- *Greenhouses south of Karak*
- *Bedouin tents throughout Jordan*
- *Dana Nature Reserve* (colorful gardens in the sandy desert?)
- *The Siq* (this will require some creativity! Perhaps an arrow pointing to the Lost City?)
- *Music and stars in the Wadi Rum* (perhaps some singers, or musical notes?)
- *Burdah Rock Bridge* (remember to make it high among the rocks!)

Travel Notes: Geographers write what they've seen in order to share the adventure with others—and so they can revisit the places in their memories! **On the next page of your travel log, record three important sights you want to remember from your photos of Jordan.**

~art ~books ~food ~music ~poetry
. . . .

Bringing It Home
Simple ideas to bring the world to your door

Books:

Jordan (Enchantment of the World) *by* Leila Merrill Foster

The Enchantment of the World series provides well-written overviews of various countries. Children will get a taste for the history, geography, politics and religion of Jordan in this book by Leila Foster. *Good for all ages.*

The Space Between Our Footsteps *by* Naomi Shihab Nye

An anthology of poetry focused on 19 countries of the Middle East. Themes of homeland, family, nature, war, and love are all explored in this collection. Colorful paintings are interspersed throughout the book making this a treat for eyes as well as ears. ***older readers Grades 7+*

Jordan: Past and Present *by* E. Borgia

Explore ancient Jordan, Petra and Amman in this clever book. Illustrations show ruins in the present day and then overlays show the ruins at the height of their beauty. *A treat for all ages.*

Poetry:

In that good and distant city
in a courtyard full of grass
all things sing
and everyone dances

~Ibrahim Nasrallah

Ibrahim Nasrallah was born in a Palestinian refugee camp in Jordan in 1954. Mr. Nasrallah is a poet, novelist, professor, painter, photographer, and journalist. He has won many awards for his poetry.

~art ~books ~food ~music ~poetry

. . . .

Bringing It Home

Simple ideas to bring the world to your door

Food:

Have you ever unpacked a bag of groceries and found that on the trip home the loaf of bread got squished and unusable? Bedouins in the Middle East - who pack up their homes and travel all the time - came up with an ingenious way to solve this problem. They make **pitas**! Pita bread is a staple in nearly all Arabic countries. A flat round bread, it is easily made, very portable, can be sliced in half for sandwiches or even used in place of a fork and spoon for eating other foods!

Why don't you try making some of your own?

- *1 package of yeast*
- *1/2 cup warm water*
- *3 cups all purpose flour*
- *1 1/4 teaspoon salt*
- *1 teaspoon granulated sugar*
- *1 cup lukewarm water*

Pour yeast into warm water, stir until dissolved. Add sugar and stir until it is also dissolved. Stand for 10-15 minutes until water is frothy.

Combine flour and salt in large bowl and make a well in the center of the mixture. Pour the yeast mixture into the well.

Slowly add an additional 1 cup of warm water, and stir until the dough is elastic.

Remove dough from bowl, place on floured surface and knead for 10-15 minutes or until no longer sticky and dough is smooth and elastic. Place dough in large bowl coated with olive oil, turning once to coat top. Cover and let rise in warm place until doubled in size. (1 hr – 3 hrs depending on temperature of room.)

Gently deflate dough after it has doubled and roll it into a long rope. Pinch off 10-12 small pieces and place on a floured surface. Allow to rest, covered with a towel for 10 minutes. Place a baking sheet in the oven and preheat to 500 F with rack on lowest oven rung.

Roll each ball of dough into ¼ inch thick circles (about 5-6 in [12-15 cm] across). Place circles on hot baking sheet and bake for 4 minutes until the bread puffs up. Turn over and bake for an additional 2 minutes. Remove pitas with a spatula and gently push down on the puffed up part. Store in plastic bags.

Go into all the world...

a walk of prayer

*Didn't we discover Jordan to be a land of sights and sounds of the Bible? From Bedouin tribes to friendly Jordanians in the capital city of Amman, the people of Jordan warmly welcomed us to walk ancient ways to wondrous places. We found that Jordan is full of **boys and girls** who are much like us. They were created by a God who loves them dearly—just as He loves you.*

Will you and your family join me in praying for the Jordanian people?

Lord, give us Your love for the peoples of the world, and help our family to live in a way that shows our love for them.

Father, Jordan is a country of influence among the Middle East. May You grant her people wisdom as they work for peace.

~We pray for **the many refugees** who come from across the Middle East to Jordan seeking peace. We ask that You bless the country of Jordan for being a place of shelter. May those who enter her borders find jobs, food, and shelter to provide for their families. May they also find rest.

~We pray that this dry country may have enough **water resources** to meet the needs of the families who live in Jordan. May they have tools to be wise stewards of their current water supplies, and may You bless Jordan with resources to develop further water supplies.

~We pray that you may **prosper the families** of Jordan, a country with few natural resources, little water, and little land suitable for agriculture. Everything every nation, family, person has is a gift from Your hand. Thank you for meeting the needs of Jordanians.

~We thank You for the freedoms that Christians have in Jordan. We ask that You would preserve those freedoms and make an even broader way for those who long to serve You. May **Christians** boldly worship You and lift up Your name.

~We ask that You would be with the many **young people** who live in Jordan. May they grow in wisdom. We ask that You raise up peace-loving leaders from among these young people and help them to influence the future direction of the Middle East.

We love you, Lord, and the people who are living in Jordan today. May the Light of our Savior dawn over all nations today. Draw us all closer to You, Father. In Jesus name, Amen.

Appendix
~Fast Facts~

Turkey resides in two continents: Asia and Europe. It borders Bulgaria, Greece, Georgia, Armenia, Iran, Azerbaijan, Iraq and Syria; the Black Sea, Aegean Sea, Sea of Marmara and Mediterranean Sea. Capital city: Ankara

Remember: *Ankara, Istanbul, Bosphorous Strait, Anatolian Plateau, Mt. Ararat, Lake Van, Haran, Tarsus, Izmir, Ephesus, Lake Tuz, Cappadocia, Fairy Chimneys*

Israel resides at the convergence of Africa, Europe and Asia. It borders Lebanon, Syria, Jordan and Egypt. It also borders the Mediterranean Sea. Capital city: Jerusalem

Remember: *Galilean Hills, Judean Hills, Samarian Hills, Sea of Galilee, Coastal Plain, Haifa, Tel Aviv, West Bank, Jerusalem, Negev Desert, Jordan River and Valley, Dead Sea*

Egypt resides in Africa, although it is considered a Middle Eastern country. It borders Libya, Sudan, and Israel; the Mediterranean and the Red Seas. Capital city: Cairo

Remember: *Sinai Peninsula, Suez Canal, Eastern Desert, the Nile River and Delta, Cairo, Giza, Alexandria, Western Desert, Black and White Desert, Great Sand Sea*

Iraq resides in Asia. It borders Kuwait, Saudi Arabia, Jordan, Syria, Turkey and Iran. It also borders the Persian Gulf. Capital City: Baghdad

Remember: *Baghdad, Babylon, Nineveh, Ur, Zagros Mts., Mosul, Kirkuk, Najaf, Tigris and Euphrates River, Marshes, Basrah, Persian Gulf*

Saudi Arabia resides on the Arabian Peninsula but is considered part of Asia. It borders Jordan, Iraq, Kuwait, Qatar, Bahrain, United Arab Emirates (UAE), Oman and Yemen. It also borders the Persian Gulf and the Red Sea. Capital city: Riyadh

Remember: *Jeddah, Hijaz Mts., Mecca, Medina, Asir Mts., Abha, Najd, Riyadh, Al Hasa, Rub'al Khali (the Empty Quarter), Ghawar, the Persian Gulf*

Jordan resides on the Arabian Peninsula, but is considered to be part of Asia. It borders Syria, Iraq, Saudi Arabia and Israel. It also borders the Dead Sea and the Gulf of Aqaba. Capital city: Amman

Remember: Amman, the King's Highway, the Highlands, the Jordan Rift Valley and River, Mt. Nebo, Petra, Wadi Rum Desert, Mt. Nebo

Appendix

Definitions

Turkey Chapter 1 – Directions to Eden, Please?

- **Definitions:**
  - **Bazaar** — A bazaar (the Persian word for "market") is a market lining a street with shops and stalls, especially in the Middle East
  - **Climate** — The meteorological conditions, including temperature, precipitation, and wind, that characteristically prevail in a particular region
  - **Continent** — One of the principal land masses of the earth
    (The seven continents are Africa, Antarctica, Asia, Australia, Europe, North America, and South America)
  - **Dam** — A barrier constructed across a waterway to control the flow or raise the level of water
  - **Geography** — The word "geography" comes from the Greek language and simply means "to write about the earth"
  - *Kilim* — A kilim is a brightly colored Turkish rug, woven with geometric designs
  - **Lake** — A large inland body of fresh water or salt water
  - **Plateau** — An elevated, comparatively level expanse of land; a tableland
  - **Sea** — The continuous body of salt water covering most of the earth's surface
  - **Strait** — A narrow channel joining two larger bodies of water
  - **Temperate** — Characterized by moderate temperatures, weather, or climate; neither hot nor cold

Turkey Chapter 2 – Houses for sale: An Ark, a Beehive, a Fairy Chimney, and a Salt Pan!

- **Definitions:**
  - **Algae** — Primitive, mainly water-dwelling organisms without roots, stems or leaves
  - *Ayran* — Traditional Turkish drink made of yogurt and water
  - **Basalt** — A dark, volcanic rock with a glassy appearance
  - **Combine** — A harvesting machine. It cuts, threshes and cleans the grains
  - **Flood** — Water overflowing onto land that is usually dry
  - **Mountain** — A land mass that rises out of the earth's surface. It usually has steep sides and is larger than a hill   *Abbr.* **Mt., Mtn.** or **Mount**
  - *Pide* — A round, flat Turkish wheat bread
  - **Plain** — An expanse of level, or nearly level, land
  - **Silt** — Mud, clay or rocks left behind by a body of water
  - **Sulfur** — A yellow, nonmetallic element
  - **Textile** — Fabric manufactured by weaving or knitting

Turkey Chapter 3 – Wandering and Wrestling, Whirling and Worshiping!

- **Definitions:**
  - *Allah* — The muslim name for God
  - *Athan* — Muslim call to prayer
  - *Dervish* — A member of a muslim order, some of which perform whirling dances
  - **Islam** — The religion of muslims based on the teachings of Muhammed
  - **Minaret** — A slender tower with balconies, attached to a mosque
  - **Mosque** — A muslim house of worship
  - *Muezzin* — The muslim official who calls worshippers to pray five times a day
  - **Ramadan** — The ninth month (Islamic calendar), in which muslims fast from sunrise to sunset
  - *Seker Bayrami* — Four-day family holiday immediately following Ramadan. Traditionally children are given candy and simple gifts

Israel Chapter 1 — Houses for Sale: An Ark, a Beehive, A Fairy Chimney, and a Salt Pan!

- **Definitions:**
  - **Christianity** — The Christian religion, based on the life and teachings of Jesus
  - **Coastal** — Land running alongside an ocean or large body of water
  - **Convergence** — A meeting place, or the point of meeting
  - **Current** — Continuous, onward movement of a body of water
  - **Elevation** — Height, or the raising of the land
  - *Felafel* — Ground chickpeas and spices shaped into balls and fried
  - **Greenhouse** — A structure for growing plants, usually made of plastic or glass for controlling temperatures
  - **Gorge** — A deep, narrow pass or valley with steep sides
  - **Harbor** — A sheltered area in a body of water allowing ships to anchor.
  - *Ketubah* — A Jewish wedding contract
  - **Judaism** — The Jewish religion, based on the Torah and the Talmud
  - **Mediterranean Climate** — The particular, usual weather of the Mediterranean region Generally defined by dry summers, wet winters and mild temperatures
  - *Mizrach* — "East"; a sign hung on a wall to remind Jewish families to pray east – towards Jerusalem
  - **Mountain** — A landform rising above the surrounding countryside, with steep sides
  - **Plain** — A broad, flat, low-lying expanse
  - **Port** — An area on the water's edge for receiving ships and their cargo
  - *Tehina* — a sauce of ground sesame seeds common in the Middle East
  - **Wadi** — A dry, rocky, river bed that remains dry until the rainy season

Israel Chapter 2 – The Extraordinary Ordinary: Farms in the Desert and the Healthy Dead Sea

- **Definitions:**
  - **Aquifer** — An underground pool of water
  - *Bedouin* — A member of the Arab nomadic desert tribes
  - **Brackish-water agriculture** — Brackish water is saltier than fresh water, yet not as salty as sea water. Agriculture is the process of raising plants for food and products
  - **Calcium carbonate** — Colorless or white crystalline compound used in manufactured products such as chalk or medicine
  - **Coral reef** — A massive rock-like structure built by the secretions of calcium carbonate from millions of very small marine animals
  - **Desalination** — The process of removing salt from water or soil
  - **Desert** — A dry, sandy geographical region with little rainfall, extreme temperatures, and sparse vegetation
  - **Erosion** — The wearing away of soil and rock by natural processes
  - **Evaporation** — The process by which water transforms to vapor
  - **Fault line** — A line indicating a crack in the earth's crust, created by motion in the crust
  - **Fertilizer** — Natural or synthetic compounds worked into the soil to stimulate plant growth
  - **Fossil** — A remnant of a plant or animal from long ago, such as a skeleton or leaf imprint, preserved in the earth's crust
  - *Halvah* — A treat made of crushed sesame seeds and honey
  - **Irrigation** — The watering of crops with a source other than rainfall
  - **Karst crater** — A bowl-shaped depression made in the earth by water pressure
  - *Kibbutz* — A community farm or settlement in Israel
  - **Loess** — A yellowish or gray fine-grained soil which is very fertile when watered
  - **Migration** — The movement of animals or people from one location to another
  - **Mineral** — An inorganic element, such as calcium, iron, potassium, sodium, or zinc, that is essential to the nutrition of humans, animals, and plants
  - **Mirage** — An optical illusion that creates the appearance of water from a long distance
  - **Natural resources** — Resources that are a part of creation, such as water, wood, minerals
  - *Neghev* — Hebrew word meaning dry
  - **Plates** — Sections of the earth's crust
  - **Potash** — One of many compounds containing potassium; used as fertilizer
  - **Pita** — Round, flat Middle Eastern bread, also called pocket bread

- o **Rift** — A narrow chasm in a rock, or the breaking of friendly relations
- o **Tap** — Another word for the source or beginning of a river
- o **Tourist** — A person who travels for recreation
- o **Sea level** — A complex measurement of the sea's level, used to determine land elevation
- o **Strike-slip fault zone** — An area in which the fault is nearly vertical, with the walls on either side tending to move left and right

Israel Chapter 3 – Howdy Pilgrim!
- • **Definitions:**
  - o **Arch** — A structure, usually made of stone, shaped like an inverted U and supporting the weight above it as in a doorway or a bridge
  - o **Beatitude** — A declaration of blessing made by Jesus in the sermon on the mount
  - o **Dome** — A vaulted roof, usually in a half-moon shape
  - o **Limestone** — A common sedimentary rock used as a building stone
  - o **Mosaic** — A picture or design made from arranging small pieces of stone or tile
  - o **Pilgrim** — One who travels to far off lands or journeys to sacred places
  - o **Octagonal** — Having eight sides and eight angles
  - o **Roman bathhouse** — A building used by the Romans for bathing
  - o **Sepulchre (or sepulcher)** — A burial chamber
  - o **Shrine** — A building that houses items considered holy
  - o *Souq* — An Arab market
  - o **Western Wall** — A section of the second Jewish Temple that is still standing and a pilgrimage site for Jews
  - o **Via Dolorosa** — The path Jesus walked to His crucifixion

Egypt Chapter 1 – Wearing Egypt
- • **Definitions:**
  - o **Canal** — An artificial waterway
  - o **Canyon** — A narrow chasm with steep cliff walls
  - o **Cartouche** — An oval shape enclosing hieroglyphics representing a Pharoah's name
  - o **Chasm** — Deep, steep sided opening in the earth
  - o **Cliff** — A high, steep face of rock
  - o **Compass** — A device with a magnetic needle, used to determine geographic direction
  - o **Dredger** — A machine used to deepen waterways
  - o **Gulf** — A large area of ocean (or sea), partially enclosed by land
  - o **Isthmus** — A narrow strip of land that connects two larger masses of land
  - o *Mag'ad* — 'Sitting place' section of the Bedouin tent
  - o *Maharama* — 'Place of women' in a Bedouin tent, where women cook, receive female guests
  - o *Ma'nad* — A woven curtain dividing a Bedouin tent
  - o **Manuscript** — A book or document written by hand
  - o **Monastery** — A community of monks, bound by religious vows and living together in at least partial seclusion
  - o **Peninsula** — A large section of land jutting out into a body of water
  - o **Pollution** — The contamination of soil, water and air with harmful substances
  - o **Pyramid** — A massive monument of ancient Egypt having a rectangular base and four triangular faces ending in a single point, built as a tomb for the Pharoahs
  - o **Ravine** — A deep narrow valley made by running water
  - o *Senet* — An ancient Egyptian board game
  - o *Tamiya* — Egyptian meal made of fava bean patties

Egypt Chapter 2 – Navigating the Nile
- • **Definitions:**
  - o *Burqa* — A loose, long garment worn by Muslim women that covers the entire body, including the face
  - o **Dam** — A large barrier across a waterway that controls the flow of water
  - o *Fellahin* — A farm worker in an Arab country
  - o *Felucca* — A sailing vessel used on the Nile or Mediterranean Sea

- o *Galabea* — An ankle-length, loose shirt
- o **Parasite** — An organism that grows and feeds on another organism but does not contribute anything to its host
- o **Reservoir** — A natural or artificial lake for storing water
- o *Zabbaleen* — People who work as garbage collectors in Cairo

Egypt Chapter 3 – Digging for Good Dirt
- **Definitions:**
  - o **Caravan** — A group of travelers, traveling together
  - o **Crystal** — A transparent mineral
  - o **Delta** — The triangular area where a river divides before entering another body of water, rich in sediment
  - o **Depression** — An area that is lower than its surroundings
  - o **Dune** — A hill of wind-blown sand
  - o *Khamsin* — A hot northern wind that creates a sandstorm in the desert
  - o **Limestone** — A common sedimentary rock often used as a building stone
  - o **Mecca** — The birthplace of Muhammed, the founder of Islam, and a pilgrimage site in Saudi Arabia
  - o **Monastery** — A community of monks, bound by religious vows and living together in at least partial seclusion
  - o **Oasis** — An area of water and green plants in the desert
  - o **Quartz** — A very hard mineral found in many different types of rocks, usually colorless or white
  - o **Sheaf** — A bundle of cut grass or straw bound in the middle with twine or straw
  - o **Sickle** — A tool with a semicircular blade used for cutting tall grasses
  - o **Silica** — White or colorless crystalline compound
  - o **Spring** — A small, natural stream of water
  - o **Topsoil** — The upper layer of soil
  - o **Turban** — A long scarf worn by Muslims that is wrapped around the head
  - o **Water table** — The level below ground that is completely saturated with water

Iraq Chapter 1 – Tell-ing the Past
- **Definitions:**
  - o *Abaya* — Traditional long, black cloak worn by Arab women
  - o **Archaeologist** — A person who studies the life and culture of peoples of the past
  - o *Cuneiform* — Early wedge-shaped writing system used in Mesopotamia and Persia
  - o *Halal* — Meat that has been prepared according to Islamic law
  - o *Haram* — "Forbidden" under Islamic law
  - o **Inscription** — Words engraved or carved on something
  - o *Kebabs* — Cubed meat cooked on a skewer
  - o *Shamal* — Summer wind
  - o *Sharqi* — Southeasterly wind from the Persian gulf in winter
  - o *Souk* — An Arab market
  - o *Tell* — Mounds, especially in the Middle East, made up of the rubble of ancient cities
  - o *Ziggurat* — A pyramid-like tower from Babylonian times

Iraq Chapter 2 – River Ride
- **Definitions:**
  - o **Foothills** — Hills found at the base of a larger mountain range
  - o **Gorge** — A deep, narrow valley with steep sides
  - o *Kibbeh* — Small dumplings filled with minced lamb or beef, nuts, raisins and spices
  - o *Kurds* — A nonArab minority group that lives a largely pastoral or agricultural life
  - o *Madrasa* — School
  - o *Matzgouf* — A grilled fish dish made of carp with peppers, onions and spices
  - o **Muslin** — A sturdy cotton fabric
  - o *Ostath* — School teacher
  - o **Pollarding** — Cutting back the limbs of tree to promote a bushier growth

- o **Precipitation** — Any form of water that falls to the earth's surface
- o **Steppe** — A vast grass-covered plain
- o *Throbes* — An ankle length robe with long sleeves worn by men
- o **Tributaries** — Streams that flow into larger bodies of water
- o *Zlabiya* — A sweet pastry that looks like a pretzel

Iraq Chapter 3 – Mixing Water and Oil?
- **Definitions:**
  - o **Alluvial** — Relating to sediment deposited by flood waters
  - o *Bunni* — A carp-like fresh water fish
  - o **Distributary** — A river branch that flows away from the main river
  - o **Irrigation** — To water dry land with artificial means through ditches, pipes or streams
  - o *Ma'dans* — A semi-nomadic Iraqi people who until recently lived in the marshlands
  - o **Marshes** — Many times a transition area between water and land; a wet, soft land area
  - o *Mashuf* — A long, flat-bottomed boat made of reeds
  - o *Mudhif* — A cathedral-like house for Ma'dan tribal gatherings
  - o **Oil** — An organic substance far underground that is used for fuel and plastics
  - o **Organic** — Coming from a living organism
  - o **Pore** — A small open space in a rock
  - o **Sediments** — Small bits of organic material, such as rock, carried by water
  - o *Sheik* — A leader of an Arab family or village
  - o **Soil salinity** — The measure of salt in soils

Saudi Arabia Chapter 1 – Migrations, Mecca and Mosques
- **Definitions:**
  - o **Aniconism** — The Muslim law forbidding representation of living creatures in art work
  - o *Egal* — A black cord used for tying on the gutra
  - o *Gutra* — Red and white checked head scarf worn by Saudi men
  - o *Hajj* — The annual Muslim pilgrimage to Mecca
  - o *Hijaz* — Mountain range on Saudi Arabia's west coast
  - o *Ihram* — A state of spiritual preparation for male pilgrims before they enter Mecca
  - o *Ka'abah* — A cube believed by Muslims to be built by Abraham and Ishmael, and viewed as the holiest site in Mecca
  - o **Meteorite** — A mass of matter fallen to earth from space
  - o *Mutawa* — The religious police

Saudi Arabia Chapter 2 – Treasures of a Hidden Kingdom
- **Definitions:**
  - o **Anhydrite** — A light colored, or colorless mineral
  - o **Bay** — A body of water nearly enclosed by land but with a mouth opening to the sea
  - o *Dahb* — An Arabian lizard that lives in the desert without drinking water
  - o *Dahl* — A sinkhole in the sand
  - o **Calligraphy** — Fine handwriting as an art form
  - o **Escarpment** — A steep slope
  - o **Gulf** — A large area of ocean nearly entirely landlocked except for access through a strait
  - o **Incense** — An aromatic substance that is burned to produce a pleasant scent
  - o *Izars* — A garment tied to the waist and covering the lower half of the body
  - o **Kestrel** — A small falcon
  - o **Monsoon** — Very heavy seasonal rains
  - o **Pinnacle** — The highest point
  - o **Precipice** — An extremely steep rock, such as a cliff face
  - o **Ramparts** — A means of protection or defense using an embankment
  - o **Terrace** — A raised area of earth with steep or sloping sides
  - o **Turrets** — A small tower on a building

Jordan Chapter 1 – The Highway Men Came Riding:
- **Definitions**

- ○ ***Argeeleh*** — A device that Arab men use for smoking
- ○ **Caracal** — A wild cat
- ○ **Cistern** — A container for water
- ○ **Economy** —— The organizing of people as consumers, workers, business owners to generate wealth for a community
- ○ **Ibex** — A wild goat
- ○ ***Keffiyeh*** — A cloth headdress worn by Arab men

Jordan Chapter 2 – Rock of Ages

- • **Definitions**
  - ○ ***Mansaf*** — A national dish of lamb, goat's milk, rice and pine nuts
  - ○ ***Rababa*** — A one string violin
  - ○ ***Shabbaba*** — A sort of flute made from a metal pipe

Photo Credits

All photos that are used with permission are duly noted throughout the text, with each photographer still holding copyrights. All other photos are in the public domain through Stock.Xchnge or Commons.Wikipedia and are licensed under ***GNU Free Documentation License*** or *Creative Commons Attribution 2.0* License
Travel log photo - sxc.hu Bringing It Home - sxc.hu , Prayer Walk – sxc.hu

Turkey 1:
Wikipedia:
Flag, Grand Bazaar, Bosphorous Bridge,Ataturk Dam
Stock exchange:
Young girl , Trazban region, Kilim

Turkey 2
Wikipedia:
Map, ayran, Lake Tuz
Cappadocia Pictures

Turkey 3
Wikipedia:
Izmir (Yilmaz Ugurlu)
Worshipper in mosque, Interior of Hagia Sophia, Turkish folk dancers, Tea glass
Stock exchange:
Mosque

Israel 1
Wikipedia:
Flag, Wildflowers, Tel Avivs, Haifa, Paper cutting, Hebrew letters
Stock exchange:
Jaffa tower, Beachcoast
Flikr: Young boy

A special thanks for their kind generosity:
Burak Sansal - www.AllAboutturkey.com
Galen Fry – www.galenfrysinger.com
Robin Searle – www.travelblog.org/Middle-East/Jordan

Israel 2
Wikipedia:
Negev, Bedouin, Ramon crater photographs, Elat, Fish, Underwater observatory, Fault Lines, Mount Hermon, Jordan River, Sea of Galilee, Kibbutz, Kibbutz dome, Floating on Dead Sea, Scene over Dead Sea, Sea of Galilee
Israel 3
Stock Exchange
Pilgrim,
Wikipedia
Bethlehem street , Church of the Nativity, Church of the nativity door, Mosaic, Jerusalem gate, Jerusalem, Market man, Western Wall, Dome of the Rock, Via Dolorosa, Holy Sepulcher entrance, Institute, Bagel and Lox, Hamentaschen
Egypt 1
Stock Xchnge
Egypt boy, Sinai Resort, Underwater Sinai, Rugged Sinai, Bedouin necklaces, Bedouin Man, Egyptian Man
Wikipedia
Tut's mask, Suez map, Suez boat Hurghada beach
Egypt 2
Stock Xchng:
Man, Egyptian Boy, Pyramid Sphinx, Cairo
Wikipedia:
Map, *Felucca,* Nile, Egyptian women
Abu Simbel, Aswan Dam, House Tour boat, Valley of the Kings, Tut's Chamber, Traffic in Cairo, Egyptian Museum, Cairo houses

Jeffrey Scott Tynes – www.natashatynes.com
Brian McMorrow – www.pbase.com/bmcmorrow/jordan

Egypt 3
Stock Xchng:
Egyptians with cart, Egyptian boy on bike, Sitting camel
Wikipedia
Alexandria Library, Coptic Museum,
Bahariya, White Desert, Egypt glass
Iraq 1
Wikipedia:
Boys, Flag, Map, Tower of Babel Ishtar Gate, Detail of Gate, Ashubanipal
Group of Children
Iraq 2
Wikipedia:
Flag, Kurd Musician, Mosul, Al – Hadba
Dolma, Tikrit Palace, Al- Najaf, Shatt Al-Arab
Iraq 3
Wikipedia:
Group of Children, Shatt Al Arab River
Saudi Arabia 1
Wikipedia:
Map, Flag, Grand Mosque at Hajj
Jordan 1:
Wikipedia:
Flag, Map, Amman, Theater in Amman
Stock Exchange:
View from Mount Nebo
Jordan 2:
Wikipedia
Mansaf, Bedouin Man lighting fire

US Soldiers – www.savvyskull.com
Dr. Carl Rasmussen – www.holylandphotos.org

About the Authors

Ann Voskamp has been lost all of her life. Which is a good reason to write about geography. She was a lost young teen when God graciously found her. She was lost behind long hair and glasses, wandering the library stacks, when her future husband found her. And her children now usually find her curled up on the couch, calling them to come get lost in a good book with her.

As a high school student, she proposed that Mr. Hammond's World Geography class sponsor a child through **World Vision**, a sponsorship which Mr. Hammond's class then annually honoured. As her fascination with geography and God's glorious globe continues decades later, so too does Ann's support of World Vision, the whole of the royalties of A Child's Geography donated to their work around the world.

Photo Credit: 12-year-old Caleb Voskamp

With a background in Education and Child Psychology from York University and the University of Waterloo, Ann's educational pursuits have focused on elementary education, her passions on the Maker of heavens and earth. This project marries both.

She and her best-friend husband raise corn, six kids, and soybeans, as full-time farmers in Ontario, Canada. She writes of their life at www.aholyexperience.com .

Tonia Peckover loves words; all her life she has been traveling and dreaming through the pages of books. Stories of colorful locales and fascinating people fired her imagination as a young teenager and propelled her forward at a church camp altar call to tell God she'd go anywhere He sent her - even Africa. In His wisdom, He sent her to rural Oregon instead. That is where Ann found her, scribbling words on the internet, dreaming of taking God's love into every exotic, captivating corner of the world. A Child's Geography brings together her passions for both and, through World Vision, allows her to invest in people all over His earth.

Tonia and her husband, Mark, live in a kooky old farmhouse on the edge of a forest where they raise ducks, enjoy the rain and homeschool their four soccer-crazy children. She writes lots more words at studyinbrown.com

QUICK ORDER FORM

Would you like your own copy of this book? Or perhaps the first volume in this series entitled **A Child's Geography: Explore His Earth**? Simply indicate the products that interest you and get in touch with us in one of the ways below.

☐ A Child's Geography: Explore His Earth - $32.95

☐ A Child's Geography: Explore the Holy Land - $34.95

☐ Or request a free catalog and sampler CD which contains samples and entire ebooks which represent our line of quality history and geography resources meant to educate and entertain your students.

Fax Orders: Fax this form to (210)568-9655
Telephone Orders: Call 1(877)697-8611 with your credit card in hand
Mail Orders: Send this form to:
Knowledge Quest, Inc.
P.O. Box 789
Boring, OR 97009
(210)745-0203

Name:_____
Address:_____
City:_____State:_____Zip:_____
Telephone:_____
Email:_____

Subtotal for books indicated above:
US Shipping, please add $5 for single title and $2 for additional title:
Total amount enclosed:

Payment:
☐ check
☐ credit card (indicate type)

Card number:_____
Name on card:_____Expiration date:_____

Yes, we do sell wholesale as well. Need to contact us? Send an email to orders@knowledgequestmaps.com or visit us online at www.knowledgequestmaps.com